PUSHKIN: A BIOGRAPHY

PUSHKIN

A Biography by David Magarshack

GROVE PRESS, INC.
NEW YORK

All the quotations in this book have
been translated by the author

CONTENTS

ILLUSTRATIONS

Acknowledgements are due to the Mansell Collection for permission to reproduce plates 3, 6, 8, 9 and to the Radio Times Hulton Picture Library for plates 10 and 25.

Some people say: what does it matter to a reader or to a critic whether I am handsome or ugly, whether I am a nobleman of ancient lineage or not, whether I am good or bad, whether I grovel at the feet of the mighty or refuse even to bow to them, whether I am a gambler or not, and so on. Let my future biographer, if the good Lord sends me one, take care of all that.

Pushkin (Refutation of Criticisms, 1830)

A true biography of Pushkin will be impossible for a long time . . . because of the so-called proprieties.

Turgenev to Annenkov (Pushkin's first biographer)
October, 1852

PART ONE

1799-1817

The Young Poet:
Childhood and Lycée

I

Alexander Pushkin, 'a poor descendant of mighty forebears', as he described himself in his *Little House at Kolomna* (1830), or more picturesquely in his poem *My Pedigree*, 'the detritus of a decrepit aristocracy', was very proud of his ancient lineage. He wrote of his father's family in his auto-biographical sketch in 1834:

We are descended from the Prussian [actually, Czech] Radshi or Rachi, a highborn gentleman ('an honest man', the Chronicle described him), who settled in Russia during the reign of Alexander Nevsky . . . Among the small number of noble families who survived the disfavour of Ivan the Terrible the historians also mention the Pushkins . . . During the interregnum a Pushkin was put in command of an army and performed his duty honourably . . . Four Pushkins signed the document electing the Romanovs to the Russian throne . . . During the reign of Peter the Great, Fyodor Alexeyevich Pushkin was executed for taking part in a plot against the Tsar. My great-grandfather, Alexander Petrovich, was married to the younger daughter of Count Golovin, the first to be decorated with the Order of St Andrey. He died very young, having murdered his pregnant wife in a fit of madness. His only son, Lev Alexandrovich, served in an artillery regiment and remained loyal to Peter III during the rebellion of 1762. He was im-prisoned in a fortress but set free two years later. After that he lived in Moscow and on his estates. My grandfather was a passionate and cruel man. His first wife died in a dungeon in one of his country houses where he had thrown her for an imaginary or real affair with a French-man, a former tutor of his sons, whom he very feudally hanged in the backyard. His second wife suffered a great deal at his hands. One day he told her to dress and drive with him on a visit to some neighbouring squires. My grandmother, who was pregnant, did not feel well but she dared not refuse. On the way she felt the pains of childbirth. My grandfather told the coachman to stop and she gave birth in the carriage – to my father, I believe. She was brought back home more dead than alive and put to bed in her finery and wearing her jewels. All this I have learnt in a rather roundabout way. My father never spoke of my grandfather's eccentricities and our old servants died long ago.

Pushkin resented the fact that, as he put it, 'today our nobility is to a large extent composed of new families who have sprung into prominence during the reign of the emperors.' He resented even more, though he dared not say it, the fact that the 'emperors', that is to say, Catherine II, Paul I, Alexander I, and Nicholas I, were even greater upstarts than the new nobles; not only was their claim to the throne of the Romanovs completely bogus but it resulted from the murders of Peter III and Paul I, in which both Catherine and Alexander had taken an active part.

Pushkin's ancestry on his father's side was therefore a contributory cause of his detestation of the ruling classes of his day, which was to lead him into a head-on collision with the high society 'mob' as well as with Alexander I and Nicholas I. On the other hand, his ancestry also led him to deny that he 'ever shared with anyone a democratic hatred of the nobility', which he regarded as 'a necessary and natural social class of a great civilised nation'. He was sorry to see the old Russian noble families wiped out or falling, like his own, into decay, and becoming, like himself, 'an object of derision among recently ennobled men of obscure origin and even among some idle buffoons'.

But there was a touch of the tarbrush in Pushkin's ancestry which one of these 'idle buffoons', Faddey Bulgarin, editor of the semi-official *Northern Bee*, an agent of the secret police and one of Pushkin's bitterest enemies, was only too happy to bring to the notice of his large number of readers. 'In one paper (almost an official one),' Pushkin wrote in the autumn of 1830, 'it was said that my great-grandfather Abram Petrovich Hannibal . . . was bought by a skipper for a bottle of rum. If my great-grandfather was bought, it was probably cheaply, but he was bought by a skipper every Russian speaks of with respect,' that is to say, by no less a person than Peter the Great. Who Hannibal, Pushkin's great-grandfather on his mother's side, was has never been ascertained. It was natural for his descendants to claim that he was the son of an Abyssinian prince who had been kidnapped and sold to the Sultan of Turkey, then abducted by the Russian ambassador and sent as a gift to Peter the Great. Pushkin never mentions his great-grandfather's Abyssinian origin, but merely describes him as 'the son of a reigning Negro princeling'. He first mentions Hannibal, a common name among Negro slaves, in a footnote to the fiftieth stanza of the First Canto of *Eugene Onegin*, written during his exile in Odessa, when he was making all sorts of plans for escaping from Russia:

> It is time to leave the tedious shore
> Of an element inimical to me,
> And amidst the southern swells,
> Beneath the skies of my Africa
> Sigh for sombre Russia. . . .

To the last line Pushkin added the following footnote:

On his mother's side the author is of African descent. His great-grandfather, Abram Petrovich Hannibal, was kidnapped from the shores of Africa in his eighth year and brought to Constantinople. The Russian ambassador obtained his freedom and sent him as a present to Peter the Great who had him baptised in Vilno. His brother followed him to Constantinople and then to Petersburg with an offer of ransom, but Peter I refused to return his godson. In his old age, Hannibal remembered Africa and the luxurious life of his father and his nineteen brothers, of whom he was the youngest; he remembered how they used to be taken to their father with their hands tied behind their backs while he alone remained free and used to go swimming beneath the fountains of his father's house; he also remembered his favourite sister, Lahan, swimming in the distance after the ship in which he was sailing away.

At the age of eighteen Hannibal was sent by the Tsar to France, where he began his military service in the army of the Regent; he returned to Russia with an injured head and the rank of French lieutenant. Since then he remained continually near the person of the Emperor. In the reign of Anna, Hannibal, a personal enemy of her favourite Buehren, was sent to Siberia on some plausible pretext. Bored with the loneliness of the place and the harshness of the climate, he returned to Petersburg of his own accord and appeared before his friend Field Marshal Muennich. Muennich advised him to go into hiding immediately. Hannibal retired to his estates where he lived during the reign of Anna, while nominally still in the service in Siberia.

Hannibal's subsequent career is related at great length in Pushkin's autobiographical sketch (1834):

> When the Empress Elisabeth ascended the throne, Hannibal (who lived in retirement on his estate) sent her a message with the words from the Gospels: 'Remember me when thou comest into thy kingdom.' Elisabeth at once summoned him to her court, promoted him to the rank of brigadier and soon after to the rank of Major-General and General-in-Chief. She also presented him with several estates in the Pskov and Petersburg provinces [including Pushkin's mother's estate of Mikhailovskoye which is so inextricably bound up with Pushkin's biography]. . . . During the reign of Peter III, Hannibal retired. He died in his ninety-third year in 1781. He wrote his memoirs in French, but in a fit of panic, to which he was subject, ordered them to be burnt in his presence together with other precious documents.

In his autobiographical sketch, Pushkin again mentions the arrival of Hannibal's brother in Petersburg, but as no mention of it can be found in any contemporary account, the whole incident was most probably invented to bolster up Hannibal's claim to his princely descent.

Hannibal had one thing in common with Pushkin's paternal grandfather: his family life, too, was unhappy:

> His first wife [Pushkin writes], a woman of Greek origin, was a great beauty. She bore him a white daughter. After divorcing her, he forced her to take the veil. He gave her daughter, Polyxena, an excellent education and a rich dowry but refused to see her. His second wife, Christina-Regina Scherberg, married him while he was commandant in Reval and bore him a great number of black children of both sexes.

Pushkin was rather proud of Hannibal's eldest son, Lieutenant-General Ivan Hannibal, the founder of the city of Kherson. Pushkin's own grandfather, Osip Abramovich, served in the navy. His marriage, too, was unhappy. He married Maria Alexeyevna Pushkin, the daughter of one of his father's uncles. Pushkin writes:

> The wife's jealousy and the husband's infidelities were the cause of constant unpleasantness and quarrels, culminating in divorce. My grandfather's African character, his fiery passions, coupled with his terrible rashness, led him into most extraordinary delusions. He married

a second wife after presenting a false certificate of his first wife's death. My grandmother was forced to petition the Empress, who at once intervened. My grandfather's new marriage was declared illegal, my grandmother was given back the custody of her three-year-old daughter and my grandfather was ordered to join the Black Sea fleet. My grandfather died in 1807 on his Pskov estate [Mikhailovskoye] as the result of an intemperate life. Eleven years later my grandmother died on the same estate. Death united them. They are buried side by side in the Svyatogorsk monastery [where Pushkin, too, was buried thirty years later beside his mother].

Pushkin knew only his great-uncle, Artillery General Peter Abramovich Hannibal, second son of Abram Hannibal, who owned the estate of Petrovskoye, a few miles from Mikhailovskoye. He visited him in 1817 and again in 1824, hoping to get some family documents from him. Peter Hannibal was known in the district for his incontinent life (like many another Russian landowner he kept a harem of young serf girls). When Pushkin saw him in November, 1824, about a year before his death, his pleasures were confined to drink. Pushkin noted in his diary:

> He ordered vodka, poured out a glass for himself and told the servant to offer me a glass. I emptied it at a gulp without pulling a face which, it seems, greatly pleased the old Negro. A quarter of an hour later, he again called for vodka and repeated this five or six times till dinner.

Pushkin got his documents, such as they were, including, it is believed, Hannibal's biography by an anonymous German.

Pushkin made several unsuccessful attempts to write his autobiography. In 1830 he jotted down what he called the 'synopses' of its first six chapters. The synopsis of the first chapter reads:

> My father's family – his education – French tutors – father and uncle in the guards – their literary acquaintances – grandmother and her mother – their poverty – Ivan Abramovich – father's wedding – death of Catherine II – birth of Olga – father's retirement, leaves Moscow – my birth.

Pushkin's father Sergey (1770–1848), as well as his uncle Vasily (1767–1830), served for a short time in guards regiments. Their family owned many estates which by the time of Pushkin's birth had fallen into decay. His father as well as his uncle had had a good education, which in those days meant an almost entirely French upbringing. Their literary acquaintances included some of the most prominent writers and poets in Russia, such as Nikolai Karamzin, the founder and leader of the sentimental movement, Ivan Dmitriev, one of Karamzin's more gifted followers and a Minister of Justice, Vasily Zhukovsky, the founder of the romantic movement, Konstantin Batyushkov, one of the most outstanding romantic poets of that time, and Alexander Turgenev, a graduate of Goettingen University and Director of the Department of non-Greek Orthodox denominations, who was to become one of Pushkin's staunchest friends.

Sergey Pushkin was described by Ivan Liprandi, one of Pushkin's Bessarabian friends, as having 'the exquisite manners of an old Marquis' and talking 'a highly polished eighteenth-century French'. Stepan Shevyryov, poet and critic of a later generation, who knew Sergey Pushkin in Moscow, described him as 'a man of limited intellect' who was fond of high society life, 'like his brother Vasily, who boasted of his excellent Russian chef Vlas, whom he had renamed Blaise'. Sergey Pushkin depended for his livelihood entirely on the income from his estates but, like many another absentee landlord, was extremely feckless, with the result that his income dwindled and he was forced to look for a wife with a competence, or the promise of a competence, of her own. It was at this point that Pushkin's uncle Ivan Hannibal stepped in and arranged the marriage between Sergey Pushkin and his niece, Nadezhda Hannibal, the daughter of Maria, the jilted wife of Osip Hannibal. At the time, it is true, Maria and her daughter were very poor and lived with Maria's mother, Sarah Pushkin, in a small provincial town. But Nadezhda stood to inherit her father's five thousand acre estate of Mikhailovskoye in the Opochka district of Pskov province, and that was not an inconsiderable attraction for a man in Sergey Pushkin's straitened circumstances.

The wedding of Sergey Pushkin and Nadezhda Hannibal took place in Petersburg on September 26, 1796. Sergey was twenty-six and Nadezhda twenty-one. A week before their wedding, Sergey resigned his commission in the army, retiring with the rank of Major. Their first child, Olga, was born in Petersburg on December 20, 1797. The family then settled in Moscow where Sergey obtained a job in the Army Commissariat. Alexander Pushkin was born on May 26 (June 6, N.S.), 1799, in a wooden house in Nemetskaya (German) Street (now renamed Baumann Street in honour of a young revolutionary killed during the 1905 revolution). Christened in the Parish Church of the Epiphany a few days later, Pushkin was named Alexander after his great-grandfather. His paternal grandmother, Olga, arrived at the christening in a large old-fashioned coach, with liveried footmen hanging on behind and a postilion riding in front. She had been against her second son's precipitous marriage to 'the beautiful creole', the granddaughter of a 'dubious' and far from wealthy 'blackamoor'. She had rarely condescended to visit the young couple, but the birth of her first grandson brought about a reconciliation with her son.

After spending part of the autumn and winter of Mikhailovskoye, the Pushkins left for Petersburg, where Pushkin seems for the first time to have been confronted by the Russian monarchy in the person of Paul I. The Tsar stopped the carriage in which Pushkin was being taken for a drive by his nurse, and sternly reprimanded her for not taking the cap off the baby's head when the monarch happened to pass by.

2

The synopsis of the second chapter of Pushkin's proposed autobiography gives very meagre information about the first eleven years of his life. It reads:

> First impressions. Yusupov park. Earthquake. My nurse. Mother's departure for the country. First troubles. Governess. Early love. Birth of Lev. My unpleasant memories. Nikolai's death. Monfort. Rousselot. Unbearable situation. Passion for reading. I am taken to Petersburg. The Jesuits. Turgenev. Lycée.

On their return to Moscow at the beginning of 1801, the Pushkins lived in a house in Greater Kharitonov Lane, which was not far from the house of Sergey Pushkin's mother. Olga Pushkin was old and ailing and in need of constant care. At the beginning of 1802, the Pushkins moved to the other end of Greater Kharitonov Lane into a wing of the great Yusupov Palace where they lived till 1803. Yusupov Palace survived the Fire of Moscow and still exists. During Pushkin's childhood its owner was Prince Nikolai Borisovich Yusupov, a man of 'enlightened' views, a disciple of Voltaire and Rousseau, which did not prevent him from being a most ruthless serf owner. He was a great lover of the theatre and was famous for his ballet of serf girls and for his serf actors and musicians. His theatre, at the other end of a winter garden, was full of exotic plants, with parrots, fastened by iron chains, swinging from bars, and cages with golden and silver pheasants. According to one of Pushkin's contemporaries, the enchanted gardens of the wizard Chernomor in *Ruslan and Lyudmila* were very like the winter garden.

In inviting Sergey Pushkin to live with his family in a wing of the palace, Prince Yusupov was no doubt counting on the assistance Sergey might render his theatrical company. Sergey was well known not only for his knowledge of French literature, but also for his love of the theatre.

The 'earthquake', which Pushkin mentions, took place in Moscow on

October 14, 1802. Pushkin was only three and a half at the time, old enough for the mild earth tremor, occurring at night, to have left a lasting impression on him.

As a little boy, Pushkin greatly enjoyed his walks through Moscow. His constant companion was Nikita Kozlov, the serf who was his valet all through his tempestuous life and who accompanied his coffin to his last resting place in the Svyatogorsk monastery. Unlike the other house serfs, Kozlov was literate and it was he who first taught Pushkin to read and write Russian. Pushkin used Kozlov as the prototype of Savelyitch, the faithful servant of Grinyov, the hero of Pushkin's last story *The Captain's Daughter*. Nikolai Sushkov, a Moscow writer, records:

> As far as I remember, Kozlov was constantly in attendance on Pushkin in Moscow, where the mischievous and sharp-witted little boy was already accumulating early impressions, running about and clambering on to the belltower of Ivan the Great and getting familiar with all the by-ways of our ancient capital.

Moscow, at the beginning of the nineteenth century, was more like a large village than a capital city. The noblemen who wished to settle there bought so-called 'wastelands' on which they built mansions of two or three storeys, which were often surrounded by very large gardens with ponds, summer houses and marble sculptures and behind which were kitchen gardens, orchards, hot-houses and outbuildings of all sorts. Most of these houses were situated along the Rivers Moskva and Yauza. The Moscow noblemen were mostly grandees who had fallen into disfavour at court, or high-ranking civil servants who had failed in their careers in Petersburg. Some of them were fabulously rich and led a life of extravagant luxury, their houses filled with innumerable household serfs, serf actors, serf dancers and orchestras of serf musicians. They gave banquets famous more for the quantity than the quality of their dishes and balls to which 'the whole city' was invited. Next to the wealthy noblemen there was an even larger number of poorer ones. These came to Moscow from their estates for the winter months, eager to strike up an acquaintance with the grandees, gain admittance to the Noblemen's Assembly, or find husbands for their marriageable daughters. The Moscow season lasted from November to February. It was famous for its balls, masquerades, charades, tableaux vivants and drives in sledges filled with masked young men and girls.

All this must have imprinted itself on Pushkin's memory, for in a poem
to Nikita Vsevolozhsky, one of his close Petersburg friends, written in
1819, he could recall the characteristic features of 'old lady Moscow'
during the first decade of the century:

> Moscow charms by her various
> And irrepressible multiformity,
> Her old-fashioned luxurious living, her feasts,
> Her brides, her church bells,
> Her amusing, light-hearted bustle,
> And her innocent prose and verse.
> There at noisy parties
> You will see pompous idleness,
> Affectation in fine lace,
> Stupidity in gold spectacles,
> The gaiety of dull nobility,
> And boredom with cards in hands . . .

Sixteen years later in his essay *A Journey from Moscow to Petersburg*,
Pushkin gave a more detailed description of the Moscow of his childhood:

A long time ago Moscow was full of retired wealthy noblemen,
grandees who had left the court, men of independent means with no
care in the world, passionately addicted to harmless gossip and cheap
hospitality; a long time ago Moscow was the gathering place of the
entire Russian nobility who came from all over Russia to spend the
winter there; resplendent young guards officers came flying from
Petersburg. Music resounded at every corner of the ancient Russian
capital and there were crowds everywhere. In the ballroom of the
Noblemen's Assembly there were about five thousand people twice a
week. It was there that young people struck up acquaintances and
weddings were arranged. Moscow was famous for her marriageable
young ladies, like Vyazma for her honey cakes. Moscow dinners were
proverbial. The innocent eccentricities of Muscovites were regarded
merely as a sign of their independence. They lived after their own
fashion and amused themselves as they liked, caring little what their
neighbours thought of them. Sometimes a wealthy eccentric would
build himself, in one of the chief streets, a Chinese palace with green
dragons and wooden mandarins under gilt parasols. Another would

drive through the Maryinsky Copse in a carriage of pure, hallmarked silver. A third would put five Negroes at the back of his spacious four-seater sledge and drive with his huntsmen and runners along the summer streets, his sledge drawn by half a dozen horses harnessed in single file. Imitating Petersburg fashion, the smart ladies outdid each other in the dresses they wore. Haughty Petersburg laughed from afar and did not interfere with old lady Moscow's fun.

Pushkin's parents threw themselves into Moscow's gay and expensive life without a thought for their own future or the future of their children. Olga and Alexander were turned over to the care of nursemaids and, when they grew up, French tutors and governesses, and they spent most of their time among the numerous household serfs.

Pushkin's younger brother Lev, who was born in April, 1805, has this to say about Pushkin's childhood:

> My brother's education had very little *Russian* about it: he heard only French spoken; his tutor was a Frenchman, a rather intelligent and educated man; my father's library consisted only of French books. The young child spent sleepless nights in his father's study, devouring one book after another. Pushkin had a prodigious memory and at the age of eleven he knew the whole of French literature by heart.

Pushkin's sister Olga is a little more accurate in her description of her brother's childhood:

> It goes without saying, that the children spoke and were taught only French. Alexander was rather lazy, but he early showed his love for reading. At the age of nine he loved to read Plutarch, the *Iliad* and *Odyssey* in French translations. Not satisfied with the books given him, he often stole into our father's study and read other books: my father's library consisted of French classics and the writings of the French philosophers of the eighteenth century.

Between the ages of nine and eleven Pushkin was also reading the large collection of pornographic books in his father's library which were hidden in a 'secret' bookcase. They were mostly by French and Russian erotic writers, such as Alexis Piron who, Pushkin wrote in a footnote to the Second Canto of *Eugene Onegin*, 'is only good in those poems which cannot even be hinted at without offending propriety.' The secret bookcase also contained the pornographic poems of Ivan Barkov who was so popular that, as Pushkin observed in a letter to his friend, the poet and critic Prince Peter Vyazemsky on July 10, 1826, 'all obscene poems went under his name'.

The Pushkin household was always full of domestic serfs, who, no doubt, helped to drain the meagre income of their master. The young girl serfs were usually set to work in the so-called 'maid's room', where Pushkin, who was often to be found there, got his first introduction into the mysteries of sex, as indeed did most of the young boys in noblemen's houses of that time. His reading of the pornographic books, so carefully collected by his father, furthered his education in sex matters, but it also rid him of the prurience and prudery which seems to afflict so many of his editors and critics.

Through his brother Vasily, Sergey Pushkin had the widest connections with the literary world of Moscow. The best poets, writers and playwrights gathered in Sergey Pushkin's study in the evenings. Sergey Pushkin records:

> In his very early childhood he [Alexander] showed great respect for writers. Before he was six, he already realised that Nikolai Karamzin was quite a different kettle of fish from the others. One evening Karamzin stayed a long time in my study; all that time Alexander sat facing him, listening to his conversation without taking his eyes off him.

Pushkin would sit unobserved in his father's study, hiding behind an armchair until he was discovered and sent to bed.

Pushkin's French tutors never stayed long, chiefly because his father could not afford to pay them regularly. By the time he was ten Pushkin had had three French tutors: Count de Monfort, Rousselot and Chedel. His sister had an English governess, a Miss Bailey, who was also supposed to give Pushkin English lessons. Pushkin did not show any particular zeal in his studies with his tutors. It was different with his nurse, Arina Rodionovna, who was to share his seclusion in Mikhailovskoye during the years of his exile.

Arina was a serf of Pushkin's grandmother, Maria Hannibal, and became the nurse of all the Pushkin children. Pushkin's sister wrote about her:

> She was a real representative of all Russian nursemaids; she had a

masterly way of telling fairy stories, she knew all Russian folk beliefs and superstitions and her speech was interspersed with Russian sayings and proverbs.

Pushkin's grandmother Maria Hannibal, too, helped to counter the influence of the French education of the children. 'Maria Hannibal,' Pushkin's sister records, 'spoke and wrote excellent Russian, which evoked great admiration from Baron Delvig, one of Pushkin's closest friends.' The stories told by Arina Rodionovna and Maria Hannibal left an indelible impression on Pushkin. He described it in his unfinished and posthumously published poem *Dream* (1816):

> I love the memories of my childhood years.
> O, how can I keep silent about my granny,
> About the delights of the mysterious nights,
> When wearing a cap and her old-fashioned dress,
> Having frightened away the evil spirits with a prayer,
> She would make the sign of the cross over me devoutly,
> And begin telling me in a whisper,
> Of dead men, of Bova's exploits . . .
> Terrified, I did not dare to stir,
> Holding my breath, I would curl up under the blankets,
> Not feeling my arms or my head.
> A single candle in a clay candlestick under the ikon
> Dimly lit up the deep wrinkles,
> The precious antique, my grandmother's cap
> And her wide mouth, in which two teeth chattered.
> Everything aroused an involuntary panic in my breast.
> I trembled – and quietly at last
> The heaviness of sleep would fall upon my eyes.
> Then in a crowd from the azure height,
> Winged dreams on a couch of roses
> Magicians, enchantresses would fly down
> Bewitching my sleep with deceits.
> I would lose myself in a transport of sweet reveries;
> In primeval forests, amidst Muromsk deserts,
> I would come across dashing Polkans and Dobrynas,
> My young mind whirling in fancies . . .

Pushkin was very fond of Maria Hannibal, but, as he confessed in his long poem *The Little Town* (1815), he was much happier when he ran away from his lessons to the room of his nanny Arina where he had not

> to kiss hands or scrape his feet [but] could spend an idle hour with my kindly old nanny, drinking aromatic tea . . . She does not have to curtsey to me, but at once tells me the latest news, for she collects all sorts of stories from all over the place, finds out everything, gets to know everything: who has died, who has fallen in love, whom his wife, as the fashion is, has furnished with a pair of horns, in what kitchen-garden the cabbage has gone to seed, that Foma has beaten his wife for no reason, that Antoshka has broken his balalaika – the old woman tells me everything, while knitting a skirt she goes on chatting. . . .

Arina's room was also a safe refuge from the 'troubles' and 'unpleasant-ness' that beset his childhood. He very early discovered that he was an unloved and unwanted child. His sister writes:

> Until he was six, there was nothing exceptional about him; on the contrary, he drove our mother to despair by his taciturnity and his clumsiness which was caused by his being a very fat boy. Mother used to take him for walks almost by force and make him run about and that was why he preferred to stay with our grandmother, climbing into her basket of sewing and watching her do her needlework . . . It was only after the age of seven that he became very active and playful. . . .

In fact, his mother hated him: he reminded her too much of her father whom she detested. She did not even bother to conceal her dislike and often slapped his face. Sergey Pushkin remarked that his son Sashka reminded him of the child of an aborigine. Pushkin was a stranger in his own home. He used to appear at breakfast looking like a hunted wolf cub, and kissed his mother's hand as though under compulsion. Very early and without mercy he passed a verdict on his parents: he never forgot how one day his father rushed into the nursery to hide himself from an impor-tunate creditor. His sister Olga, the favourite of his parents, alone seemed to enjoy Sashka's escapades and his quarrels with his mother and his tutor Rousselot. She listened at the keyhole to Rousselot's reprimands, her mother's screams, and Pushkin's defiant and contemptuous snorts. There was also the terrible scene at one of his dancing lessons at the fashionable establishment of M. Iogel. In a fit of sudden disgust with her son, who always felt constrained in her presence, she rose from her seat, seized him by the ear and flung him out of the room. 'Monster!' she muttered.

Alexey Vulf, the son of Mrs Osipov and one of Pushkin's close friends, described the visit in 1842 of Pushkin's brother Lev to his mother's estate of Trigorskoye, where Pushkin had spent so many happy days during his exile to Mikhailovskoye. 'He visited us,' Vulf writes, 'and wished to have a look at the grave of his mother and his brother who now lay under one stone, much nearer to one another after death than they had ever been in life.'

An even happier escape from his 'intolerable position' at home during the summer months was in his grandmother's country house at Zakharovo, an estate about thirty miles from Moscow, which Maria Hannibal had acquired in 1804. The country house, with its two wings and flower gardens, was situated within a large linden park. It stood on a hill at the foot of which was a big pond. The other side of the pond was covered by thickets of pine trees, behind which the village of Zakharovo could be glimpsed. From 1805, the Pushkins began spending their summers there. Alexander loved the countryside around the estate. In his *Epistle to Yudin*, one of his schoolfellows, written in 1815 when he was sixteen, Pushkin left this description of 'my' Zakharovo:

It is reflected in the mirror of waters, with its fences, its bridge over the river and its shady groves. My house is on a hill; from the balcony I can go down into the gay garden, where Flora and Pomona together offer me their gifts of flowers and fruits, where the dark line of old maple trees rises to the very sky and the poplars rustle mysteriously. There I would hasten at dawn with a humble spade in my hands, or walk across the meadows, along a twisting path, or water the tulips and the roses and – feel happy in this morning's work. There beneath a spreading oak tree, I would become immersed in pleasant dreams with La Fontaine and Horace. Nearby a brook ran along noisily between its moist banks, hiding its bright current vexatiously in the neighbouring woods and meadows. But it is noon. In the light dining room, the round table is gaily laid; there is bread and salt on the clean tablecloth; the steam rises from the cabbage soup; the glasses are filled with wine and a pike lies stretched out on the tablecloth. Breaking the silence, the neighbours enter in a noisy crowd. They sit down; we listen to the tinkling of their

glasses; everyone praises Bacchus and Pomona and, with them, the
beautiful spring.

In the same poem, incidentally, Pushkin recalls his 'early love'. He was
nine at the time and it was at the dancing lessons at Iogel's that he met
eight-year-old Sofia Sushkov, the 'love' of his 'golden childhood years, the
friend of my heart'. At the age of sixteen he still saw her 'sweet spectre
everywhere . . . in the darkness of gloomy midnight, in the hours of golden
sunrise, at the end of a dark avenue in the hush of the evening . . .'

Pushkin enjoyed the feeling of freedom in Zakharovo. He loved his long
country walks, his games with the peasant children in the birch woods and
the entrancing stories told by the old peasants. In the village or in front
of the country house the village girls used to dance in a ring in the evenings. On June 24, the mysterious St John's Eve, the village girls twined
wreaths and threw them in to the 'mirror of the waters' of the Zakharovo
pool while singing the customary songs.

On Sundays and church holidays the whole family went to church to
Great Vyazyomy, the estate of Prince Boris Golitsyn, a friend of Sergey
Pushkin, whose great country house the Pushkin family visited several
times in summer. Pushkin's seven-year-old brother Nikolai, who died in
the summer of 1807 in Zakharovo, was buried under the central apse of
the church. Zakharovo was sold three years later.

According to Arina's daughter, Maria, Pushkin visited Zakharovo
shortly after his engagement in 1831, drove quickly through the estate to
see the places that were familiar to him from early childhood and told
Maria that things were no longer as they used to be.

Pushkin's parents had at first planned to send him to the Jesuit boarding
school in Petersburg, but they heard of the foundation of the Lycée. The
opportunity it presented of getting rid of their troublesome son for seven
years and having him educated at the government's expense made them
change their minds. They soon managed to have him admitted to the
Lycée through the good offices of Alexander Turgenev. In July, 1811,
Pushkin left for Petersburg with his uncle Vasily and a new and exciting
life lay ahead of him.

3

The synopses of the chapters of Pushkin's proposed autobiography dealing with his life at the Lycée are very brief and cover only the first five years:

1811: My unce Vasily Lvovich. – Dmitriev. Dashkov. Bludov. Row with Anna Nikolayevna. – High society life. – *The Lycée*. Opening. The Emperor. Malinovsky, Kunitsyn, Arakcheyev. Our masters. My position. Philosophic thoughts. Martinism. We kick out Piletsky. 1812: No entries for the dramatic year of the French invasion of Russia. 1813: The Empress at Tsarskoye Selo. Countess Kochubey . . . 1814: Examination. Galich. Derzhavin, poem. News about entry into Paris. Death of Malinovsky. Anarchy. I am fifteen. School sanatorium. Arrival of mother. Arrival of father. Poems etc. Attitude towards school-fellows. My vanity. 1815: Examinations.

On their arrival in Petersburg on July 20, 1811, Pushkin, his uncle Vasily and his uncle's young mistress, Anna Vorozheykin, stopped at the Hotel Demut, the oldest and most fashionable hotel in Petersburg. It was to become the regular stopping place for Pushkin in later years. To defray the cost of their stay Vasily Pushkin 'borrowed' the hundred roubles his nephew had been given for 'pocket money' by his grandmother and his aunt, leaving the boy penniless when he entered the Lycée.

During his very first visit to the Lycée, Pushkin met his future classmate Ivan Pushchin who was a year older. They became close friends. In his memoirs, Pushchin describes the twelve-year-old Pushkin as 'a somewhat shy, vivacious boy with fair wavy hair and darting blue eyes'. He writes:

Occasionally I went for a walk with Pushkin in the Summer Garden. In the absence of his uncle, we often remained alone with Anna Vorozheykin, who would sometimes show great affection for us, though it also happened that she would scold us when we pestered her with our premature pranks. She took good care that our caresses should not go too far, though she liked to joke and romp with us. We greatly enjoyed the free and easy familiarity of the charming girl and the certain amount of freedom she allowed us, though quite often Pushkin would quarrel with her and she would sometimes ask his uncle to make him behave himself. Pushkin's life at home and at his uncle's house in their circle of literary men hastened his education. He despised learning of any sort and seemed eager to prove that he was good at running, jumping over chairs, ball games, etc. Occasionally we would find him immersed in thought or in reading at an age when one would hardly expect it, but almost immediately he would leave his occupations and fly into a temper merely because someone else, who in his view was not as good as he, would outrun him or with one throw drop all the skittles.

Pushkin found Petersburg quite unlike Moscow. He was accustomed to Moscow's hills, her scattered suburbs, her multitude of wastelands and her magnificent mansions with smaller houses clustered round them. But Pushkin now saw a city laid out according to a carefully worked out plan on a completely flat plain. He was struck by the perspective of long, straight streets and avenues, the granite embankments of the Neva and numerous canals, the majestic piles of palaces and the wrought-iron railings of their parks. On August 12 Pushkin passed the entrance examinations to the Lycée, receiving the following marks: Russian grammar, very good; French grammar, good; German, did not study; arithmetic, knowledge elementary; geography and history, knowledge elementary.

The solemn opening of the Lycée, situated in a wing of the Tsarskoye Selo Palace, took place on October 19, 1811, in the presence of Alexander I. The thirty boys of the first year wore their formal, full-dress uniforms, consisting of blue cotton coats, red collars, silver tabs, white trousers, white vests, white cravats, jackboots and tricorn hats. The official proceedings began with a somewhat subdued address by Vasily Malinovsky, the headmaster, and a speech by Alexander Kunitsyn, one of the masters. Pushchin writes that Kunitsyn spoke of 'the duties of the citizen and the warrior', a speech appropriate to the occasion of the approaching war with Napoleon. After the speeches a list of the names of the scholars was read out. The boys came forward, bowed to the Emperor who, Pushchin records, 'bowed very graciously to everyone of us and responded patiently to our awkward bows.' This was the only time the two Alexanders – one an all-powerful emperor surrounded by his courtiers and ministers, the other a puny, penniless, little boy whose fame was to outshine the emperor and his dynasty – stood face to face. Neither of them suspected that they would spend most of their lives hating each other.

In the evening the boys played snowball in front of the illuminated building of the Lycée. Earlier, at tea, the headmaster had told them that because of an order from the Minister of Education, the boys would not be allowed to leave the Lycée and their parents would be allowed to visit them only during the holidays.

The Lycée was to provide an all-round education to future holders of high office, and its founders intended that the students should come from the great Russian noble houses. In fact, the Russian aristocrats refused to send their children away to a boarding school for six years, preferring a domestic education for them. It was the poor noblemen, who could not afford to give their children a good education at home, who availed themselves of the educational facilities of the Lycée. Besides Ivan Pushchin, the students whose names were later to appear in Pushkin's poems included Prince Vladimir Gorchakov, a future Minister of Foreign Affairs, and two future poets: Anton Delvig and Wilhelm Kuechelbecker, the latter an eccentric boy who was soon to become the good-natured butt of his schoolfellows.

Malinovsky, the Lycée's first headmaster, was one of the most liberal pedagogues of the time. His letters, diaries and works disclose that he was a convinced opponent of serfdom and an enthusiastic advocate of 'political changes'. He was a graduate of the philosophy faculty of Moscow University and spent two years as an official of the Russian Embassy in London. His diaries are full of criticisms of the Russian autocracy and the venality of Russian officials. He was in favour of a constitutional monarchy and his views inspired the course of studies at the Lycée. He allowed the scholars complete freedom to discuss political questions and insisted, contrary to the usual practice, that there should be no corporal punishment at the Lycée.

The Lycée was divided into a lower and upper school, each covering three years of studies. The Russian master, Nikolai Koshansky, was little respected by Pushkin. In his poem *To my Aristarchus* (1815), addressed to Koshansky, Pushkin described Koshansky as 'a boring preacher', 'a gloomy censor' and 'a persecutor'. Koshansky's frequent and prolonged absences (according to the Lycée students he suffered from recurrent attacks of delirium tremens) caused long interruptions in his lectures, his place being taken by the Alexander Galich, to whom Pushkin addressed two of his epistles.

Pushkin loved to discuss literary subjects with Galich. In his diary Pushkin noted that on March 16, 1834, he was present at a literary meeting where he met Galich 'who a long time ago was my professor and encouraged me to pursue the vocation I have chosen. He made me write my *Recollections of Tsarskoye Selo* for the examination of 1814'.

David de Boudry, the French master, was so extraordinary an historical figure that Pushkin left this extensive note on him in his *Table Talk* (1820–1836):

> Boudry, Professor of French Literature at the Tsarskoye Selo Lycée, was a brother of [Jean Paul] Marat. Catherine II changed his surname at his request, adding the aristocratic *de* which Boudry was very careful to keep. He was a native of Boudry. He highly respected his brother's memory and once in the classroom, talking of Robespierre, said to us, as if it were something very ordinary: *C'est lui qui sous main travailla l'esprit de Charlotte Corday et fit de cette fille un second Ravaillac.* However, in spite of Boudry's relationship, his democratic ideas, his greasy jacket and, generally, his exterior which reminded one of a Jacobin, he was a very deft courtier on his short little legs. Boudry used to say that his brother was extraordinarily strong in spite of being so thin and so short. He told us many things about his good nature, his love for his relatives, etc., etc. As a young man, to prevent his brother from associating with prostitutes, Marat had taken him to a hospital in order to show him the horrors of venereal disease.

Kunitsyn, whose subjects were moral sciences, logic and law, exercised the greatest influence on his pupils. In his poem *19th of October* (1825) Pushkin wrote about Kunitsyn:

> He created us, he nurtured our flame,
> He laid the foundation stone for us,
> He lit the pure lamp.

Pushkin mentions Kunitsyn in another poem written in 1836 commemorating the opening of the Lycée:

Kunitsyn met us
With a greeting amidst the royal guests.

This is a reference to Kunitsyn's speech in which, taking advantage of the fact that Alexander I was still pursuing his liberal policies, he went so far as to claim that laws 'violated by those who are supposed to uphold them' could not be deemed 'sacred in the eyes of the people'. This speech made Pushkin treat Kunitsyn differently from his other Lycée masters. Pushchin records:

Pushkin paid much more attention in Kunitsyn's class than in any other classes and that, too, in his own way: he never repeated the lessons, he did not bother to take many notes and refused to copy the professor's lectures (there were no printed textbooks in those days): everything was done à livre ouvert.

A curious intruder into Pushkin's Lycée verse is his Lycée valet (each boy had a valet of his own) Konstantin Sazonov, who, during the two years he looked after Pushkin, committed several murders and robberies. In a short poem beginning with the lines: 'In the morning with a penny candle' (1816) Pushkin celebrated his own escape from so 'enterprising' a servant and promised to light a candle before 'the holy ikon' for having remained alive, though constantly 'under the scythe of death: Sazonov was my servant and Peshel – my doctor'. Peshel was the doctor who attended Pushkin in the Lycée sanatorium.

The only real conflict between the Lycée scholars and the school authorities occurred in the lower school. The boys hated their 'supervisor of studies and morals', Martin Piletsky, a sanctimonious mystic who personified the new reactionary trend in Russian internal and external policies after Alexander I's conversion to mysticism. They made Piletsky's life so unbearable that he was forced to resign at the end of 1813. Pushkin's mention, in his synopsis, of the Empress in Tsarskoye Selo is another indication of the unpopularity of Alexander I among the more radical students. The Empress was living apart from her husband, who was living openly with his mistress.

4

Pushkin amazed his classmates and teachers by his wide knowledge of French literature and his perfect mastery of French. In the 'national', that is, satirical, songs of the Lycée students, Pushkin is always described as 'the Frenchman'. This nickname, according to one of them, was given Pushkin because of his 'passion for the French language'. His other nickname of 'monkey' was given him, according to the same student, because of 'his face and certain habits', presumably his agility in jumping over chairs and on to tables. His classmates also called him 'a cross between a monkey and a tiger', a phrase used to describe Frenchmen in general, which became particularly popular after the liberation of Moscow. Announcing the liberation, Admiral Shishkov wrote: 'The French writers themselves depicted the character of their own people as the crossing of a tiger with a monkey'. Pushkin, no doubt, knew the source of this expression. It arose from a phrase used by Voltaire in a letter to a correspondent on August 30, 1769: '*La nation passe un peu pour être une jolie troupe de singes; mais parmi ces singes, il y a tigres, et il y en a toujours eu.*'

During Malinovsky's headmastership the Lycée régime was exceedingly strict. The boys were wakened by the ringing of a bell at six o'clock, they had lessons from seven to nine, followed by breakfast at nine and a walk in the park, more lessons from ten to twelve, another longer walk from twelve to one, luncheon at one, more lessons from two to five, tea at five, followed by a third walk, then homework and, on Wednesdays and Saturdays, dancing or fencing. At half past eight a bell announced supper, followed by games in the hall till ten, then evening prayers and bed. This timetable did not vary, except for the subjects of study.

The boys' rooms were on the third floor of the Lycée, an annexe of the Imperial Palace, the other adjoining wing of which was occupied by the ladies-in-waiting of the Empress. Every boy had a little room of his own, furnished, according to Pushchin, with an iron bedstead, a chest of drawers, a tall writing desk, a mirror, a chair, a washstand and a bedside table. There was an inkstand and a candlestick with a pair of snuffers on the desk. Pushkin occupied room number 14 and his next-door neighbour in room 13 was Pushchin.

One of Pushkin's early Lycée poems *To my Sister* (April, 1814), contains the following description of his room:

> A latch on the door . . .
> A rickety chair, unupholstered,
> And a wobbly bed, a vessel filled with water,
> A reed pipe.

The dim corridor with the little rooms at either side and the Lycée's strict régime made Pushkin describe himself as 'the Tsarskoye Selo hermit – rhymester' and compare the Lycée to a monastery:

> Alas, in a monastery,
> At the dim light of a candle,
> Alone I write to my sister.
> Everything is quiet in my sombre cell.

With his Lycée 'cell' Pushkin always associated his first 'meetings with his Muse'. He wrote in the Eighth Canto, Stanza III, of *Eugene Onegin* (omitted in the final edition of the poem):

> In those days, in the twilight of the woods,
> Near the waters flowing in the stillness,
> In the corners of the Lycée corridors
> The Muse began to appear to me.
> My student's cell,
> Hitherto a stranger to gaiety
> Suddenly was filled with light!
> In it my Muse opened the feast of her fancies.

The first stanzas of the Eighth Canto of *Eugene Onegin* give a pretty detailed account of Pushkin's life at the Lycée, which, perhaps, explains why Pushkin decided to re-write them in his fair copy. Different versions of the same stanzas provide glimpses of different aspects of Pushkin's life and interests. In one, he talks of enjoying reading *Yelisey*, a bawdy parody of the Russian classical school by the popular eighteenth-century Russian poet Vasily Maykov, and cursing Cicero, in another of 'secretly' reading

Apuleius and yawning over Virgil. He preferred 'a well-aimed ball' to any
'rare poem'; he was 'lazy, obstinate, sly, frank, subdued, unruly, sad,
silent', and only occasionally 'talkative and sociable'. Pushkin was not
particularly popular either with his classmates or with his teachers.
Pushchin writes in his memoirs:

> From the very beginning Pushkin was more irritable than any other
> boy. He did not win general sympathy. By his misplaced and inappro-
> priate jokes and his clumsy, biting remarks he would put himself in a
> difficult position from which he was unable to extricate himself. There
> was in him a mixture of bravado and shyness. What he lacked most of
> all was tact.

Another of his Lycée classmates recalls Pushkin's complete indifference
to his studies. During the mathematics lessons he used to jot down his
ideas, 'gnawing at his pen with impatience and knitting his brows and
panting, and reading to himself what he had written "with a fiery gaze".'
The professors and the tutors, the Lycée memoirist adds, did not like
Pushkin, but they feared his epigrams and his jokes at their expense.
What Kunitsyn thought of Pushkin's progress becomes clear from his
report of November 19, 1812:

> Alexander Pushkin is very intelligent, subtle and witty, but not at all
> diligent; he is capable of absorbing only the easiest subjects demanding
> the least possible effort. That is why his progress is not particularly
> significant, especially in logic. He has a vivacious nature, but he is
> secretive and at the same time quick-tempered.

The first Lycée report describes Pushkin as 'thoughtless and flighty,
skilful in French and drawing, lazy and backward in arithmetic'. The
report of Chirikov, the art master, for 1812 reads: 'Very talented and
diligent, but hasty and inconsiderate; his progress is not therefore as
noticeable as the progress of some of his classmates'. On September 30,
1813, Chirikov wrote about Pushkin: 'Thoughtless, frivolous, untidy,
negligent; however, good-humoured, diligent, courteous, has a special
passion for poetry'. On September 23, 1814, the same master still described
Pushkin as 'thoughtless, frivolous and sometimes short-tempered; well-
mannered, witty and careful', but stressed his gift for poetry: 'Has a
particular leaning towards poetry. Gives hope for improvement'.

Koshansky, the Russian master, reported on March 15, 1812:

Alexander Pushkin possesses more taste than industry and, therefore, even small difficulties can stop him but not keep him back: for, incited by a feeling of competition and mindful of his own benefit, he wishes to put himself on an equal footing with the best pupils. His progress in Russian is brilliant rather than thorough.

The great political events during Pushkin's first years at the Lycée were, of course, Napoleon's invasion of Russia and the Fire of Moscow. In an unfinished poem on the anniversary of the Lycée written only a few months before his death, Pushkin later described 'the storm of 1812' when 'one host after another marched' past the gates of the Lycée and 'we bade farewell to our brothers, and, feeling vexed, went back to the abode of learning, envying those who had marched past us to die. . . .'

The entry of the Russian troops into Paris, which Pushkin mentions in his synopsis, took place on March 19, 1814, a year fraught with many other dramatic events in the life of fifteen-year-old Pushkin. On March 12 headmaster Malinovsky had died. His death was followed by two years of 'anarchy' under the acting head, the German master F. M. Hauenschild, a 'pedant', as Pushkin described him in a poem, and hated by all the boys. On April 12 Pushkin's mother and sister Olga paid a visit to the Lycée. Pushkin had not seen them for about three years, during which they had been evacuated from Moscow and followed Sergey Pushkin to Warsaw, where he had obtained a job. The 'French marquis' himself joined his wife and children in Petersburg in October, where they were to settle permanently in Kolomna, one of Petersburg's least desirable suburbs inhabited by low-grade civil servants and all sorts of penurious folk. Sergey paid a visit to the Lycée on October 11. Beyond Pushkin's brief record of the fact of his parents' visit, nothing more is known of this family reunion.

Four weeks before his father's visit, on September 5, 1814, Pushkin was involved in a characteristic escapade that nearly ended in his being sent down from the Lycée. Together with his 'dear friend' Pushchin and the son of the late headmaster Malinovsky, Pushkin obtained a bottle of rum, some eggs and sugar and prepared the potent punch known as 'gogel-mogel'. They were discovered by the ever watchful Hauenschild, who sent in a report to Count Alexey Razumovsky, Minister of Education, who, in turn, sent 'a formal reprimand'. The three culprits were ordered to kneel at morning and evening prayers for two weeks, to occupy the 'last' places at the dining table and to have their names entered in 'the black book', which might well have deprived them of their graduation certificates. Pushkin was the least concerned of the three. He wrote two poems about the unfortunate party. In *Recollection* addressed to Pushchin and published posthumously, he described the party at great length in a style rather more grandiose than the occasion warranted:

> Do you remember how we drowned our sorrows in foaming wine? How we indulged ourselves lazily in our dark corner? Do you remember the whispering of our friends round the punch glasses, the menacing stillness . . . the flame of our cheap pipes? . . . Suddenly, the terrible voice of the pedant . . . And in a trice the bottles are broken, the glasses thrown out of the window, the floor covered in punch and wine . . . O, my friends, I swear to you, every year in my leisure hours I shall celebrate at table . . . this sweet conspiracy of Bacchus. . . .

It may well have been his father's visit and the scolding he must have given the young poet for his disgraceful behaviour four weeks earlier, that induced Pushkin to write *The Feasting Students*, a rollicking poem in which he re-lived his drinking party. He recited it to a group of his closest friends who came to see him at the Lycée sanatorium where he was confined between October 12 and 14, suffering from a cold. Pushchin records this event:

> After evening tea we went to see him in a crowd together with our master Chirikov. The reading began: 'Friends, the hour of leisure has come, everything is quiet, everything is at peace . . .' and so on. General attention, hushed silence, now and then interrupted only by some exclamations. Wilhelm Kuechelbecker begged us not to interrupt. He was listening enraptured to every line of the poem. At last the final stanza is reached: 'Writer, for your sins you seem more sober than anyone else: Wilhelm read us your poem so that I may fall asleep the faster.' At this unexpected appeal, we forget the poet and fling ourselves on poor old Kuechelbecker, the enthusiast for old Russian prosody. What a kind fellow our Kukhlya was! Recovering from his excitement, he implored Pushkin to recite his poem again, for already then he was getting deaf in one ear.

Much more exciting was the occasion when Pushkin recited his *Recollections at Tsarskoye Selo*, the first poem to be published in 1815 under Pushkin's full name. It was Galich who suggested to Pushkin that he should write a poem for the final examinations of the lower school, which were to take place in October, 1814. The examinations were, however, postponed and took place between January 4 and 8, 1815. Before permission was granted for Pushkin's poem to be read it was first examined by the school authorities and sent to the Minister of Education for his approval. Pushchin recalls that 'Pushkin read his poem with quite extraordinary animation. Listening to the familiar verses sent a shiver down my spine'. The poem was, therefore, well known to Pushkin's classmates before the examinations. It is generally assumed that the poem was written in imitation of Gavrila Derzhavin, Russia's greatest eighteenth-century poet. But Pushkin's dependence on Derzhavin is not particularly striking. There is not a single rhyme in the poem which could be mistaken for a direct imitation of Derzhavin's rhymes. Pushkin, no doubt, unconsciously imitated several of his predecessors, particularly Batyushkov, whom he greatly admired. But for all that his poem is full of original touches. It was recited by Pushkin on January 8 in the presence of high officials, the archbishop, a large number of scholars and professors and, last but not least, the aged Derzhavin himself. In the Eighth Canto (Stanza II) of *Eugene Onegin*, Pushkin recalled the occasion in two lines:

> Old Derzhavin noticed us
> And blessed us before descending to his grave.

Pushkin left the following description of his recitation of the poem in his *Reminiscences* (1835):

I saw Derzhavin only once in my life, but I shall never forget that occasion. It was on January 8, 1815, at a public examination in the Lycée. When we learnt that Derzhavin was coming, we were all excited. Delvig went out on the stairs to wait for him and kiss the hand that wrote *The Waterfall*. Derzhavin arrived. He entered the entrance hall and Delvig heard him ask the doorman: 'I say, my good man, where is the privy here?' This prosaic question disillusioned Delvig, who changed his mind and went back to the examination hall. Delvig told me this with remarkable good humour and cheerfulness. Derzhavin was very old. He was in uniform and wore plush boots. Our examination tired him very much. He sat with head propped on his hand. His face was expressionless, his eyes dull, his lip sagging. The portrait that shows him in nightcap and dressing-gown is very like him. He dozed until the beginning of the examination in Russian literature. Then he came to life, his eyes sparkled; he was completely transformed. It was, of course, his poems that were read, his poems that were analysed, his poems that were continuously praised. He listened with quite extraordinary animation. At last I was called. I recited my *Recollections at Tsarskoye Selo* while standing within two paces of Derzhavin. I am incapable of describing the state of my mind: when I reached the verse where Derzhavin's name is mentioned, my adolescent voice rang and my heart throbbed with inexpressible rapture . . . I do not remember how I finished my recitation; I do not remember where I had fled to. Derzhavin was delighted; he demanded to see me, he wanted to embrace me, they looked for me but they could not find me. . . .

5

Several descriptions of Pushkin were left by his friends and contemporaries, but the most striking one was left by himself in a French poem, *Mon Portrait*, which he wrote at the Lycée in 1815:

I am a young scapegrace who is still at school; I am not stupid, I speak with little constraint and no affectation. There never was a chatterbox nor a Doctor of Sorbonne more tiresome and more clamorous than my own person. My figure cannot be compared with those who are tall. My complexion is fresh, my hair fair and wavy. I like society and its noises; I hate solitude; I abhor quarrels and controversies and – study. I love games ... Yes, that is how God made me and how I want to appear: a veritable demon of mischief, a veritable monkey face, a little too thoughtless. Yes, indeed, such is Pushkin.

> *Vrai démon pour l'espièglerie,*
> *Vrai singe par sa mine,*
> *Beaucoup et trop d'étourderie.*
> *Ma foie, voilà Pouchkine.*

From early childhood, Pushkin was very troubled by his appearance. He was about five foot three inches tall, slender and extremely agile. He could never resist a pretty face but, alas, his looks made him rather unlucky in love. In an epistle to one of his classmates written shortly before his exile from Petersburg at the age of twenty, Pushkin described himself as 'an ugly offspring of Negroes, brought up in savage simplicity'. He goes on to say that he can attract 'a young beautiful girl' only by the 'wild frenzy of desire. So a young nymph, stealthily and without realising it, sometimes gazes at a fawn, her cheeks aflame in spite of herself'.

The first girl Pushkin fell in love with at the Lycée seems to have been Countess Natalya Kochubey, who lived in Tsarskoye Selo in the summer of 1813. As she was only twelve at the time, the affair could hardly have gone too far and should be mentioned merely because Pushkin mentions her in his synopsis under the same year. Another Natalya, who had charmed Pushkin in 1813 and to whom he addressed a rather coy poem, ending with the line: 'Know Natalya – I am a monk,' was the serf actress of Count V. Tolstoy's, whose serf theatre in Tsarskoye Selo the Lycée students were occasionally permitted to visit. To judge from the poem, Pushkin never met his 'charming priestess of Thalia'.

A much more genuine feeling was aroused in Pushkin by Yekaterina Bakunin, a lady-in-waiting and a sister of one of his classmates. Pushkin was sixteen and Yekaterina twenty at the time. In his diary on November 19, 1815, Pushkin left the following cryptic entry about this mysterious affair (it has been suggested by some biographers that Pushkin had actually been Yekaterina's lover):

> So I was happy, so I enjoyed myself,
> Was drunk with quiet joy and delight . . .
> But where has the swift day of merriment gone?
> Rushed away with the flight of a dream,
> The delight of enjoyment has faded,
> And once again there is the shade of dull boredom around me!

I was happy! No, I was not happy yesterday; in the morning I was tormented by expectations, standing with indescribable agitation at the window and looking at the snow-covered road – she was not to be seen! At last I lost hope. Then all of a sudden I happened to meet her on the stairs, – delightful moment! How sweet she was! How becoming was that black dress of charming Miss Bakunin! But I did not see her for eighteen hours – oh! what a situation, what torment! But for five minutes I was happy. . . .

The only direct mention of this early affair in Pushkin's poems is a rather innocuous quatrain written on the occasion of Yekaterina's name-day. Pushkin declares that there is no reason why he should sing her praises on her name-day since she was no more charming on the day of St Catherine than on any other day.

An analysis of Pushkin's first raptures of love was made by Pushkin himself in the expunged first stanzas of the Fourth Canto of *Eugene Onegin*:

> At the beginning of my life the charming, sly, weak sex ruled me. Its arbitrary will was the only law I set myself at the time. My soul

had only just begun to burst into flame when woman appeared to me as a kind of pure divinity. Possessing my feelings and my mind, she shone with perfection. Before her I melted in silence; her love seemed to me an unattainable rapture. To live, to die at her sweet feet – I desired nothing more.

Then suddenly I would hate her and tremble and shed tears, seeing her, with anguish and horror, as a creature of malicious and mysterious forces; her piercing looks, her smile, her voice, her talk – everything in her was poisoned, filled with malice and treachery, everything in her thirsted for my tears and moans, fed on my blood . . . then suddenly I saw in her the marble before Pygmalion's prayer still cold and mute, but presently warm and alive.

The radical changes in life at the Lycée introduced by Yegor Engelhardt, the new headmaster, on his appointment in February 1816, made it possible for Pushkin to gain the experience he lacked for the further development of his genius. Engelhardt relaxed the rules which forbade students to leave without official permission and supervision. He invited the students to his house and organised parties and theatrical shows for them.

Pushchin writes in his memoirs:

With the appointment of the new headmaster, our school life assumed a different character. In the evenings Engelhardt organised meetings in the hall in which he took part personally; in his house we became familiar with the manners of high society and we also found pleasant female society there. In summer during our vacation month of July, our headmaster took us on long country walks in the vicinity of Tsarskoye Selo, which sometimes lasted two days; in winter we drove outside the town in troikas to lunch or tea; in the park we tobogganed or skated. In all these diversions his family took part as well as the ladies and young girls of his acquaintance and sometimes our relatives who came to visit us.

Pushchin adds an odd note about Engelhardt's relationship with Pushkin. 'Pushkin,' he writes, 'never wanted to see him [Engelhardt] in his true light and avoided any friendly contact with him. There was something here which he refused to discuss with me.' Pushkin refused to discuss with his friend his affair with Maria Smith, a young French widow who kept house for Engelhardt and who was suspected of being his mistress. Pushkin dedicated several erotic poems to her, including one in French entitled *Couplets*. He wrote this in reply to Maria's French poem to him in which she declared her admiration for his talent. This exchange of French 'couplets' took place in 1817 at a time when the young widow already began to look favourably on Pushkin's attentions. In the same year Pushkin wrote several other poems in Russian to Maria Smith, who figures in them under the name of Lida or Lila. These poems are remarkable for their genuine feeling and are quite different from the mawkish love poems he wrote earlier. In one of them, entitled quite openly *To a Young Widow*, he implores Maria not to utter 'soft moans' in her 'light sleep' when feeling tired with 'voluptuousness'. He asks her why it was that when he was experiencing 'the quick swoon of love' he sometimes noticed tears in her eyes. He wonders whether she is still thinking of her dead husband and assures her that the dead do not care for 'spring roses, the noise of feasts, or the timid call of a mistress'.

In his much more outspoken *Letter to Lida* (1817) Pushkin speaks of leaving his 'prison' as soon as the 'Arguses' are asleep and hastening to her room where 'by my swift steps, my passionate silence, my fearless, trembling hands, my ardent breath and my hot caressing lips, you will recognise your lover . . .' Did Engelhardt, as some of Pushkin's biographers surmise, discover Pushkin and Maria in bed one morning and was that the real reason why the two could not get on? Be that as it may, the fact remains that Engelhardt dismissed his young French housekeeper abruptly, thus putting an end to Pushkin's Lycée love lyrics.

Another more authenticated incident of Pushkin's love quests brought even Alexander I on the scene. It concerned Princess Varvara Volkonsky, a far from beautiful thirty-five-year-old lady-in-waiting to the Empress. In the dark corridor of the annexe to the palace one evening Pushkin mistook the princess for her pretty maid Natasha and with his natural impetuosity rushed up to her and began kissing her. The outraged princess complained to the Empress who referred the matter to the Emperor. Alexander I came to see Engelhardt about it. His Majesty seemed, however, more amused than shocked. '*La vieille*,' he remarked uncharitably to the headmaster, '*est peut-être enchantée de la méprise du jeune homme, entre nous soit dit.*' The matter was allowed to drop, but Pushkin could hardly be expected not to have the last word in a French quatrain addressed to the Princess Volkonsky:

On peut très bien, Mademoiselle,
Vous prendre pour une maquerelle,
Ou pour une vieille guenon,
Mais pour une Grâce. – oh, mon Dieu, non!

As for Engelhardt, this incident must have further exacerbated his feelings towards the young poet, particularly as he was just then shown a highly unflattering caricature Pushkin had drawn of him. His opinion of Pushkin was, therefore, somewhat biased as can be gathered from the following note in German found among his private papers:

> Pushkin's highest and final aim is to shine and especially through his poetry. He reduces everything to that and occupies himself lovingly with everything that has a direct bearing on it. Yet I do not think he will ever succeed in providing a firm foundation even to his poems, for he shuns every kind of serious study and, besides, his poetic spirit is not one that penetrates deeply, but is an absolutely superficial French spirit. All this is really the best one can say about him, if, indeed, this can be considered something good. His heart is cold and empty, empty of love and empty of any religious feeling, for which he feels no need; it is perhaps as empty as no youthful heart has ever been. All the most tender and youthful feelings are defiled in his imagination, which is stained with all the vices of French literature he knew partly or wholly by heart when he joined the Lycée – a worthy addition to his former education.

Engelhardt, however, was fair enough to protest energetically when it was suggested that Pushkin should not be allowed to sit his final examinations because his name had been entered in the 'black book'. When three years later Pushkin was threatened with exile to Siberia, it was Engelhardt again who interceded on his behalf with Alexander I.

6

Much more important to Pushkin's future development even than the relaxation of school discipline by Engelhardt and his first love affairs, was his close association with the outstanding writers of the day. Karamzin and Zhukovsky, with Pushkin's uncle Vasily, were the leading lights of the Arzamas Society of Obscure People, founded to combat the reactionary Association of the Lovers of Russian Letters led by Admiral Alexander Shishkov, a minor poet and president of the Russian Academy of Sciences. Pushkin met Zhukovsky for the first time in September, 1815. By that time Pushkin was the author of twenty published poems. Pushkin recalls their meeting in his epistle to Zhukovsky (1816):

> Can I forget the hour when before you
> I stood in silence, and with lightning speed
> My soul flew to your lofty soul
> And, uniting mysteriously, was aflame in rapture.

From a boy of sixteen to a famous poet twice his age such 'rapture' is perhaps excusable. Zhukovsky himself announced his 'pleasant acquaintance' with 'our young miracle worker Pushkin', in a letter to Vyazemsky on September 19, 1815:

> I spent a minute with him in Tsarskoye Selo. What a charming vivacious creature! He was delighted to see me and pressed my hand to his heart. He is the hope of our literary club. The only thing I am afraid of is that, imagining himself to be mature, he may prevent himself from growing to maturity. We must all unite to help this future giant to grow up. He will outstrip us all. He must not go on studying as we did! I am afraid for him in that deadly Lycée – they teach badly there! Learning, if badly presented, loses its charm to a young, ardent soul which finds it much more pleasant to create than to work hard and gather material for a solid edifice. He will exhaust himself. I wish I

could transfer him for three or four years to Goettingen or some other German university. Even Dorpat is better than Tsarskoye Selo. He wrote an epistle to me which he handed to me personally. It is beautiful. It is one of his best works. But in his other poems, too, one can see an extraordinary talent. His soul needs nourishment! At the moment he is wandering round other men's ideas and pictures, but when he lays in a supply of his own—you will see what will come of it. I will send you the epistle later.

The epistle mentioned by Zhukovsky is unknown. In his diary Pushkin, in an undated entry of 1815, mentions the fact that Zhukovsky promised to present him with his works. Zhukovsky sent Pushkin the first volume of his collected poems before its publication on December 7, 1815.

Zhukovsky's idea of sending Pushkin to Goettingen or some other German university seems rather absurd when one considers how little regard Pushkin had for academic studies, or, indeed, 'learning' in general. Pushkin himself may later have regretted his lackadaisical attitude towards his studies, but the experience of life he had gained during his last three years at the Lycée was much more important to him as a creative artist than any book knowledge he might have acquired. His complete indifference to his studies becomes all too clear from his marks for the last quarter from October to December 1816. These were: encyclopedia of human rights, 4 (bad); political economy, 4 (bad); military science, 0; applied mathematics, 4 (bad); general political history, 4 (bad); statistics, 4 (bad); Latin, 0; Russian poetry, 1 (excellent); aesthetics, 4 (bad); German rhetoric, 4 (bad); French rhetoric, 1 (excellent); diligence, 4 (bad); conduct, 4 (bad).

All the subjects were uniformly bad except military science and Latin, which he seemed to have completely ignored, and Russian and French poetry in which he excelled.

Karamzin settled with his family in Tsarskoye Selo in the summer of 1816 and during the summers of 1816 and 1817, Pushkin was an almost daily visitor at their house. Karamzin was fifty at the time, his wife, Catherine, half-sister of Prince Vyazemsky, was thirty-six and their two daughters, Sofia and Catherine, were fourteen and ten respectively. Mikhail Pogodin, historian and author, wrote in his life of Karamzin:

Every day after his lessons Pushkin used to visit the Karamzins. He spent the evenings at their house, told stories, made jokes and burst into loud peals of laughter, but he liked to listen to Karamzin and used to control himself immediately Karamzin looked severely at him or his wife said something to dampen his enthusiasm.

In a letter to Vyazemsky, Karamzin wrote: 'The students of the Lycée visit us: Pushkin is witty.' Gorchakov wrote in a letter to a friend: 'Pushkin spent all his free time this summer in Karamzin's house so that he never even thought of writing poems, but as Karamzin is leaving Tsarskoye Selo for good, there is hope that quite soon we shall again hear the pleasant and familiar voice of our domestic lyre.'

Pushkin's attitude to Karamzin was ambivalent: he abominated Karamzin's reactionary politics and he thought very little of his poetry and sentimental tales, but he admired him as an historian. Karamzin was just then working on the last volumes of his *History of the Russian State* and he could not help discussing his political views with Pushkin. Pushkin wrote in one of his autobiographical notes:

One day Karamzin began to expound in my presence his favourite paradoxes. Challenging him, I said: 'So you prefer slavery to freedom, do you?' Karamzin flushed and called me his calumniator. I said nothing, respecting the anger of a beautiful soul. We changed the subject. Soon Karamzin felt sorry and, as he said goodbye to me, he reproached me, as though apologising for his outburst: 'You said something to me today which neither Shikhmatov nor Kutuzov [two members of Shishkov's Association] would ever have said to me.' In the whole course of our six years' acquaintance, it was only then that he mentioned his enemies in my presence . . . Once on his way to the Palace in Pavlovsk he cast a sidelong glance at me as he was putting on his sash and could not help laughing. I guffawed and both of us burst into loud laughter.

On another occasion Karamzin was less restrained. 'He said to me one day (he favoured me with his attention and often contested my views),' Pushkin writes, 'that if we had been granted freedom of publication of books, he would have emigrated to Constantinople with his wife and children.'

The relations between Karamzin and Pushkin were further complicated by personal antipathy: Pushkin, who lacked a mother's love and therefore felt greatly attracted to women much older than he, fell violently in love with Karamzin's wife. Catherine Karamzin treated Pushkin's infatuation with a mixture of amused understanding and genuine sympathy that removed the sting of wounded pride from a boy of seventeen who was all too conscious of his inordinate vanity. Indeed, Catherine Karamzin was one of the very few chaste married women Pushkin knew. Her fidelity and loyalty so impressed him that many years later he was to make them into the dominant traits of the character of Tatyana, the heroine of *Eugene Onegin*. Catherine Karamzin remained one of Pushkin's closest friends, although it does not seem likely that he ever discussed his works or his views with her. It was Catherine he asked to give him her blessing on his deathbed.

In Karamzin's house Pushkin met Peter Chaadaev, the born rebel who was to write the *Philosophic Letters*. At the time he was serving in a Hussar Guards regiment stationed in Tsarskoye Selo. Chaadaev had fought all through the Napoleonic campaigns and distinguished himself in the battle of Borodino. It was to Chaadaev that in 1818 Pushkin wrote one of his most popular and most widely circulated political poems, in which he called upon his friend 'to devote the beautiful impulses of his soul to our country' and to believe that 'the star of enchanting happiness will rise', that 'Russia will awake from her slumbers' and that 'on the wreckage of the autocracy they will inscribe our names'. Chaadaev introduced Pushkin to other hussar officers of his regiment, including Nikolai Raevsky, the younger son of General Nikolai Raevsky, one of the heroes of the Napoleonic campaigns, with whom he was to travel to the Caucasus and the Crimea. Some of these hussar officers formed the first secret political society with the aim of abolishing serfdom and introducing a more liberal régime in Russia. According to Pushchin, 'our constant talks [with the hussars] turned on social problems and the evils of the existing order of things and the possibility of changing it. Pushkin always agreed with their ideas and in his own way expressed them in his poems and prose.'

Pushkin reaffirmed his loyalty to the 'sacred fraternity' of the radical movement in his poem to Kuechelbecker written shortly before leaving the Lycée:

> Wherever I may happen to be: whether in the
>   brunt of deadly battle,
> Or near the peaceful banks of my native stream,
> I shall remain faithful to you, sacred fraternity.

Another result of Pushkin's friendship with the hussars was that he became their boon companion in their wenching and gambling. The changes introduced by Engelhardt made this possible. According to Modest Korf, Pushkin's classmate:

> During the first three or four years at the Lycée we were not allowed to leave the building by ourselves so that when our parents or relatives came to see us they were made to sit with us in the hall or, if we happened to be out on a walk, they had to run after us in the park. Our supervisor and tutors were considered to be much better guardians of our morals than our parents . . . Afterwards everything was changed and in our free time we used to visit not only our music master at his house, but also other respectable houses. At first we were only allowed to visit our friends the hussars during holidays, but even this restriction was abolished and we could go out when we liked and come back sometimes late at night. I believe that some of us were even absent the whole night. A small tip to the doorman settled the matter because our tutors and servants were already all asleep.

Another of Pushkin's schoolfellows, Komovsky, writes:

> *Outside* the Lycée he [Pushkin] was acquainted with several desperate hussars who lived at the time in Tsarkoye Selo. Together with them, a secret kept from the school authorities, he liked to offer up sacrifices to Bacchus and Venus, chasing after the beautiful actresses of Count Tolstoy . . . In these adventures his whole passionate and voluptuous African nature came to the fore. One touch of the hand of a dancing partner produced such an electric effect on him that it involuntarily drew everybody's attention . . . His eyes blazed, he panted and snorted, like an ardent horse in the midst of a herd of young mares.

Pushkin's friendship with the hussars was reflected in some of his so-called 'hussar' poems, such as *The Tear* (1815), in which a hussar tells a lover to be ashamed to cry because a girl has jilted him, and *The Moustache: A Philosophic Ode* (1816). This is a humorous paean to the hussar's moustache, which the brave warrior keeps twirling in the dread hour of battle and when alone with a beautiful woman, 'with one hand roaming in ecstasy of voluptuous love over a lovely breast and with the other twirling his portentous moustache.' As for the 'desperate' or, in other words, immoral company he kept, Pushkin in his epistle to one of his hussar friends did not deny the hussar's predilection for 'Comus and Love', but also stressed that it was possible 'to live in friendship with poems and cards, with Plato and a wineglass' and that one could 'conceal a lofty mind and heart under the light veil of playful adventures'.

In the spring of 1817 the Lycée students began to prepare for the final examinations and make plans for their future careers. Some chose the civil service and others the army. Pushkin, bound by his friendship with the hussars, had been dreaming of an army career. In his *Epistle to Galich* (1815) he was already talking of the approaching 'stern hour' when he would leave 'the pleasant shelter of his cell', throw off his 'Tartar dressing gown' and don 'narrow riding breeches', twirl his 'proud moustache', attach 'a pair of shining epaulettes' to his shoulders, and – 'I – the nursling of the Muses – in a crowd of warring cornets.'

Pushkin's parents, however, were not particularly happy about his plans to join the cavalry and Pushkin thought it necessary to prove the advantages of military service in his epistle to his uncle of 1817: 'What can be more charming and more lively than war, battles and conflagrations . . . and what more enviable than . . . not very intelligent, moustachioed hussars?' Pushkin himself did not seem to be quite convinced by his own arguments, for he reverted again to thoughts of 'solitude and freedom' as the poet's true calling. In his farewell epistles to his fellow students the theme that a poet's career must be service to poetry becomes more emphasised.

Pushkin passed his final examinations in May, 1817. He did excellently in literature (French and Russian) and fencing, well in Latin, State economy and finances, moderately well in Scriptures, logic, moral philosophy and Russian civil and criminal law, and 'also studied' history, geography, statistics, mathematics, and German. On June 9, 1817, Pushkin graduated with the rank of collegiate secretary, the lowest rank in the civil service, and was nominally attached to the Ministry of Foreign Affairs.

7

'I began writing at the age of thirteen and publishing almost at the same time,' Pushkin wrote in 1830. 'A great many things I should like to destroy as unworthy even of my talent whatever that may be. Some of it lies heavy on my conscience like a reproach. At any rate, I can hardly be held responsible for the re-publication of the sins of my adolescence.'

Pushkin was not so harsh about his early work in the first five expunged stanzas of the Eighth Canto of *Eugene Onegin*, written almost at the same time:

In those days in the shadows of the vaulted woods, near waters flowing in the stillness, in corners of the Lycée corridors, the Muse began to appear to me. My student cell, which knew no gaiety till then, was suddenly flooded with light – in it the Muse opened a feast of her fancies. Farewell, cold studies! Farewell, games of my first years! I was changed. I was a poet. Within me only sounds overflowed, lived, ran into sweet measures. Everywhere by my side, tireless, my Muse would sing and sing again to me (*amorem canat aetas prima*), always of love and of love. I echoed her – during their leisure hours my young friends were fond of listening to my voice. With indulgent souls devoted to our fraternal union, they presented me with my first wreath, so that their poet might adorn his bashful Muse with it. O, the triumph of innocent days! Your dream is sweet to my soul. And the world welcomed me with a smile. First success inspired me, old Derzhavin noticed me and on the brink of his grave blessed me. Dmitriev was not my detractor, and the guardian of Russian life [Karamzin], leaving his scrolls, would listen to me and caress my timid Muse, and you, deeply inspired poet of everything that is beautiful, you, idol of virginal hearts [Zhukovsky], was it not you who, carried away by sympathy, held out a hand to me and summoned me to pure fame.

Some works which Pushkin wrote at the Lycée are not extant. In his diary Pushkin noted on December 10, 1815:

Yesterday I wrote the third chapter of [a novel] *Fatam or Man's Reason: Natural Law*. S.S. [Stepan Frolov, a fellow student] read it and in the evening I put out the candles and lamps in the hall with my classmates. An excellent occupation for a philosopher! In the morning I read *The Life of Voltaire* [by Antoine Condorcet?].

I have begun a comedy – don't know whether I'll finish it. The day before yesterday I wanted to begin an heroic poem, *Igor and Olga*, but instead wrote an epigram on Shakhovskoy and Shishkov . . .

In the summer I shall write *A Picture of Tsarskoye Selo:* 1) A picture of the Park; 2) A day in Tsarskoye Selo. The Palace; 3) Morning Walk; 4) Evening Walk; 5) Inhabitants of Tsarskoye Selo

These are the chief subjects of my daily notes. But that is all *in the future*.

Nothing definite is known of any of these juvenile works.

Of the 130 poems which Pushkin wrote at the Lycée only about thirty were published between 1814 and 1817. Some of them were discovered long after Pushkin's death. His great satire *The Shade of Fonvizin* was discovered as late as 1935. His unfinished early poem *The Monk* was also only found in 1920, among the papers of Prince Vladimir Gorchakov. This anti-religious poem contains several independent episodes mostly of a traditional mythological character with a strong erotic flavour. According to the literary tradition of the day, eroticism was used in poems to defy the ascetic ideals of the Church. *The Monk* was followed by *Vova*, written probably in 1814, since it refers to Napoleon as 'the Emperor of Elba'. *Vova*, too, remained a fragment. It begins with the political theme of a usurped throne: King Dadon, who personifies tyranny and lawlessness, obtains his crown by killing the lawful king Bendokir 'the feeble-minded'. This reference to the murder of a feeble-minded king may well have been an allusion to the murder of Paul I. A third poem, *The Dream (A Fragment)*, written in 1816 and published posthumously, seems to be a 'fragment' of another long poem Pushkin intended to write under the title of *Indolence Justified*. In 1817 at the Lycée Pushkin began writing *Ruslan and Lyudmila*.

In the list of his Lycée poems, which Pushkin compiled at the end of

1816, they are divided into 'epistles', 'lyrical poems', 'elegies' and 'epigrams and inscriptions'. This division is in accordance with the eighteenth-century poetical tradition which Pushkin himself was soon to abandon. Among the 'epistles' is Pushkin's first published poem, *To My Versifier Friend*, published in Karamzin's *European Herald* on July 4, 1814. The poem, a satire against the members of Admiral Shishkov's 'Association', is a clever imitation of Vasily Pushkin's satirical epistles which go back to the satires of Boileau.

While both Batyushkov and Zhukovsky accepted the social inequalities of their time and preferred to overlook the iniquities of serfdom, the sixteen-year-old Pushkin did not hesitate to condemn these in his next satirical epistle *To Licinius* (published in *The Russian Museum* on May 22, 1815). The poem speaks of 'the corrupt city . . . where everything is venal: laws, honour and duty', and ends with the line: 'Rome grew great by freedom and was ruined by slavery.' The poem, however, is not revolutionary since in Pushkin's view at the time, the only remedy against tyranny is retirement to the countryside, where 'in a shady grove, on the shore of the sea . . . in a beautiful and bright house we shall rest in our old age in the stillness of solitude . . .'

Quite a different type of epistle is the poem *On the Return of the Emperor from Paris in* 1815, published later under the title *To Alexander*, commissioned by Prince Razumovsky, the Minister of Education, on the occasion of the Emperor's return from Paris. After expressing his hatred of Napoleon (a view that was to undergo a radical change later), Pushkin concluded the poem with a rather oddly utopian vision of eternal peace:

> And the golden times of peace will come, the helmets will be covered with rust, the steel arrows hidden in the quivers will forget their flight, the happy husbandman, ignorant of all trouble, will draw his plough made keen by peace across the meadow; and the flying ships, inspired by trade, will cut across the free ocean with their prows.

The last long epistle written in the Lycée at the end of 1816 is signed 'Arzamas Member' and is addressed to Zhukovsky, secretary of Arzamas. The poem is another attack on Shishkov's 'Association' which is described as 'a refuge of the enemies of enlightenment'.

In his early poems Pushkin is inclined to ridicule the laborious writing of verse as a pedantic occupation. In conformity with the sentimental school of poets, Pushkin at first regarded the poet's chief task to be the extolling of the joys of life, that is, the gentle joys becoming to an indolent poet-dreamer which were to be found in love, friendship and feasts. Joy and gaiety should be the poet's accompaniment to the day of his death: 'Gaiety be our true companion to the grave and let us die to the clinking of full glasses,' he writes on May 4, 1815, in his *Epistle to Pushchin*. In his poem *My Will and Testament. To my Friends* (1815) he calls upon his friends to gather round his tomb 'in a joyous crowd' and let their 'chisel' inscribe on it: 'Here dozes a young sage, a nursling of Apollo and voluptuousness.' *My Epitaph* (1815) is written in the same spirit: 'Here Pushkin lies buried: he spent his gay life with his young Muse in love and indolence. He did no good deed and yet at heart, I vow, he was a good man.'

An occasional note of despondency and gloom does break in, however, in Pushkin's so-called 'Ossianic' poems. The Napoleonic Wars made Russian writers conscious of their nationhood and they were only too eager to free themselves from the dominance of French literature and, at the same time, get rid of the overworked Olympian gods. The Ossianic poems came to their rescue. For one thing, the northern landscapes of the Ossianic poems were nearer to them than the Mediterranean landscapes of the classics. The feeling of melancholy that pervaded the Ossianic poems was also more in accord with the general sentiment of those days. These landscapes are to be found in Pushkin's poems 'In Imitation of Ossian'. The same landscapes can also be found in Pushkin's *Recollections at Tsarskoye Selo, Napoleon on Elba* and other poems. The theme of the gaiety of life disappears, in its place is the dominant mood of sadness, anguish and gloom. In *The Singer* (1816), written in the spirit of a melancholy, sentimental lovesong, the poet talks of young boys with 'gentle eyes full of anguish'. The poet is still depicted as indolent, but he is no longer the same. In *I thought that love had died forever*, Pushkin declares that he wished once more 'to sing the praises of Bacchus and Delphira,' but his 'tired hand lay, langorous', on his 'disobedient lyre'. Experience reveals to him the emptiness of his old themes. In a poem addressed to Alexander Shishkov, a minor poet, written in 1816, Pushkin renounces his past:

I could not forever luxuriate in a delightful state of blindness. I can already discern the tedious light of cold truth . . . An officious follower of Bacchus, I used to extol wine in watery poems . . . scolded bad writers in bad verse, or twined a wreath to friendship – and friendship yawned . . . I was awakened involuntarily by stern *experience*.

For over a year and a half (1816–1817) Pushkin wrote only gloomy elegies. There were, it is true, no more descriptive passages with the moon peering through torn clouds upon gloom-sodden woods. In them nature was more diversified. In *An Autumn Morning* (1816), for instance, it is the dawn that inspires Pushkin to write the beautiful poem in which he describes how he re-visits the places where he used to meet Yekaterina Bakunin, but no longer finds 'the barely visible traces of her beautiful foot' on the banks of the stream. The memory of his 'mistress' fills him with melancholy thoughts as he watches 'the cold hand of autumn' baring the tops of linden and birch. But it was not long before Pushkin felt the limited nature of his elegiac moods. He began to wonder what the real purpose of poetry was, and he could not help feeling that his inspiration was fruitless and false. But these themes of disillusionment do not completely kill his faith in poetry's final victory. In his poem written in the album of one of his classmates, *In Illichevsky's Album* (1817), Pushkin admits that he would prefer 'the immortality of my works to the immortality of my soul'.

At the Lycée Pushkin still bowed to the authority of 'the great age'. He still accepted Boileau's code of poetic art. *To My Versifier Friend* is constructed in accordance with all the rules of a satirical epistle. The French writer he admired most, however, was Voltaire, 'the son of Momus and Minerva, the malicious bawler of Verney, the first poet among poets . . . who, brought up by Phoebus became a poet from childhood, most read by all, least boring of all, the rival of Euripides, the tender friend of Erato, the grandson of Ariosto-Candide's father – he is everything, he is great everywhere.' Traces of Pushkin's admiration for Voltaire's *La Pucelle* can even be detected in *Ruslan and Lyudmila*. Another French writer Pushkin greatly admired was Louis Gresset (1709–1777), author of the malicious and spirited poem *Ver-vert* about a pet parrot in a nunnery. Evariste Parny is another French poet who influenced Pushkin's early poetry, particularly his Ossianic poems written in direct imitation of Parny's similar poems. Pushkin mentions Parny again and again in his poems, though already in the Third Canto of *Eugene Onegin* he declares: 'I know the pen of tender Parny is no longer fashionable nowadays.' It was Parny who, by emphasising the poet's personal feelings and attitude towards nature, was chiefly responsible for Pushkin's new conception of the elegy as an expression of the poet's innermost feelings which he still further elaborated in his lyrical poems written at the beginning of the 'twenties, in which there are similar moods of disillusionment based on 'nature and man's inner world'. Towards the end of his Lycée period Pushkin was very careful to avoid the fashionable clichés introduced by the Russian lyric poets under the influence of the Ossianic poems. His poems do not describe anything that does not correspond to the autumn landscape of Tsarskoye Selo, 'the familiar hills and the solitary voice of the brook, the woods, bared by the cold hand of autumn', 'the yellow leaf whirling day and night', 'the mist over the chilled waves', 'the howling of the wind', 'the grey lake', and so on – all of them descriptive echoes of the two parks of the Lycée. Indeed, in his poem *Tsarskoye Selo* (1819) the descriptive passages reproduce in a masterly fashion the world in which he grew up. These memories of Tsarskoye Selo will occur again and again throughout his life, ending in the famous descriptive passages of *Eugene Onegin*.

PART TWO

1817-1820
The Young Rebel: Petersburg

I

Pushkin wrote in his diary on November 24, 1824:

On leaving the Lycée I left almost at once for my mother's estate [of Mikhailovskoye], Pskov Province. I remember how much I enjoyed life in the country, the Russian bath, strawberries, etc., but I liked all this for a very short time. I loved and still love noise and crowds and I agree with Voltaire that the country *est le premier*. . . .

Pushkin graduated on June 9, 1817, and left for Mikhailovskoye some time between June 8 and 10, staying in the country till the end of August. Before leaving for Petersburg, he wrote a short farewell poem in the album of Mrs Praskovya Osipov. 'Perhaps,' he wrote, as it turned out, prophetically, 'I shall return to your fields once more and walk under the canopy of your lime tree, a worshipper of friendly freedom, gaiety, grace and intellect.'

In Petersburg Pushkin lived with his parents who occupied a first floor, seven-roomed flat in a three-storied basement house in the unfashionable suburb of Kolomna. Modest Korf, who lived next door, writes:

The flat was always in a state of chaos: one room was full of expensive antique furniture, another had no furniture in it at all, not even chairs; numerous ragged and always drunken house-serfs; large ramshackle coaches with gaunt old jades, gorgeous dresses and a perpetual shortage of everything beginning with money and ending with glasses.

Pushkin occupied the smallest room, which he described in his epistle to his old classmate, Vasily Engelhardt, as 'cramped and simple'. Vasily Ertel, a librarian at the Petersburg Public Library, who was taken to meet Pushkin by Delvig and Yevgeny Baratynsky, one of the more talented young poets of the period, has left the following description of Pushkin's room:

We went up the stairs, a servant opened the door and we entered Pushkin's room. A bed stood near the door and on it lay a young man in a striped Bokhara dressing gown and a skull cap. On a table near the bed lay sheets of paper and books. The whole room struck one as the living quarters of a young man about town who was used to the poetic disorder of a scholar . . .

Pushkin never invited any of his aristocratic friends to his home, where he had to put up with constant scenes from his parents. His father even begrudged him his fare to town: 'When ill, in autumn slush or hard frosts, I took a cab from Anichkov Bridge, father would abuse me for 80 kopecks,' Pushkin wrote to his brother bitterly on August 25, 1823. It was in that 'cramped and simple' room, however, that he wrote most of his poems, including his *Ode to Liberty* and *Ruslan and Lyudmila*. Pushkin described his life in Petersburg as 'dissipated', a description in which most of his friends and biographers concur. For a young man of his age and his environment, he certainly experienced the 'joys of life' to the full, though Bacchus and Aphrodite so frequently mentioned in his poems of this period were not his only companions. According to Modest Korf, Pushkin excelled everyone at the Lycée 'by his sensuality' and later on 'gave himself up to every kind of depravity, spending days and nights in an uninterrupted round of Bacchanalian orgies. It is amazing,' Korf went on, 'how his health and talent could withstand such a mode of life which was quite naturally accompanied by frequent infamous diseases which often brought him to the brink of the grave'. But even Korf had to admit that Pushkin's 'dominant passion' was poetry. Pushkin's closest friends, including Prince Vyazemsky and Alexander Turgenev, seemed to take a kind of vicarious pleasure in reporting to each other Pushkin's adventures in the sleazier parts of Petersburg. In the summer of 1817 Turgenev wrote to Vyazemsky: 'The cricket [Pushkin's Arzamas nickname] jumps about on the boulevards and in brothels, but for all his dissolute life, he is finishing the fourth canto of his poem [*Ruslan and Lyudmila*].' In August 1818 Turgenev reported to Vyazemsky: 'Pushkin tells Zhukovsky that he spent sleepless nights visiting brothels and playing cards.' In the summer of 1819 Turgenev again referred to Pushkin's nocturnal life: 'Pushkin has caught a cold while waiting in the rain at the door of a prostitute who did not let him in because she did not want to infect him with her illness. What a struggle between generosity, love and dissipation!'

Pushkin himself left the following candid description of his life in a letter written on October 27, 1819, to Pavel Mansurov, a member of the Green Lamp literary circle to which he belonged:

We have not forgotten you and at half past seven each day we remember you in the theatre with handclappings and signs and say – Pavel, our darling, what is he doing now in Great Novgorod? Is he envying us? Is he crying for Krylova, with his back passage of course. Every morning the winged maiden [a pun on Krylova's name: *krylo* – a wing in Russian] flies to rehearsals past the window of our Nikita [Vsevolozhsky, at whose sumptuous apartment the meetings of the Green Lamp took place]; as before, telescopes are raised towards her, pricks, too. But alas, you do not see her, she does not see you. Let's leave elegies my friend. Let me tell you about our fellows as behoves an historian. Everything is going on as before; the champagne, thank God, is magnificent, the actresses likewise, the one gets drunk, the others get fucked, amen, amen. That's how it should be. Yuryev [a member of the Green Lamp], thank God, is rid of the clap. I am just starting a little one; I. must be thankful for that. Nikita is gambling; the air is thick with chalk! Money is strewn all over the place. Sosnitskaya [an actress] and Prince Shakhovskoy are getting fat and stupid – but I'm not in love with them – nevertheless, I did call for him to take a bow for his bad comedy and for her – for her mediocre playing. Tolstoy [Yakov Tolstoy, chairman of the Green Lamp] is sick – I shall not say what of – there are, as it is, too many claps in my letter. The Green Lamp needs snuffing badly – I am afraid it is about to go out. A pity, there's plenty of oil (i.e. our friend's champagne). Are you writing to me, my dear fellow? . . . Tell me about yourself – about the military settlements. I need all that because – I love you and hate despotism. Goodbye, my sweetie. A. Pushkin.

It was not only Vsevolozhsky who raised clouds of chalk while playing cards. Even at that early date, cards became Pushkin's 'fiery passion', as he called it in one of the expunged stanzas of the Second Canto of *Eugene Onegin*:

Neither the gifts of liberty
Nor Phoebus, nor fame, nor feasts,
Could have lured me in former days

From a game of cards;
Pensive, all night till daybreak,
I used to be prepared in former days
To seek an answer to Fate's will:
Would the Jack come up on the left?
Already the church bell was ringing for mass,
Among the torn decks
The tired banker was dozing,
While, with furrowed brow, pale and vigorous,
And full of hope, closing my eyes,
I set upon the third ace.

'A modest hermit,' he goes on to say, he no longer 'betted on a dark card, having left the chalk in peace.' But that was a wish rather than a fact, for Pushkin never gave up gambling. In the late 'twenties Xenophon Polevoy, journalist and critic, paid Pushkin a visit at the Hotel Demut, where the poet occupied a small suite of two tiny rooms. He found him sitting at a table with an acquaintance playing cards. Polevoy writes in his reminiscences:

> It was then impossible to talk to him. After a few words I went away, leaving him to carry on with the game. It is a well known fact that he played for high stakes and more often than not lost everything he possessed. It was pitiful to look at that extraordinary man in the clutches of so coarse and stupid a passion.

The Green Lamp succeeded Arzamas as a literary circle of the more radical members of the Russian nobility. By the time Pushkin joined Arzamas after leaving the Lycée, the goose dinners, the red caps and the facetious attacks on Shishkov's reactionary Association had lost a great deal of their attraction. The attempt of the younger Arzamas members, especially Nikolai Turgenev, Alexander Turgenev's revolutionary brother, to breathe new life into it by introducing political subjects merely hastened its dissolution. The older members, including Zhukovsky, were confirmed conservatives and supporters of the autocracy. The Green Lamp suffered from no such cleavage of opinion. Meetings began in the winter of 1818–1819. They took place twice a week in a drawing room where a green lamp hung from the ceiling. The green colour was taken by the members to symbolise 'hope' and its light stood for 'enlightenment'. 'Light and hope' became the motto of the society. Each member wore a ring with the seal of the lamp. Most of them were young army officers and writers, the latter including Pushkin, Delvig and Gnedich, translator of the *Iliad*. At the meetings, the members read their works, talked politics, debated and joked. In his *Epistle to N.N.* (that is to say, to Engelhardt, a member of the Green Lamp, written at the beginning of July, 1819) Pushkin declared that the aims of the Green Lamp were 'to speak with an open heart about the fool, the wicked grandee, the inveterate groveller, the heavenly king and, sometimes, the earthly one'. According to Arkady Rodzyanko, a member of the Green Lamp who was to become famous as a pornographic poet, the poems which were 'continually' read at those meetings 'were directed against the Emperor and the government'. Pushkin addressed many epistles to its members, most of them describing the various kinds of pleasures they indulged in. On September 26, 1822, Pushkin enquired nostalgically in a poem enclosed in a letter from Kishinev to Yakov Tolstoy:

Do you still burn our Lamp, friend of feasts and late nights? Do you still bubble over, golden chalice, in the hands of gay wits? Are you still the same, my friends of merriment, friends of Aphrodite and Poetry? Hours of love, hours of hangovers, do they still fly at the call of freedom, indolence and idleness? In my tedious exile, every hour of grief I fly to you enviously, I imagine you, I see you. . . .

By that time the Green Lamp no longer existed. It was dissolved after the mutiny of the Semyonovsky Regiment in 1820, when the Petersburg police was beginning to show too much interest in societies that had no official permit.

2

Like the other members of the Green Lamp, Pushkin was a keen playgoer.
In his descriptions of high society life in Petersburg at the end of 1819,
Pushkin allots an important place to the theatre. He makes Onegin, 'the
theatre's malicious lawgiver, inconstant admirer of enchanting actresses,
honorary citizen of the footlights,' fly to the theatre where

> everyone, breathing freedom, is prepared (for the sole purpose of being
> heard) to clap an *entrechat*, to hiss Phaedra, Cleopatra, call out Moina
> [heroine of one of Vladislav Ozerov's plays]. A world of magic! There
> in olden days the bold sovereign of satire, the friend of freedom,
> Fonvizin shone, as well as imitative Knyazhnin: there Ozerov shared
> with young Semyonova the involuntary tributes of public tears and
> handclappings; there our Katenin resurrected Corneille's grand genius;
> there caustic Shakhovskoy produced the noisy swarm of his comedies;
> there Didelot crowned himself with glory – there, beneath the shelter
> of the footlights, my young days were spent.

Pushkin used almost the same words some years earlier to describe his
own friends of the Green Lamp: 'And you, citizens of the stage, malicious
chroniclers of the theatre, inconstant adorers of enchanting actresses.'

One of the major Russian playwrights whose plays were performed on
the Petersburg stage between 1817 and 1820 was Vladislav Ozerov. He
was the author of a number of pseudo-historical plays, the most popular
of which was *Oedipus in Athens* (1804). The play was produced by the
playwright Prince Alexander Shakhovskoy and its scenery was designed
by Alexey Olenin, an expert on Greek and Roman archaeology and
Director of the Petersburg Public Library. Both Shakhovskoy and Olenin
were also responsible for the great success of Ozerov's Ossianic play
Fingal. Ozerov introduced a great number of topical themes in his plays
with allusions to Alexander I and Napoleon.

Pavel Katenin was an adherent of the classical school of poetry, a translator of Corneille and author of many tragedies, poems and articles. Like Pushkin, he was a great theatre-goer. Pushkin often visited Katenin's quarters in the barracks of the first battalion of the Preobrazhensky Regiment in Million Street. In *Eugene Onegin* Pushkin refers to Million Street and to the late hours at which he used to leave Katenin's quarters when 'everything was still, only the sentries called one to another, and the distant clatter of some cab resounding suddenly from Million Street'. In his reminiscences, Katenin recalls Pushkin's first visit to his rooms:

> My visitor met me at the door, offered me his stick with its thick end and said, 'I came to you as Diogenes to Antisthenes: Give me a beating, but teach me.' I replied: 'To educate an educated man is to spoil him,' and taking him by the arm led him to my rooms. A quarter of an hour later the ceremonies were over, our conversation became animated, time passed imperceptibly and I invited him to dine with me. Someone else came in and my new friend left late at night.

It was Katenin who in 1818 introduced Pushkin to Shakhovskoy's 'garret', as Shakhovskoy's third floor apartment was known. Most of his visitors were actors, actresses, writers, scholars, and army officers, who were confirmed playgoers and used to go there straight after a performance. Alexandra Kolosova, a celebrated actress of that period, met Pushkin at Shakhovskoy's 'garret'. In her memoirs she writes:

> Shakhovskoy's friends, including Griboyedov, Katenin, Andrey Zhandre (Gendre) [the author of several plays adapted from the French], tried their best to be pleasant to Pushkin, but treated him as grown-ups would treat a young boy. Pushkin thought a lot of their views and seemed to be proud of their friendship. He did not occupy the first place in their circle and was hardly ever listened to. Only occasionally, when the theatre and literature were discussed, did the future genius amuse them with some witty remark or some impromptu poem, which showed his fine aesthetic taste.

Pushkin (in a letter to Katenin in September, 1825) referred to one of the evenings at Shakhovskoy's 'garret' as 'one of the happiest evenings of my life'.

Kolosova described Pushkin as not particularly handsome, but very agile and animated. He looked almost a boy. In large gatherings he was sullen and taciturn. Kolosova writes in her memoirs:

Sasha Pushkin used to visit us and amuse us by his childish tricks. He kept jumping about, changing seats, rummaging in my mother's workbasket, removing the balls of wool from my embroidery, mixing up my mother's cards when she was laying out patience. My mother would threaten to punish him by cutting off his long claws, as she called his nails. 'Take hold of his hand,' she said to me one day, picking up a pair of scissors, 'and let me cut them off.' I took hold of Pushkin's hand but he started screaming and moaning and complaining of being ill-used so that in the end he made us all laugh . . . After a serious illness in 1818 his head was shaved and he had to wear a wig, which did not particularly enhance his original looks. In our box at the Bolshoi Theatre one evening he took off his wig and began fanning himself in the most pathetic scene on the stage so that it was impossible to look at him without laughing. The reason why Pushkin was so angry with me was because of an absurd misunderstanding. Speaking of Pushkin at Shakhovskoy's, Griboyedov called him *un sapajou*, but Pushkin was told that it was I who had called him that.

Pushkin never forgot a personal slight and he wrote a short epigram on Kolosova in 1819, when she appeared in the name part in *Esther*, the tragedy by Racine translated by Katenin. 'Everything,' Pushkin wrote, 'charms us in Esther: her entrancing speech, her dignified steps, her purple gown, her black tresses reaching to her shoulders, her sweet voice, her looks of love, her white arms, her painted brows, and – her enormous feet!' Actually, as Kolosova icily remarks, she had very small feet, though it is true that her feet might have appeared to Pushkin, who adored tiny feet, as rather large, but hardly enormous.

Pushkin was much nastier to Kolosova in an article he wrote in 1820 under the title of *My Remarks on the Russian Stage*. He went out of his way to praise the acting of Yekaterina Semyonova, Kolosova's chief stage rival with whom, according to Gnedich, he was in love at the time. Semyonova, he wrote, is 'always free, clear, her movements noble, her voice pure, even and pleasant and her moments of true inspiration frequent'. Kolosova, who appeared for the first time 'in the modest garb of Antigone and won the applause of the entire theatre', Pushkin found infinitely inferior to Semyonova:

Three times Kolosova played three different parts with equal success. But how did it all end? Admiration for her talent and beauty grew less and less marked, the applause died down, and people stopped comparing her with the incomparable Semyonova; soon she began to appear before an empty house. At last, on her benefit night, when she played the part of Zaira [in Voltaire's tragedy of the same name], everyone fell asleep and only woke up when the Christian Zaira, murdered in the last act, reappeared in a rather boring farce, wearing a raspberry coloured *sarafan* and a gold band round her hair, and began dancing a Russian dance . . . If Kolosova [Pushkin fired his last poisoned shaft] will show less interest in his Majesty's aides-de-camp and more in her parts, if she will correct her monotonous singsong, her harsh screams, her Parisian pronunciation of the letter 'r', very pleasant in a private room but inappropriate in a tragic scene, if her gestures will be more natural and not so affected, if she will try not to imitate the expression of Semyonova's face, but will instead acquire a profound conception of her parts, there is hope that with time we shall have a truly good actress, charming not only in herself but also in her fine intellect, her art and her indisputable talent.

The article, written specially for Semyonova, was never published. Semyonova handed it to Gnedich, her dramatic tutor, among whose papers it was found with the following note: 'This article was written by Alexander Pushkin at a time when he was trying to impress Semyonova, who handed it to me.'

Kolosova met Pushkin again in 1827 at a performance of Marivaux's comedy *Les Fausses Confidences*, in which she played the lead. 'We made it up,' Kolosova writes in her memoirs, 'and we became great friends.' Kolosova was at the time married to Vasily Karatygin, the great Russian actor, with whom Pushkin, too, made friends. At the beginning of the 'thirties he read his historical play *Boris Godunov* at their house.

Commenting on Pushkin's sensitiveness to any intentional or unintentional slight, Vyazemsky, who knew him better than any of his other friends, writes in his memoirs:

In ordinary life Pushkin was quite unusually kind-hearted and good-humoured, but in certain circumstances he never forgot an injury not only by ill-wishers but also by friends. A scratch inflicted on his vanity, whether intentionally or unintentionally, did not heal very quickly. He kept a written account of his debtors, real or imaginary, and was only waiting for the right moment to repay them in full. The

Sword of Damocles was never removed from the head of the guilty party until the sentence was carried out. He wrote the names of the people, who were waiting their turn to be struck down, on little scraps of paper. Sometimes he even noted down carefully the date of their punishment. It all ended in a few blobs of ink.

Between 1817 and 1820, Pushkin also saw more than fifteen ballets produced by Charles Didelot, French dancer and chief choreographer of the Petersburg Bolshoi Ballet. Pushkin wrote in a note to Stanza XXX of the First Canto of *Eugene Onegin:*

The ballets of M. Didelot are full of liveliness, fancy and extraordinary charm. One of our romantic writers finds much more poetry in them than in the whole of the French literature.

Didelot's early ballets were all based on mythological themes. An example is *Acis and Galatea*, in which the famous ballerina Avdotya Istomina, whom Pushkin mentions in *Eugene Onegin*, made her début on August 30, 1815.

Pushkin's conduct at the theatre was in no way different from the rowdy conduct of the left-wing spectators who occupied the left side of the stalls and never hesitated to express their views. Pushchin writes in his reminiscences:

It is hardly worth mentioning the scenes created by Pushkin in the theatre. One evening, for instance, a young bear had broken his chain in Tsarskoye Selo and ran along a dark avenue where he could easily have come across the Emperor. Fortunately, a keeper raised the alarm in time and the bear was destroyed. Pushkin, who on that evening arrived at the theatre after the first act, was asked why he was so late. He related the incident with the bear, declaring in a loud voice 'There is at least one good fellow left in the world and he is a bear'. On another occasion he shouted for everyone to hear: 'It's quite safe now: the ice is going down the Neva,' meaning that no one need be afraid of being sent to the Peter and Paul Fortress for expressing disloyal views. All this, of course, is nonsense, but it is a sort of nonsense which sounds very much like an attempt to provoke the authorities and was repeated as such, giving rise to all sorts of talk which had further developments; here, too, a certain aim was achieved in which he took part unconsciously.

According to Rodzyanko, it was also in the theatre that Pushkin showed round a portrait of Louvel, the murderer of the Duce de Berry, with the inscription: 'A lesson to Tsars.' The Duce de Berry was killed on February 13, 1820, so that this incident must have occurred towards the end of Pushkin's first Petersburg period.

In August 1819 Pushkin's uninhibited behaviour at the theatre nearly led him to fight with a man who had objected to his loud interruptions during the performance. The incident is related by Ivan Lazhechnikov, the author of *The Palace of Ice* and other historical novels, who was spending a few days in Petersburg at the time:

As soon as I entered my room, three unknown young men followed me in from the hall. One of them was a very young man, slender, short, curly-headed, with a Negro profile. He was wearing a frock coat. His companions were two handsome cavalry officers, who were rattling their sabres and jingling their spurs. The young civilian approached me and said in a soft, insinuating voice: 'Could you tell me, sir, whether Major Deniseyevich lives here?' 'Yes,' I replied, 'I'll ask one of the servants to call him.' Deniseyevich came in and asked Pushkin drily what he wanted. 'You ought to know that,' Pushkin replied. 'You asked me to call on you at eight o'clock.' (Here he took out his watch.) 'It is a quarter to eight now. We have just time to choose our weapons and fix the place.' 'That was not why I asked you to call on me,' said Deniseyevich. 'I merely wanted to point out to you that a young man like you should not shout in the theatre and prevent the people near him from listening to the actors on the stage, that such behaviour is improper . . .' 'You have already admonished me yesterday in the presence of many people. I'm not a schoolboy and I have come to discuss quite a different matter with you. A few words will suffice: here are my two seconds. This gentleman here (he pointed to me) will, I am sure, not refuse to act as your second.'

'I cannot fight you,' said Deniseyevich. 'You are a young man whom nobody knows and I am a high-ranking officer.'

'I am a Russian nobleman,' said Pushkin. 'My friends here will vouch for me and you ought not therefore to be ashamed to fight a duel with me.'

One of Pushkin's seconds told me that in the theatre Pushkin kept yawning, hissing and exclaiming in a loud voice: Disgusting! The

Major who sat beside him and who was enjoying the play, lost patience
and said to Pushkin that he was preventing him from listening to it.
Pushkin gave him a sidelong glance and resumed his noisy demonstration. It was then that Deniseyevich told him that he was going to call
the police to turn him out of the theatre.

'We shall see,' said Pushkin coolly and went on with his rowdy
demonstration.

After the play, Deniseyevich stopped Pushkin in the corridor.
'Young man,' he said, shaking a finger at him, 'you did not let me listen
to the play. That is indecent and impolite.'

'I admit I am not an old man,' said Pushkin, 'but, my dear sir, it is
even more impolite to tell me this here and with such a gesture. Where
do you live?'

Lazhechnikov concludes his illuminating account of this hardly creditable, but characteristic incident by saying that 'It all ended happily with
an apology.'

An incident no less revealing happened a year earlier and illustrates
another side of Pushkin's character: his deep-seated superstitiousness,
implanted in him in early childhood chiefly by his nurse Arina. Like his
heroine Tatyana, Pushkin believed in 'dreams and fortune telling' and
was worried by all sorts of 'signs and omens'. Like her, he was full of
'forebodings' when he happened to meet a priest or monk or when a hare
ran across his path. Shortly before the Decembrist revolt he was saved
from disaster by the appearance of a priest and a hare which made him
change his mind about going to Petersburg. A much more lasting impression was made on him by a German woman palmist he had gone to
consult in 1819 with a friend, an army officer. According to Pushkin's
brother, the palmist told him that he was going to have a talk with a senior
officer about joining the army and that he would receive a letter containing
money. She also foretold his exile and warned him that the man who
would eventually kill him would be tall and fairhaired. On leaving the
theatre that evening Pushkin, according to the same source, met General
Alexey Orlov, commander of the Emperor's bodyguard, who discussed
with him his intention of leaving the Foreign Office and joining the army.
On his arrival home he found a letter with money from one of his classmates in repayment of a gambling debt. Next day Pushkin was shocked to
learn that the army officer, who had also been foretold a violent death by

the palmist, had been knifed to death by one of his non-commissioned officers. Pushkin became so convinced of the truth of the fortune-teller's predictions that he avoided being left alone with tall, fairhaired men and never showed any fear of an opponent in a duel who was neither tall nor fairhaired. Ironically enough, the man who mortally wounded him in a duel was tall and fairhaired, but Pushkin was so mad with jealousy and so set on killing his rival that he forgot all about the fortune-teller's prophecy.

3

Pushkin was exiled first to the South of Russia and then to Mikhailoskoye by the order of Alexander I, who could not forgive him the reference to the assassination of his father, Paul I, in the *Ode to Liberty*. In the imaginary conversation with Alexander I which Pushkin wrote in French in 1824, he makes the Emperor say to him: 'I notice that you have tried to blacken me in the eyes of my people by spreading a stupid slander [that is to say, his personal involvement in the assassination] and that you have not had sufficient respect for truth and personal honour even in an Emperor.'

There was certainly some substance in the Emperor's fear that Pushkin's poem, which contained a veiled threat to the throne if the monarch did not obey the laws of the land, might help to spread the rumours of his involvement in his father's assassination. These rumours were so persistent because, instead of being put on trial, the assassins were promoted in the service. Pushkin never forgot that damning fact. During his exile in Kishinev he was invited to a dinner given by one of the divisional generals to another general who had just received a high decoration. The dinner took place on March 23, the anniversary of the assassination of Paul I. The host happened to be one of the assassins. Pushkin, whose sympathies were entirely with the members of the secret Southern Society, who plotted the overthrow of the monarchy, found the temptation too strong. He got up, raised his glass and, turning to their host, said aloud: 'To the twenty-third of March!' A shocked silence fell on the assembled company of high-ranking army officers. But the general was quick to save the situation. 'Good heavens,' he said to Pushkin with a smile, 'how did you know that today is my niece's name-day?' A roar of congratulations greeted the news. They all raised their glasses and drank to the non-existent name-day of the general's non-existent niece.

On April 14, 1820, Alexander I ordered General Miloradovich, the military governor of Petersburg, to carry out a search of Pushkin's room and to arrest him. The detective given this job did not find Pushkin at home. 'When I returned home late at night,' Pushkin told the poet Fyodor Glinka, who served under General Miloradovich, 'my old valet told me that an unknown man came to see me and offered him five roubles to let him read my poems. My faithful valet did not agree and I instantly burned all my papers. I have now been summoned to Miloradovich. I know him by reputation, but I do not know what is going to happen or how to deal with him.' Glinka advised Pushkin to go and see Miloradovich and to trust 'the nobility of his soul'. Pushkin went at once to see Miloradovich. Miloradovich told Glinka:

> The poet looked very self-possessed. When I asked him about his papers, he replied, 'Count, all my papers have been burnt. You will find nothing in my place but, if you wish, everything is *here* (he pointed to his forehead). Tell them to give me some sheets of paper and I will write out everything that has ever been written by me, everything, that is, that has not yet been published.' He was given pen and paper and sat down and wrote and wrote, filling a whole book. Here it is [Miloradovich said), Have a look at it. Tomorrow I shall take it to the Emperor. Pushkin made an excellent impression on me as an honourable man.

Miloradovich assured Pushkin that the Emperor would 'forgive' him, but Alexander I did not. According to Pushchin, Alexander I stopped Engelhardt in the park of Tsarskoye Selo and told him that he, the Emperor, intended to exile Pushkin to Siberia. 'He has flooded Russia with outrageous poems,' Alexander I said. 'All our young men know them by heart. I like his frank behaviour with Miloradovich, but that does not make things any better.'

Engelhardt was shocked by the Emperor's intention to destroy Pushkin:

> It is, of course, as your Majesty pleases, but you must forgive me if I permit myself to put in a word for my former pupil. He has quite an extraordinary talent, which is still in the process of development and which requires to be treated mercifully. Pushkin is already an ornament of our modern literature and there are great hopes for his future. Exile to Siberia may have a disastrous effect on the ardent character of the young man. I think, Sire, that your generosity is much more likely to put some sense into his head.

The intercession of Pushkin's other friends, including Glinka, Chaadaev, Zhukovsky, and Karamzin made Alexander I change his mind. Instead of Siberia, Pushkin was exiled to the South of Russia, ostensibly as an official attached to the Chancellery of General Ivan Inzov in Yekaterinoslav (now Dnepropetrovsk).

But before Pushkin left Petersburg on May 6, 1820, a story that he had been flogged during the interview with Miloradovich gained wide currency. It had a shattering effect on Pushkin who was only too well aware of his ambiguous position in Petersburg high society. 'A radical in his views,' Pushchin writes in his reminiscences, 'Pushkin cut a rather poor figure in the company of some of his aristocratic friends. He had a pitiful habit of dancing attendance in the theatre on General Orlov, General Kiselev and other aristocrats who listened to his witticisms and jokes with patronising smiles.' It was this position of a down-at-heel nobleman of ancient lineage fawning on the arrogant representatives of the new aristocracy that accounted for Pushkin's morbid sense of honour. It drove him to challenge to a duel the man whom he suspected of spreading the story.

The identity of that man has remained one of the unsolved mysteries of Pushkin's biography. A puzzling passage in a letter Pushkin wrote on March 24, 1825, is believed to indicate that his opponent might have been Kondraty Ryleyev, the poet who was hanged for his part in the Decembrist insurrection of December 14, 1825. Pushkin's letter was addressed to Alexander Bestuzhev, another writer involved in the Decembrist plot, who was to become famous as a romantic novelist under the pen-name of Marlinsky:

> Where did you get the idea that I flatter Ryleyev? I express my opinion about his *Meditations* loud and clear. The same is true about his other poems. I know very well that I am his teacher in poetry, but he goes his own way. He's a poet at heart. I really am afraid of him and I am very sorry that I didn't shoot him dead when I had an opportunity to do so – the devil alone knows why I didn't.

Pushkin could have shot Ryleyev only in a duel. Was there a duel between Pushkin and Ryleyev, who might have repeated the rumour about the flogging merely as another proof of the Tsar's iniquitous régime? Or was the duel merely planned but did not take place? Or, again, was the person with whom Pushkin fought a duel not Ryleyev but someone else?

Pushkin refers to this duel in his unposted letter to Alexander I written in French between July and September, 1825:

Rash speeches and satirical poems turned the attention of society upon me, and slanderous stories were spread about me to the effect that I had been taken to the secret police headquarters and flogged there. I was the last to hear these slanderous allegations, which seem to have been common knowledge and I felt myself dishonoured in public opinion. I gave way to despair. I fought a duel – I was twenty in 1820 and I was wondering whether I should not commit suicide or kill V. [?]. In the first instance, I should have merely confirmed the slanderous stories which dishonoured me. In the second, I should not have revenged myself because there was no question of an insult, but I should have committed a crime. I should have made a sacrifice to the opinion of society, which I despise, of a man upon whom everything depended and whose gifts involuntarily inspired respect in me. Such were my reflections. I confided them to a friend who agreed with me entirely. He advised me to take steps with the authorities for the sake of rehabilitating myself, but I felt the utter uselessness of it. It was then that I decided to include in my speeches and writings so many improprieties and insolences that the authorities would be forced at last to regard me as a criminal; I hoped to be sent to Siberia or to be confined in a fortress, as a means of restoring my honour.

Who the mysterious V. was has never been established. It has even been suggested that Pushkin contemplated assassinating the Emperor. It is not clear whom Pushkin meant by his friend: Chaadaev or Nikolai Raevsky or perhaps both? In his epilogue to *Ruslan and Lyudmila*, written during his exile, Pushkin recalls the last days of his life in Petersburg, 'the injuries of enemies . . . and the noisy slanders of fools,' and declares that it was friendship, 'the tender comforter of my sickly soul' that averted 'the gathering storm' and brought back 'peace to my heart'. By his reference to friendship averting the storm, Pushkin most probably meant a friend who interceded on his behalf with the Tsar, in which case it could only have been Chaadaev who did so through Karamzin. On the other hand, Pushkin wrote in his dedication to Nikolai Raevsky of *The Caucasian Captive*:

When I was perishing, innocent and cheerless, and listened to the whisper of slander on all sides, when the cold dagger of treachery and the heavy dream of love tormented me and filled me with cold despair, I found peace beside you; my heart found rest – we were fond of one another – and the storms abated their fury and I blessed the gods in a peaceful haven.

In his letter to his brother in 1820, Pushkin reaffirms the important services Nikolai Raevsky had rendered him, but fails to specify what those services were.

As for the mental agony which Pushkin suffered shortly before his exile, it would seem from his *Epistle to Chaadaev* (April 6, 1821) that it was Chaadaev who had helped him through the crisis. 'O, unfailing friend,' Pushkin writes, 'you knew my heart in the flower of my youth. You saw how in the excitement of passions, I was secretly pining away and you supported me in a moment of disaster and brought hope and peace to your friend . . .' Was Pushkin recalling his decision to commit suicide, which he mentioned in his letter to Alexander I, and was Chaadaev instrumental in averting that? Again and again, Pushkin harked back to the insult he could not forget – the treachery of his friends who had turned away from him during the agonising days that followed his interview with Miloradovich, 'the fleeting friends of my fleeting youth', as he expressed it. He remembered them again in *Eugene Onegin* (Canto Four, Stanza XVIII–XIX), when he wrote about Onegin's enemies and friends 'which is perhaps one and the same thing' and declared that 'everyone has enemies in the world, but may the Lord save us from our friends', for 'there is no slander more despicable which your friend would not repeat with a smile in a circle of decent people', while professing that he was 'ready to die for you'.

A few days after leaving Petersburg, Pushkin learned that Count Fyodor Tolstoy was giving all sorts of lurid accounts of his supposed flogging. The count was a somewhat flamboyant figure in Petersburg high society, known as 'the American', because he had been dumped for insubordination on one of the Aleutian Islands during a voyage round the world. During the next six years Pushkin tried to improve his shooting in the hope of challenging Tolstoy to a duel immediately upon his return from exile. 'Tolstoy,' he told his brother, 'will not kill me, for I shall be killed by a fairhaired man as the sorceress foretold.' On his arrival in Moscow, in September, 1826, he did actually challenge Tolstoy, but friends managed to bring about a reconciliation between them.

A contributory cause of Pushkin's agony of mind before his departure from Petersburg on May 6, 1820, was an unhappy love affair which he mentions again and again in his poems written between 1820 and 1822. While a great deal is known of Pushkin's 'dissipations' during the three years of his first Petersburg period, very little is known of his serious attachments during this time. In his memoirs Vyazemsky mentions that 'during the honeymoon months of his entry into the fashionable world' Pushkin was in love with Princess Eudoxie Golitsyn. Karamzin also mentions this in a letter to Vyazemsky on December 24, 1817. 'The poet Pushkin has fallen head over heels in love in our house with the pretty Golitsyn and now spends all his evenings at our place. He tells lies from love, he's angry from love, but still does not write from love.' Karamzin, Zhukovsky, Vyazemsky, Alexander Turgenev and other close friends and patrons of Pushkin were constant visitors of the Princess's drawing-room. Princess Golitsyn was almost twenty years older than Pushkin, but it would seem that her beauty and originality had captivated his imagination. He dedicated a poem to her in which he declared that he almost grew to hate his native country because there he could not find 'a citizen with a noble soul or a woman with a fiery, intoxicating and living beauty', but having visited the Princess the day before, he was now 'reconciled to his country'. But Pushkin could not stomach the Princess's conservative politics and described her ironically as 'poetic, unforgettable, constitutional, anti-Polish, heavenly'. He remembered her in his exile. 'Away from Princess Golitsyn's fireplace,' he wrote to Alexander Turgenev on May 7, 1821, 'one can freeze even under the skies of Italy.'

Anna Kern was another much younger woman who made a deep impression on Pushkin in 1819. She was the nineteen-year-old niece of Praskovya Osipov, and was married to a middle-aged brigadier. Pushkin met her one spring evening at the hospitable house of Alexey Olenin on the Fontanka Embankment. Anna Kern had just arrived from the remote province of Poltava and was too interested in Petersburg high society to pay any attention to Pushkin. She left the following description in her memoirs of her first meeting with the poet: 'In Olenin's house they used to play all sorts of interesting games, mostly *charades en action*. One evening I met Pushkin there, but did not pay any attention to him since I was completely occupied with the charades.' Krylov, who was also present on that occasion, was made to read one of his fables as a forfeit. He chose *The Ass and the Peasant*, a fable in which he, a faithful member of Admiral

Shishkov's Association, derided Pushkin's uncle Vasily in the guise of an ass hired by a peasant to guard his kitchen garden, who took his duties so seriously that he kept stamping all over the place and destroying all the vegetables. 'The ass,' Krylov wrote, 'was a creature of the most honest principles,' a phrase that Pushkin mischievously introduced in the first sentence of *Eugene Onegin* as 'My uncle – a man of the most honest principles'.

During the game, Anna Kern had to play the part of Cleopatra. When she held the basket of flowers, Pushkin came up to her, glanced at the basket and, pointing to her cousin, Alexander Poltoratsky, said: '*C'est sans doute Monsieur qui fera l'aspic.*' Anna found it 'rather insolent' and walked away without reply. At supper Pushkin tried to attract her attention by 'all sorts of flattering exclamations', such as, '*Est-il permis d'être aussi jolie?*' Then he started a jocular conversation about who was going to get into heaven or hell. There were going to be lots of pretty women in hell, Pushkin said, so that one could play charades there. He then asked Anna 'whether she would like to go to hell?' Anna Kern replied 'very seriously and a little drily' that she did not want to go to hell. '*Je me revise,*' Pushkin countered. 'I do not want to go to hell although there will be pretty women there.' When Anna left Olenin's house, her cousin sat down beside her in the carriage and Pushkin, who was standing on the front steps, followed her with his eyes.

They were to meet again seven years later when, overcome by the memory of their first meeting, Pushkin wrote one of his most famous lyrics to her.

But it was neither Eudoxie Golitsyn nor Anna Kern who engaged all his thoughts and feelings before his departure from Petersburg, and who, as he expressed it in *Eugene Onegin*, rendered him 'stupid and mute' in her presence. In his famous poem, beginning with the lines: '*Pogaslo dnevnoye svetilo*' (The orb of day has set), written at night on board a naval brig that was taking him from Theodossia to Gurzuf, Pushkin recalls 'the insane love of former years' and everything that made him 'suffer' and everything that was 'dear' to his heart, 'the agonising deception of desires and hopes' and 'the deep wounds of love'. In *The Caucasian Captive* (1821), whose hero, like Pushkin, was the victim of an unhappy love affair, Pushkin talks of being tormented by 'the painful dream of love', and in his next narrative poem, *The Fountain of Bakhchisaray* (1823), he wrote:

I remember the gaze so dear to me . . . all the thoughts of my heart fly to her . . . it is for her I long in my exile . . . Madman, do not revive the vain yearning, you have paid your tribute to the mutinous dreams of unhappy love – come to your senses; how long are you to kiss your chains and trumpet your madness through the world with your immodest lyre ?'

Pushkin scholars have sought in vain to identify the object of Pushkin's great love. It was only recently that sufficient evidence has come to light which points to Princess Sofia Potocki. Sofia was only seventeen when she first came out in the Petersburg winter season of 1818–1819. Her beauty evoked general admiration. Pushkin, who admitted that he could not help admiring the perfect beauty of a woman's face, could not but be fascinated by the young Polish girl, who had already captured the fancy of Prince Vyazemsky. Pushkin had described his Petersburg love as 'rejected'. This is not to be wondered at since at that time Sofia had fallen in love with one of Pushkin's aristocratic friends, General Pavel Kiselev, a brilliant guards officer, a man under thirty who was soon to be appointed Chief of Staff of the Second Army in the South of Russia. She became engaged to Kiselev in April, 1821, and married him in Odessa the following August. She was known to be greatly interested in literature. She was also a personal friend of several well-known poets of the time, including the Polish poet, Adam Mickiewicz. The newlyweds settled in Tulchino, a Ukrainian township which belonged to the Potocki family, and which Pushkin visited twice during his Bessarabian exile. Pushkin disliked Kiselev. As early as 1819, he declared in one of his epistles to General Alexey Orlov, in connection with his plans to join the army, that he could place no hope on General Kiselev, because he was 'a courtier' and because his promises were 'worthless'.

Sofia Potocki told Pushkin of the legend, current in her family, about a young 17th century Princess Potocki, who was captured by the Crimean Khan Girey and kept prisoner in his harem at the Palace of Bakhchisaray – the subject of one of Pushkin's most popular narrative poems. In some of the rough drafts of *Eugene Onegin*, Pushkin, in a reference to the Bakhchisaray fountain, hints at his unhappy love affair: 'Were those the thoughts that occurred to me when I heard your haunting sounds and when before you in silence I recalled [Sofia] Potocki?' The last line he afterwards altered to 'I imagined Zarema', one of the heroines of *The Fountain of*

Bakhchisaray, who was the cause of the death of Maria Potocki, the other heroine. In the expunged canto of *Onegin's Travels* (1830), Pushkin again hinted that it was 'the Polish maid' whom he had in mind when writing the *Fountain*. According to Vyazemsky, Pushkin was also thinking of Sofia Potocki in his poem *Platonic Love*, a free adaptation of a poem by Parny, in the lines: 'I understood the ardour of your eyes, I understood your half-closed gaze and your pale cheeks and the languor of your steps,' and that it was to her that Pushkin appealed to realise that she would not be beautiful forever and that she was not beautiful for herself.

4

At the final Russian examination of the Lycée Pushkin read his long poem *Disbelief*. This was a plea for the agnostic who, like himself, was never comforted by 'quiet faith' (*Elegy*, 1816), but who nonetheless deserved pity rather than execration since his disbelief in God and life beyond the grave deprived him of the consolation of religion. The subject of this poem had been suggested to him by the authorities and Pushkin was, quite naturally, very careful in revealing his own views on religion. But this poem expressed, in however concealed a form, ideas that were soon to bring him to the very brink of disaster.

In Petersburg the first poems Pushkin wrote were still mostly elegies in which, as before, he extolled the kind of tender love that did not exist on earth. 'Do not ask,' he writes in one of these poems, 'why, amid pleasures, I am so often depressed by gloomy thoughts, why I look upon everything with so jaundiced an eye, why the sweet dream of life is not dear to me . . .' Alexander and Nikolai Turgenev were far from sympathetic to Pushkin's lamentations. Nikolai Turgenev had no use for 'pure art', being a typical precursor of the nihilist revolutionaries of the 'forties and 'fifties. Neither was Alexander Turgenev an admirer of Pushkin's elegiac effusions. In his epistle to Alexander, Pushkin wrote on November 8, 1817: 'Why laugh at me when with a feeble hand I wander quiveringly over my lyre, and its subdued notes merely find delicate sounds of love, the torment so dear to my heart? . . .'

What did the Turgenev brothers want Pushkin to become? The answer is clear from a note made by their youngest brother, Sergey Turgenev, in Paris in his diary on December 1, 1817: 'They wrote to me again about Pushkin as a poet of great promise. Oh, if only he were filled with liberal ideas instead of constantly bemoaning himself. Let his first song be: freedom.' It was, in fact, in Turgenev's house that Pushkin wrote his first revolutionary poem, his *Liberty: an Ode*, that was to have such dire consequences. Filipp Vigel, the Russian memoirist, gives the following account in his diary of the origin of *Liberty: an Ode*:

Of his elders Pushkin mostly visited the brothers Turgenev who lived on the Fontanka Embankment opposite the Mihailovsky Palace [which had stood empty since Paul I was assassinated there]. It was at their apartment that the highly intelligent young freethinkers often congregated. One of these, looking out of the window at the empty and abandoned palace, jestingly suggested to Pushkin to write a poem about it. Pushkin suddenly leapt on to the large table before the window, stretched himself out on it, seized a pen and paper and laughingly began to write. Having finished his poem, he showed it to his friends.

Nikolai Turgenev himself stated in a letter to Peter Bartenev, the literary historian, in May, 1867, that Pushkin composed half of the *Ode to Liberty* in his room. 'He finished it at night and brought it back to me next day copied out on a large sheet of paper.' The ode, written in December, 1817, begins with a repudiation of the poetry Pushkin had written during his last years at the Lycée: 'Run, hide from my eyes, weak queen of Cytheria! Where are you, terror of kings, proud songstress of freedom? Come, tear the wreath from me, break the pampered lyre . . . I want to sing freedom to the world, to strike down vice on the thrones.' Pushkin goes on to attack the reactionary Church sunk 'in the inspissated darkness of prejudices' and the political and spiritual oppression of the autocracy. It was only in countries where 'powerful laws' were the result of 'sacred freedom', that the people did not suffer. He went on to impress upon the ·Tsars that it was law and not nature that gave them their 'crown and throne', and that 'eternal law' was above kings. Louis XVI perished because of mistakes made by his forebears, but his execution, Pushkin claimed, was an illegal act which was avenged by Napoleon, whom Pushkin still regarded as an 'autocratic villain' and a 'reproach to God on earth'. The poem ends with a description of the assassination of Paul I, which Pushkin holds up as a warning to the Tsars that 'neither punishments, nor rewards, nor prison walls, nor altars' can protect them. He calls upon them to 'bow their heads under the safe protection of the law' that ought to become the 'eternal guardian of the throne and of the peace and liberty of the people'.

The attitude of the authorities to the Ode becomes clear from the following passage in the official letter Pushkin was given to deliver to

General Ivan Inzov, under whom he was to serve during his exile in Bessarabia:

> Some of Pushkin's poetic works and, particularly, his *Ode to Liberty* attracted the attention of the government. Among the great beauties of its idea and style, this poem reveals the dangerous principles derived from the contemporary school, or rather system, of anarchy, which is unscrupulously described as the system of human rights, of freedom and independence of nations.

This letter was approved by Alexander I who, as becomes clear from Pushkin's *Imaginary Conversation*, was incensed by the detailed description of his father's assassination at the end of the poem.

One of the most popular political poems Pushkin wrote between 1817 and 1820 was his famous *Epistle to Chaadaev*, usually dated 1818, but probably written shortly after his *Liberty: an Ode*. Pushkin was a constant visitor at the expensive suite of rooms in the Hotel Demut occupied by Chaadaev at the time. He described it in the First Canto of *Eugene Onegin* as supposedly Onegin's suite of rooms:

> Amber on pipes from Tsargrad, porcelain and bronzes on the table, and perfume, the delight of pampered senses in cut-crystal phials; combs, little files of steel, straight and curved scissors and brushes of thirty kinds for the nails and teeth. Rousseau (let me observe in passing) could not understand how pompous Grimm dared clean his nails in front of him, the eloquent crackpot. The advocate of liberty and human rights was not right in this particular case. One can be a sensible man and care for the beauty of one's nails [a hint, surely, at his own preoccupation with his fingernails]; why waste your time arguing with the age? Custom is a despot among men. A second Chaadaev, my Eugene, afraid of jealous censures, was a pedant in his dress and what we'd call a dandy. He spent at least three hours before his mirror and emerged from his dressing-room like flighty Venus when, donning a man's attire, the goddess drives to a masked ball.

Chaadaev was certainly famous for his elegance but, unlike Onegin, he was constantly preoccupied with philosophical and political problems. Indeed, he was to create a sensation in 1836 by the publication of his first *Philosophic Letter* in which he declared his preference for the Roman Church and attacked the stagnation of Russian society. For this the authorities declared him insane and put him under house arrest. In 1818 he became a member of the revolutionary Union of Welfare. Chaadaev and Pushkin used to meet, argue and discuss all sorts of questions. It was under the impression of one of their talks that Pushkin wrote his *Epistle to Chaadaev*. The poem, which was widely circulated at the time, is much more mature than *Liberty: an Ode*, but its theme is the same.

Pushkin wrote his next poem, *The Village*, at Mikhailovskoye between the middle of July and the middle of August, 1819. The innocuous first part was published in the collection of his poems in 1825 under the title of *Solitude*. It bears a striking resemblance to his earlier sentimental elegies with their usual theme of seclusion far from the city's 'pleasures and corrupt delusions'. The descriptive passages, however, are already remarkable for an objectivity that was to become characteristic of his later poems. It is quite easy to recognise the Mikhailovskoye landscape as seen from the porch of the country house:

I love the dark garden with its coolness and flowers, the field with its aromatic hayricks, the bright streams which run noisily among the bushes . . . the azure meadows between two lakes on which the sail of a fisherman sometimes shows up white in the distance and behind them a chain of hills and striped cornfields . . . in the distance scattered huts, herds wandering along the wet banks, smoking barns and windmills . . .

So far the landscape seems to be a faithful reproduction of the topographical features of the countryside around Mikhailovskoye. What follows, however, is something quite different from Pushkin's former elegiac effusions:

Here, freed from restless constraints, I study how to find bliss in truth, how to worship the law with a free soul, how not to listen to the murmurings of an unenlightened crowd, how to reply with sympathy to timid supplications, and how not to envy the fate of a villain or a fool in their unrighteous splendour.

So carefully did Pushkin conceal the political significance of his verse that the censor did not object to the publication of these lines.

The second part of the poem was circulated in manuscript copies, since no censorship would ever have allowed publication. The poem was first published in full in London in 1856 by Herzen and in Russia only in 1870. In the second part the idyllic note is replaced by an angry and rhetorical one. Pushkin paints a horrifying picture of serfdom:

Here savage landlordism, without feeling and without law, has with the help of the oppressive rod appropriated both labour, property and the husbandman's time. Stooping over the plough that does not belong to him and in obedience to the whip, haggard slavery drags itself along the furrows of the implacable landlord.

One of the most evil consequences of serfdom was the life house-serfs were forced to live in the mansions of their masters. This is how Pushkin describes the horror of a house-serf's life:

Here young girls flower to satisfy the whims of a callous villain. Young boys, the support of their ageing parents, are taken from the family cottages to multiply the crowds of exhausted slaves. O, if only my voice had the power to stir hearts . . . Will I ever, O friends, see people who are not oppressed and slavery abolished by the will of the Tsar, and will the beautiful dawn at last rise over my country, enlightened by freedom?

Much more deadly were the political satires Pushkin wrote between 1818 and 1820. In his poem *Fairy Tales* (*Noelles*, 1818), which was supposed to be a Christmas carol, Pushkin refers to the address Alexander I gave at the opening of the Polish Seym of March 15, 1818. In it Alexander promised to grant a constitution not only to Poland, but also to the rest of Russia. At the Aachen Congress the following September, Alexander I, together with the Emperor of Austria and the King of Prussia, signed a declaration in favour of the preservation of the present order and of the 'protection' of their peoples against any revolutionary movements. *Noelles*, which was another reason for Pushkin's exile two years later, begins with a withering reference to Alexander I: 'Hurrah, the wandering despot, has galloped back to Russia,' and goes on to tell of the Child Jesus weeping bitterly and all the nations after him. Mary tries to stop the Saviour's tears by threatening Him with the arrival of the Russian Tsar. The Tsar comes in and, after telling 'our Saviour' of the 'uniform' he and the Prussian and Austrian Kings made for themselves, tells his people to rejoice for he was 'well fed, healthy and fat'. 'Listen,' he says, 'what I intend to do afterwards: I shall send Lavrov [the director of the executive department of the Ministry of Police] to a lunatic asylum;

I shall restore law in place of Gorgoli [the Petersburg Chief of Police] and grant man human rights as an instance of my imperial favour and of my own free will.' The Holy Infant in the bed wept for joy, but was not sure whether Alexander was 'joking or not'. But his mother tells him to go to sleep unless he wants 'to listen to our father the Tsar telling you more fairy tales'. The poem became famous overnight. According to Ivan Yakushkin, a leading member of one of the secret revolutionary societies, 'everyone knew the poem by heart and sang it almost in the streets.'

Pushkin also wrote a number of revolutionary epigrams, such as the one on the all-powerful Arakcheyev, 'the friend and brother of the Tsar' and 'the oppressor of all Russia', a man who is 'full of malice and vengeance, a man without intellect, without feelings, without honour', and another on Alexander himself in which the Emperor is described as 'brought up under a drum', and as 'a dashing captain who ran away under Austerlitz and shook with fear in 1812', and a 'professor of drill' who 'soon got tired of army drill', and was 'just a Collegiate Assessor in foreign affairs'. One of Pushkin's epigrams on Karamzin resulted in a rift between them which Pushkin deeply regretted. 'One of the best epigrams [against Karamzin],' Pushkin wrote in an autobiographical note, 'has been ascribed to me: this is not the best feature of my life.' The epigram sums up the true political significance of Karamzin's *History of the Russian State* in the following four lines:

> In his History, elegance and simplicity
> Prove to us, without any bias
> The need for autocracy
> And the delights of the whip [*knout*].

The chief work Pushkin wrote between 1817 and 1820 was *Ruslan and Lyudmila*, his first great narrative poem. The final text of the poem must have been written after the publication of Karamzin's *History* in 1818, since some of its incidents are based on it. Pushkin left a full account of the time when he first read Karamzin's *History* and what he thought of it. He was just recovering from a serious illness. In 1826 he wrote:

Illness for a time put a stop to the mode of life chosen by me. I was suffering from typhoid fever. Leyton would not answer for me. My family was in despair; but six weeks later I recovered. During my illness my friends often visited me and their conversation helped to shorten the tedious evenings. Convalescence is a most delightful experience. I remember the impatience with which I waited for the spring, although, as a rule, that season of the year makes me feel depressed and is even harmful to my health. But during my illness I got so thoroughly fed up with the stuffy air and the closed windows that spring appeared to my imagination in all its poetic charm. It was February, 1818. The first eight volumes of Karamzin's Russian *History* had just been published. I read them in bed with great eagerness and attention. The publication of this book (as was to be expected) created a great stir and produced a powerful impression. Three thousand copies were sold in one month (which no one expected, not even Karamzin himself), an unprecedented event in our country.

By the end of October, 1818, Pushkin had completed the first two cantos of *Ruslan and Lyudmila*. 'Cricket,' Batyushkov wrote to a fellow member of Arzamas, about the middle of October, 'is about to start on the third canto of his poem. A wonderful rare talent: good taste, wit, invention, gaiety. At nineteen Ariosto couldn't have written anything better.' Batyushkov concluded his letter with the usual refrain of all Pushkin's literary friends at the time: 'I am sorry he gives himself up to a life of dissipation to the detriment of himself and us, lovers of fine poetry.' On December 3, 1818, Alexander Turgenev wrote to Vyazemsky: 'For all his dissipated way of life, Pushkin is just finishing the fourth canto of his poem.' But it was only on August 19, 1819, that Turgenev could inform Vyazemsky that 'the shaven Pushkin (Pushkin with head shaven after his serious illness), had arrived from the country and read the fifth canto of the poem. On February 25, 1820, Turgenev finally wrote to Vyazemsky that Pushkin had 'almost finished' his poem and that it was time Pushkin thought of publishing it. Turgenev wrote:

I also hope that when it is published Pushkin will derive another benefit: for seeing himself among the published authors and, therefore, authors who deserve to be respected, he will start respecting himself and become less wild in his conduct. Now he is only known from his small poems and his big escapades, but when his poem is published people, I hope, will regard him, if not as an academic wit, at least not as a rake of the first order.

The rough copy of *Ruslan and Lyudmila* bears the date: '26th at night'. On March 26, Pushkin read the poem at Zhukovsky's. In honour of that occasion, Zhukovsky presented Pushkin with his portrait with an inscription in which he acknowledged Pushkin's superiority as a poet: 'To the victorious pupil from the vanquished teacher on the great and solemn day on which he finished his poem *Ruslan and Lyudmila*. March 26, 1820, Good Friday.' Pushkin, though, was still revising the poem, for on March 28 he wrote to Vyazemsky: 'My poem is about to be finished. I shall probably finish the last canto during the next few days.' It was only on April 21 that he informed Vyazemsky that he had finished his poem. 'Only the last, that is to say, the final verse,' he wrote, 'gave me true pleasure. You will read extracts from it in the journals and receive it when published. I am so sick and tired of it that I cannot bring myself to copy it out in bits for you.'

The manuscript was not quite ready for the printers when Pushkin was forced to leave Petersburg on May 6, 1820. A day before Alexander Turgenev wrote to Vyazemsky: 'We will try to get the poem from him, read it and then consign it to immortality, that is to say, to print.' Pushkin authorised the poet and translator Gnedich to supervise the publication of his poem, which Gnedich did with some assistance from Zhukovsky.

The autobiographical epilogue to the poem with its elegiac memories and glimpses of the Caucasian mountains was written on July 26, 1820, during Pushkin's travels in the Caucasus. The prologue, full of magic and mystery and evoking a mood of wonder and expectation unequalled in any of Pushkin's poems, was written six years later, while Pushkin was under house arrest in Mikhailovskoye, and published in the second edition in 1828.

According to Pavel Annenkov, Pushkin's first biographer, Pushkin consulted all sorts of people when writing *Ruslan and Lyudmila*, including Olenin who, Annenkov writes: 'was the first to recognise the poetic merit of *Ruslan and Lyudmila*. Our poet was received at Olenin's house, as though he were a member of the family and often carried on discussions on art with Olenin.'

There is a great deal that is derivative in *Ruslan and Lyudmila*. Pushkin himself admitted the influence of Voltaire's *La Pucelle d'Orléans*, Ariosto's *Orlando Furioso*, Maykov's *Yelisey* and Bogdanovich's *Dushenka*. Traces of Russian folk tales can also be discovered in the poem. In spite of this, it is an original work in the truest sense of the word. Many attempts were made by the Russian poets of the time, including Zhukovsky, to write a romantic poem based on Russian folk lore. But the fantastic fairy tale elements in *Ruslan and Lyudmila*, the conventional character of which Pushkin himself emphasised ironically in the poem, are diametrically opposed to the medieval religious ideas and the visions beyond the grave of Zhukovsky's romantic poems. Its heroes care nothing for heaven or hell. They do not die of grief, for the instinct of life is strong in them. It is full of the joy of life which is entirely in keeping with the spirit of Russian folk tales with their happy endings, their triumphant heroes and final victory of good over evil. One of the most striking peculiarities of Pushkin's genius appears for the first time in this poem, namely, the author's own ironic comments on the events of his fantastic tale. This detached ironic attitude, which enables Pushkin to indulge in all sorts of lyrical digressions, will reappear in the first cantos of *Eugene Onegin*. It is already apparent in Pushkin's earlier lyrical poems as well as in his epistles to his friends. The same boon companions Pushkin addresses in *Ruslan and Lyudmila*: 'But you, my rivals in love, live in friendship, if you can. Believe me, my friends, if fate allots a young maid's heart to a man, she will love him in the teeth of the universe; it is silly and sinful to be angry, for did God grant us only one joy in the sublunar world? You still have left, as a solace, war, Muses and wine.' Prudish readers were appalled by the poem's eroticism, which is merely a follow-up of the erotic poems he wrote during his membership of the Green Lamp. The amorous adventures and gay parties described in those poems were to some extent meant as a demonstration against the official mysticism and sanctimoniousness at court.

The voice of the narrator of the poem divulging his plans and moods can be heard not only in the lyrical digressions, but also throughout the poem, whose characters are always described ironically. Though fairy-tale figures, they are endowed with certain features that make them much more alive than the heroes of earlier poems of a similar type, for Pushkin took great care to endow each of his characters with traits that distinguished them from each other.

Ruslan and Lyudmila, though it contains traces of the poetic diction of both Batyushkov and Zhukovsky, shows a much closer approximation to colloquial speech. The poem does not reflect contemporary life, nor does it seem to have any connection with the social and political problems which Pushkin had raised in his *Liberty: an Ode*, *The Village* and his *Epistle to Chaadaev*. This to some extent explains Pushkin's dissatisfaction with himself and his environment. 'Petersburg,' he wrote to Vyazemsky in April, 1820, 'is stifling to a poet. I crave for distant places: the southern air will perhaps revive my spirit.' His wish was fulfilled, though not in the way he planned.

PART THREE

1820-1824
The Exile

I

Let me begin with the eggs of Leda. Having arrived in Yekaterinoslav
I got bored, went for a sail on the Dnieper, had a swim and caught a
fever as usual. General Raevsky, who was travelling to the Caucasus
with his son and two daughters, found me in a Jewish hut, in a fever
without a doctor, a mug of iced lemonade beside me. His son (you know
our close friendship and his important services which I shall never
forget) proposed that I should travel with them to the Caucasian waters
and the doctor who accompanied them promised not to starve me to
death on the way. Inzov gave me his blessing and wished me a happy
journey. I lay in the carriage feeling ill, but after a week I completely
recovered. I lived two months in the Caucasus; the waters helped me
greatly, especially the hot sulphur ones. However, I also bathed in the
warm acidulous sulphur water, the iron water and the acidulous cold
water. All these medicinal springs are not far distant from one another
in the last foothills of the Caucasian mountains. I am sorry you could
not see this magnificent range of mountains; their icy summits which in
the clear dawn look from a distance like strange, many-coloured and
motionless clouds; I regret that you could not climb with me the sharp
peak of five-ridged Beshtu, of Mashuk and Iron Stone and Serpentine.
The Caucasian region, the torrid boundary of Asia, is interesting in all
respects . . .

This is how Pushkin described his journey to the Caucasus in a letter
to his brother from Kishinev on September 24, 1820. It is Pushkin's first
attempt to communicate with his family. He left fearing that, shocked by
his exile, his parents might try 'to erase' his younger brother 'from my
heart' as he wrote to Delvig on March 23, 1821. As always in Pushkin's
letters to his friends and relations, the most personal events of his life are
carefully glossed over. Pushkin had been put under the special care of
General Inzov who was entrusted with the task of leading him back to the

path of 'faith and virtue'. As a result of the special efforts of Pushkin's Petersburg friends, Inzov was also authorised to grant Pushkin leave of absence. It was arranged that Pushkin should spend some time in the Caucasus and the Crimea with the family of General Nikolai Raevsky. At the time Raevsky's wife and his two elder daughters, Yekaterina, twenty-two, and Yelena, sixteen, were in Petersburg and the General himself with his younger son, Nikolai, and his two younger daughters, Maria fourteen, and Sofia, twelve, were in Kiev. His wife and his two daughters were about to leave for the Crimea, while the General and his younger son and two daughters were to go to the Caucasus, where his elder son Alexander was undergoing a cure. It would seem that Pushkin travelled to Yekaterinoslav via Kiev where he made final arrangements with the Raevskys to travel with them to the Caucasus. A week after his arrival in Yekaterinoslav, the Raevskys joined him there and took him with them. The General's party included a Russian nurse, an English governess, a Tartar lady companion, a physician, Doctor Eustaphy Rudykovsky, and a French tutor. According to the doctor, they found Pushkin 'lying on a wooden bench in a dirty hut, unshaven, pale and thin'. The Raevsky party left Yekaterinoslav on May 26, 1820, Pushkin travelling in a carriage with Nikolai Raevsky, a Captain of a Hussar Guards regiment at the time. General Raevsky and the doctor travelled in another carriage and Raevsky's daughters, the English governess, the nurse and the Tartar lady companion in a third. On the shore of the Taganrog Bay occurred the incident which Maria Raevsky some twenty years later romanticised in her memoirs:

I remember how during this journey not far from Taganrog I was driving in a carriage with my sister Sofia, our English governess, our Russian nurse and our lady companion. At the sight of the sea, we all told our driver to stop and our whole crowd left the carriage and ran towards the sea . . . Not suspecting that the poet was walking behind us, I began to amuse myself by running after the waves and then running away from them as soon as they were about to reach me; in the end my feet got wet which, of course, I did not tell anyone about when I returned to our carriage. Pushkin found this scene so beautiful that he described it in his charming verses, poeticising my childish prank. I was only fifteen at the time:

How I envy the waves – running in stormy succession
To lie down lovingly at her feet!

How much I wished then with the waves
To touch her dear feet with my lips.
[*Eugene Onegin*, Canto One, Stanza XXXIII]

Maria Raevsky was not yet fifteen at the time. She was a rather unattractive, dark-skinned girl and if Pushkin really had her in mind in the stanza she quotes in her memoirs he would hardly have gone on to express his longing to kiss her lips 'with such anguish' or 'the roses' of her 'ardent cheeks', or her 'breasts, full of languor'. Maria certainly 'poeticised' the whole incident or, more plainly, invented it, leading many a Pushkin scholar sadly astray about Pushkin's supposed infatuation with her.

Pushkin and the Raevskys arrived in Pyatigorsk on June 6, 1820. There Pushkin met Alexander Raevsky, whom he described in his letter to his brother (quite mistakenly, as it turned out) as one who was going 'to be more than merely known'. Alexander Raevsky was four years older than Pushkin. He was a tall, thin, even bony man with a small, round, closely cropped head, a dark yellowish complexion and innumerable wrinkles and creases on his face. A cold sceptic, the sardonic expression which hardly ever left his face was emphasised by a very large mouth and thin lips. He was close shaven and wore spectacles which did not conceal the cynical gleam of his small, yellowish eyes which reminded Pushkin of the eyes of Voltaire. For the next two years Pushkin was completely under the spell of Alexander Raevsky. He even put up with Alexander's gibes at his poems. In the end, Alexander was to prove himself a treacherous friend. Pushkin drew a psychological portrait of him in *The Demon*, a poem written in 1824 after he had become aware of his friend's treachery. A year later he tried, not very convincingly, to deny the similarity between Alexander Raevsky and the Demon by the guarded statement that 'it seems to me that they [those who identified the two] must be wrong'. Pushkin describes the Demon as 'some evil genius' who began paying him visits at a time when 'lofty feelings, freedom, fame and love, and the inspiration of art stirred my blood so violently'. The Demon's 'smile, look and sarcastic speeches poured cold poison into my soul . . .' The Demon 'despised inspiration, did not believe in love . . . and refused to bless anything in nature'.

Pushkin and the Raevskys went for long trips in the surrounding countryside. They visited a Scottish missionary colony which Pushkin mentions in his unfinished poem *Tazit* (1829) in an attempt to show how the work of the Scottish missionaries conflicted with the warlike customs of the wild Circassian tribes.

After leaving Pyatigorsk, the Raevskys and Pushkin spent some time among the natives of a wild and deserted region surrounded by forests and mountains. Pushkin liked to visit Tartar villages, sometimes on horseback and sometimes on foot. On one of these trips in the mountains an old soldier told Pushkin about his life as a captive of the Caucasian mountaineers, which no doubt suggested to him the subject of his first romantic poem, *The Caucasian Captive*. Pushkin enjoyed listening to the legends and songs of the mountaineers. 'The Georgian songs,' he wrote in one of his notes to *The Caucasian Captive*, 'are mostly doleful, but quite pleasant. They glorify the brief successes of Caucasian arms, acts of treachery, murders and sometimes love and pleasures.'

Pushkin never disguised his nationalistic sentiments which during the Polish insurrection of 1830 made him use the phrase '*delenda est Varsovia*' in a letter to a friend, followed by his rabid poem *To the Slanderers of Russia*, written on August 16, 1831, shortly before the capture of Warsaw by the Russian forces. In a letter to his brother in September, 1820, he expressed the hope that not only would the Caucasus bring the Russians and Persians together 'for safe trading', but also that 'perhaps' Napoleon's 'chimerical plan of conquering India' would one day come true 'so far as we are concerned'. He greatly admired the Cossacks who stood guard 'over our possessions' and were always ready to fight:

I travelled in sight of the hostile fields of the free mountain peoples. We were surrounded by a company of sixty Cossacks and behind us a loaded cannon with a lighted slow match was being dragged . . . From the peninsula of Taman, the ancient principality of Tmutarakan, I caught sight of the shores of the Crimea . . . In Kerch . . . I expected to see the ruins of the tomb of Mithridates and the traces of Panticapaeum [where Mithridates was supposed to have committed suicide in 63 B.C.], I expected to – but all I saw was a heap of stones and rough-hewn rocks in the cemetery on the adjacent mountains. I noticed also a few steps, the work of human hands. Whether this is a tomb or the ancient foundations of a tower, I do not know. A few miles further we stopped on the *Golden Mound*. Rows of stones, a ditch now almost level with the ground – that was all that was left of the city of Panticapaeum. No doubt a great deal that is of value is hidden under the earth piled up by the centuries . . . From Kerch we travelled to Kefa [Theodossia] where we stayed at the house of Bronevsky [an ex-mayor of Theodossia], a man honoured for his incorruptibility and his poverty. From Kefa we set off by sea past the southern shores of Tauris to Gurzuf where Raevsky's family was. At night on board ship I wrote an elegy which I am sending you . . . The ship sailed alongside mountains covered with poplars, vineyards, laurels and cypresses; Tartar villages were scattered all over the place; the ship stopped in sight of Gurzuf. I spent three weeks there.

Pushkin goes on to describe 'the happiest moments' of his life, spent with the Raevsky family and how he was particularly drawn to General Raevsky whom he loved as 'a man of a clear mind, a simple and beautiful soul'. The Raevsky girls, too, Pushkin declared to be 'charming'. Even in his letter to his brother he was unable to disguise his admiration for the oldest, Yekaterina, whom he declared to be 'an unusual woman'. His cherished hope was to see again 'the southern shore and the Raevsky family'. 'Judge whether I was happy,' he wrote. 'A free, untroubled life in the circle of a charming family, a life which I love so much and which I had never enjoyed – a happy southern sky, an enchanting region, scenery which satisfies the imagination – mountains, orchards, the sea . . .'

Pushkin concluded the letter with an appeal to his brother to 'honour' poetry, 'a good intelligent old lady on whom one may drop in sometimes to forget for a moment the slanders, the newspapers and the cares and worries of life, to be cheered by her charming chatter and her fairy tales, though to fall in love with her is unwise'. After mentioning General Mikhail Orlov, who was shortly to be his successful rival by marrying Yekaterina Raevsky, Pushkin made a rather brief reference to his parents and ended by an appeal for money: 'I need money, I need it badly,' a cry for help that was to go on all through his exile and was never to be satisfied.

From Theodossia, which they left on August 18, 1820, Pushkin and the Raevskys sailed to Gurzuf on board a naval brig put at the disposal of the General. It was on board the brig that Pushkin wrote his first Crimean poem which he mentioned in his letter to his brother. This was a romantic elegy beginning with the line 'The orb of day has set'. It was remarkable not so much for its descriptive passages as for Pushkin's own feelings at the time and, particularly, for his mention of 'the insane love' he remembered and 'everything I have suffered and everything that was dear to my heart, the anguished illusions, hopes and desires'.

A much more detailed description of Pushkin's experiences in the Crimea can be found in a note he wrote in December, 1824, in the form of a letter to D [Delvig]:

From Asia we crossed over to Europe on a ship. I went at once to see the so-called Tomb of Mithridates (the ruins of a sort of tower); there I picked a flower in memory of my visit and lost it the next day without the least compunction. The ruins of Panticapaeum did not make any stronger impression on my imagination. I saw traces of streets, a half overgrown ditch, old bricks – and that was all. From Theodossia to Gurzuf I went by sea. I did not sleep all night. There was no moon, the stars glittered; in front of me in the mist stretched the southern mountains . . . 'There's Chatyrdag,' the captain said to me. I could not make it out and I was not particularly interested. I fell asleep before dawn. Meanwhile the ship dropped anchor in sight of Gurzuf. On awaking, I saw a most delightful scene. The multicoloured mountains shimmered brightly; the flat roofs of the Tartar huts looked from a distance like beehives stuck to the mountains; the poplars, like green pillars, rose gracefully between them; on the right was the enormous Ayu-dag . . . and all around the clear blue sky and bright sea and the brilliant light and the meridional air.

In Gurzuf I hardly stirred from my place; I bathed in the sea and gorged myself on grapes; I got used at once to the southern climate and enjoyed it with all the indifference and unconcern of a Neapolitan *lazzarone*. On awaking at night, I loved to hear the roar of the sea and I would listen to it for hours. A few yards from my house grew a young cypress tree; every morning I paid a visit to it. I became attached to it with a feeling that was indistinguishable from friendship. That is all that my stay in Gurzuf has left in my memory.

I travelled all round the southern shore and Muravyov's *Journey over Tauris* revived many memories; but his terrible crossing over the Kikeneis cliffs has not left a single trace in my memory. We clambered up the mountain steps on foot, holding on to the tails of our Tartar horses. This amused me very much and seemed to me to be a kind of mysterious oriental ritual. The first thing that struck me on crossing the mountains was a birch tree; a northern birch tree! My heart missed a beat; I even began to long for the dear south, although I was still in the Crimea and was still seeing poplars and vines. The St George Monastery and its steep steps to the sea left a powerful impression on me. It was there that I saw the fabulous ruins of the Temple of Diana.

It seems I am luckier with mythological legends than with historical memories. At any rate, it was there that I was inspired to write a few lines of poetry . . .

I arrived in Bakhchisaray ill. I had heard before about the strange memorial of the lovesick Khan. K . . . described it in a very poetical fashion and called it *la fontaine des larmes*. On entering the palace, I saw a crumbling fountain; from a rusty iron funnel water trickled in drops. I walked through the palace feeling greatly vexed at the neglect by which it is decaying and with the semi-European restoration of some of the tombs. N.N. almost forced me to go up a rickety staircase leading to the ruins of the harem and the Khan's cemetery, but my heart was not full of that at the time; I was in the throes of a fever.

As for the memorial of the Khan's mistress, which Muravyov speaks of, I did not remember it when I wrote my poem or I should have most certainly made use of it.

Explain to me why the meridional shore and Bakhchisaray exert such an inexplicable fascination over me. Why do I feel such a strong desire to re-visit the places I left with such indifference? Or is memory itself the strongest faculty of our mind which charms everything in its power?

The 'K . . .' in Pushkin's description of his visit to the Palace of Bakhchisaray, which was so soon to inspire him to write one of his most melodious poems, has greatly puzzled Pushkin scholars, who were hot on the trail of several promising young women. Maria Raevsky is a keen favourite of Soviet critics, chiefly it seems because she followed her husband, General Sergey Volkonsky, one of the Decembrist leaders, to Siberia. More recent research associates the mysterious 'K . . .' with Kiselev, Sofia Potocki's married name.

Although Pushkin spent only about thirty days in the Crimea, the memory of it seems to have haunted him all through his life. As late as 1830, when writing *Onegin's Journey*, the last unfinished Canto of *Eugene Onegin*, he recalled his first glimpse of the Crimea from aboard the naval brig:

You are beautiful, shores of Tauris, when seen from board ship by
the light of the morning star, as I saw you for the first time: You
appeared to me in bridal splendour: in the blue, translucent sky shone
the piles of your mountains, valleys, trees, the tracery of your villages
was spread before me and there, amid the Tartar huts . . . what ardour
was awakened in me! With what magic longing my ardent breast was
constricted . . .

Many years earlier, in the concluding stanza of *The Fountain of
Bakhchisaray*, Pushkin had described the Gurzuf landscape almost in the
same ecstatic terms:

A miraculous region! A delight to the eye!
Everything is alive there: hills, woods,
The amber and sapphire of the grape,
The warm beauty of the valleys,
And the coolness of the streams and the poplars . . .
Everything enchants the feelings of the traveller,
When in the carefree hour of the morning,
In the mountains, along the shore road
His experienced horse canters,
And the greenish waves,
Sparkle and resound
Around the rocks of Ayu-dag.

In Gurzuf the Raevskys occupied the two-storied country house of the
Duc de Richelieu, a French émigré and former Governor-General of
Novorossiysk. Pushkin and Nikolai Raevsky lived in one of the corner
rooms of this house. In Richelieu's large library Pushkin found the works
of Voltaire, André Chénier and, particularly, Lord Byron, which he read
in a French prose translation and under whose spell he wrote both
The Caucasian Captive and *The Fountain of Bakhchisaray*. In his unfinished
article on *The Refutation of Criticism* (1830), he admits that both poems
had been greatly influenced by Byron 'about whom I raved at the time'.

On a rock over the bay Pushkin found the ruins of a fort constructed by
the Emperor Justinian I. One of the towers of the fort was still standing.
Pushkin described the ruins of this fortress in an unfinished poem he
wrote in 1821:

When the moon shone over the bay,
I used to wander on the sea-shore
And contemplate in their proud decline
. . . The waves beat round the scorched ramparts
Around decaying walls and deserted turrets.

In another unfinished poem Pushkin recalled the Greek cemetery near the fortress:

Near the crumbling walls over a fallen urn
I could see through the dark woods
The vaults of rocks and the azure sparkle of the sea,
And the sky bright like joy.

There are also reminiscences of the Gurzuf cliffs in his poems *Storm* (1825), *Talisman* (1827) and others.

The Raevskys and Pushkin left Gurzuf on September 5, for Yalta, at the time a small village. They travelled to Alupka where they spent a night in a small Tartar cottage. The next night they spent in St George Monastery, described by Pushkin in his letter to D. After a visit to the Temple of Diana, Pushkin and his companions left for Bakhchisaray, where they arrived on September 7. In the Tartar language Bakhchisaray means a Palace of Gardens. Until the conquest of the Crimea by Russia, the town was the capital city of the Crimean Khans.

In the Crimea Pushkin fell desperately in love not with Maria, but with the twenty-two-year-old Yekaterina. Yekaterina struck her contemporaries not only as beautiful, intelligent and well educated, but also as cunning and masterful. The Raevsky family album has a caricature of Yekaterina, showing her standing over the kneeling figure of her husband, Mikhail Orlov, with a bunch of birch twigs in her hand. Two poems Pushkin wrote in Gurzuf refer directly to her. In the first, *Nereis*, Pushkin described how 'hidden between trees and hardly daring to breathe', he watched a sea nymph raising her 'young bosom, white as a swan, over the clear waters', and squeezing the 'foamy water in a stream from her hair'. This indiscreet, Peeping-Tom experience in six lines was published in 1824 by Alexander Bestuzhev in his journal *The Pole Star*, together with Pushkin's much longer elegy beginning with the line 'The scudding ridge of clouds is thinning out'. The elegy referred unmistakably to Yekaterina in the last three lines describing 'a young maiden' looking for a star in the twilight and calling it with her name to her girl friends. This 'sad evening star' was at first assumed by Pushkin scholars to have been the planet Venus. Since Venus could not have risen at that particular time over Gurzuf, it gave rise to a number of most ingenious academic speculations. It has more recently been identified with Jupiter, a planet Yekaterina seems to have identified with herself. Pushkin's elegy made the 'star' famous and Mikhail Orlov in one of his letters to his wife, writes that every time he sees 'that famous star' he hails its appearance from his balcony the moment it rises over the horizon.

Pushkin protested angrily to Bestuzhev for publishing the two poems without his permission. He wrote on June 29, 1824:

> Judge for yourself. I happened once to be madly in love. In such a case I usually write elegies just as another man soils his bed, but do you think it is the act of a friend to hang out my wet sheets for everyone to see? The Lord forgive you, but you have disgraced me in the current number of your *Star* by publishing the three last lines of my elegy . . . Imagine my despair when I saw them in print. The journal may fall into her hands. What will she think when she sees how readily I talk about her *with one of my Petersburg cronies*? How is she to know that I did not mention her name . . . that the devil only knows who delivered that damned elegy to you and that it is nobody's fault? I confess that I value one thought of that woman more than the views of all the journals in the world and of our entire public.

Why Pushkin should have been so upset by the publication of the three innocent last lines of the elegy is difficult to imagine unless it was the simultaneous publication of *Nereis*, in which he confessed watching Yekaterina bathing naked in the sea.

Some of Pushkin's poems written between 1820 and 1821 also refer unmistakably to Yekaterina. Pushkin for obvious reasons post-dated them to 1824. In one addressed to 'O, maiden rose', he admits that he is not ashamed to be in her chains for 'so does a nightingale in a laurel bush live in sweet bondage near the proud and beautiful rose and sings tender songs to her in the passionate darkness of the night'. In another, *To a Maiden*, he warns an 'incautious friend' to be careful not to 'observe another nor seek other eyes' in the presence of the girl who 'draws hearts to herself with unwitting force'. The supplications of 'favourites of fortune and nursling of fate' are all in vain for 'the proud maiden dislikes their feelings and, dropping her eyes, neither listens nor sees'. It is again Yekaterina's 'pride' as well as her 'smile and cunning look' that, in the poem *A Beautiful Girl Before a Mirror*, is reflected in the mirror as she 'toys with her tresses and encircles her face with flowers'. Yekaterina's 'ravishing' smile is mentioned again in *Dionaea*, the short poem Pushkin wrote a short time before Yekaterina's wedding to Mikhail Orlov in May, 1821: 'Chromides is in love with you: he is young and not once, stealthily, the two of us have observed you; you listen to him, blushing in silence, your downcast eyes are burning with desire, and long afterwards, Dionaea, your face preserves its ravishing smile.'

It was 'proud' Yekaterina again whom Pushkin recalls years later in one of the stanzas of *Onegin's Journey*:

And there among the Tartar huts . . . what ardour awakened in me! With what magical longing did my blazing breast contract! But, Muse, forget the past! Whatever feelings were hidden in me at the time, none is left: they have all disappeared or changed . . . Peace to you, anxieties of past years! In those days I seem to have longed for deserts, regions of pearly waves, the noise of the sea, piles of rocks, the ideal of a proud maid, and nameless sufferings.

When writing his tragedy *Boris Godunov* in 1825, Pushkin was thinking of Yekaterina, who was to be the prototype of the proud, cunning, masterful, and beautiful Marina Mnishek. He admitted as much in his letter to Vyazemsky on September 13, 1825: 'Today I finished the second part of my tragedy. There will be four parts altogether, I think. My Marina is a wonderful girl – a real Yekaterina Orlov. Do you know her? However, do not tell anyone about this.'

Mikhail Orlov's incompetence as a lover seems to have been common knowledge among his friends. In one of his early poems, beginning with the line: 'Orlov and Istomina in bed' (1817), Pushkin refers to the 'inconstant' general's failure to distinguish himself in 'the ardent business' of love and describes how the famous ballerina, 'not wishing to offend her lover', murmured, picking up a microscope, 'Let me have a look, dear . . .' Pushkin's resentment of Mikhail Orlov's marriage to Yekaterina Raevsky found expression in a characteristically cynical reference to the General's lack of virility. Pushkin wrote to Alexander Turgenev on May 7, 1821:

Orlov has got married. You will ask how? I don't know. Unless he mistook his bald head for the head of his prick and fucked his wife with it. His head is hard; his soul is beautiful; but what the hell do they matter? He has got married, he will put on his dressing-gown and say: *Beatus qui procul.* . . .

2

To find himself immured in Kishinev, where he arrived on September 21, 1820, must have been a terrible blow to Pushkin, especially so soon after his gay life in Petersburg and his more recent romantic journey across the Caucasus and the Crimea. Kishinev, the capital of Bessarabia, was a small provincial town of about a thousand hovels and half a dozen brick houses. Its population consisted of Moldavians with a sprinkling of Russian civil servants and army officers. Bessarabia had become a Russian province only ten years earlier and still preserved many of the characteristics of its former Turkish rule. The Moldavian grandees, some of them members of the Supreme Council of Bessarabia, still wore beards, turbans and oriental garments. The Kishinev ladies, freed from the restraint of Muslim customs, were amorous, but also a little too free with their favours as well as with their tongues.

Vladimir Gorchakov who met Pushkin a short time after his arrival in Kishinev, at the vice-governor's private theatre, left the following description of him in his diary:

My attention was drawn to a rather short young man, with quick and observant eyes, who was extraordinarily agile in his movements and who would often burst out laughing in an excess of gaiety and as suddenly fall into a brown study. The features of his face were irregular and unattractive, but his expression, when engrossed in thought, was so charming that one could not help wishing to ask him what made him brood so much. The young man wore a black frockcoat buttoned to the top and black trousers.

Nikolai Alexeyev, a civil servant on special duty at General Inzov's office, who was to become Pushkin's close friend, introduced Gorchakov to Pushkin during one of the intervals. They began discussing the Petersburg actors and actresses and Gorchakov observed how the memories of his life in Petersburg again cast a gloom over Pushkin:

In this frame of mind, Pushkin left us, made his way between the chairs with all the adroitness and refined courtesy of a man of the world, and stopped before some young woman of his acquaintance. I followed him involuntarily with my eyes and I could not help noticing that his melancholy mood suddenly vanished and that he was again talking animatedly and laughing loudly, his beautiful teeth revealing themselves in all their splendour and a smile never leaving his lips.

This transition from gaiety, manifesting itself in bursts of loud laughter, to fits of overpowering sadness was, according to Pushkin's sister Olga, usual with Pushkin, though perhaps more frequent in Kishinev. 'My disposition,' Pushkin wrote to a friend in December, 1826, 'is uneven, jealous, susceptible to offence and, at the same time, weak.'

Gorchakov wrote again of these sudden quirks of temper, on meeting Pushkin a second time, a day later at a dinner at General Orlov's at which Nikolai Raevsky and his father's two half-brothers, Vasily and Alexander Davydov, were present:

They all seemed to treat Pushkin in a very friendly fashion, except perhaps Alexander Davydov who appeared to assume a patronising air when speaking to Pushkin, which Pushkin did not seem to like very much. Pushkin had just written his ballad *The Black Shawl* [Pushkin wrote it on November 14, 1820], based on a Moldavian folk song, and they were all talking about it. Not knowing the poem myself, I could not take part in the conversation. Pushkin noticed this and promised to recite it, but after reciting a few lines, suddenly snatched up a rapier and began to play about with it, skipping about and striking poses, as though challenging an opponent. At that moment one of General Orlov's aides-de-camp came in and Pushkin, scarcely giving him time to exchange greetings with us, began asking him to have a bout with him. The officer refused. Pushkin kept insisting and, like a naughty child, began poking him with his rapier in jest. The officer pushed the rapier away with his hand, but Pushkin would not be put off and the officer began to be cross. To avoid a quarrel I again asked Pushkin to read me his Moldavian song. He at once agreed, threw away the rapier and began to recite his poem with great animation, each line appearing to inspire him. He seemed to be completely satisfied with his new work.

Next day I went to pay an official visit to General Orlov. During our interview, Pushkin entered. The General embraced him and began reciting *The Black Shawl*. Pushkin laughed and blushed.

'Do you know it already?' he asked.

'As you see,' the General replied.

'You mean, as I hear,' observed Pushkin, laughing.

The General smiled pleasantly at this remark.

'But joking apart,' he went on, 'your ballad is excellent. Every two lines of it are absolutely inimitably complete,' he concluded, assuming the profound expression of an expert patron of the arts, but at the same time glancing quickly at us.

To escape the Kishinev *beau monde*, Pushkin used to visit the Kishinev fairs and the local sporting events. In his poem *The Official and the Poet* (1821), he wrote: 'I love the excitement of the fair, the shouts, the arguments and the heated bargaining . . . I like the crowds, the rags, the noise . . . my mind here penetrates into the spirit of the common people.' He admired, in particular, the wrestling matches at the fairs and told a friend that he would like to learn the art of wrestling. According to another acquaintance, Pushkin 'used to take long walks through the city on festive days and when he came across dancing Moldavians joined them without ceremony and without paying attention to the people who used to come specially to "watch Pushkin".' At the end of the dance, he would leave the Moldavians and join the 'spectators' of the educated classes. He would tell them with relish, how much he enjoyed dancing the Moldavian national dances to the accompaniment of the Moldavian national stringed instruments.

Duels provided another distraction. A few weeks after his arrival in Kishinev, Pushkin nearly fought one with two Hussar officers at once. The incident is recounted at great length in his diary by Lieutenant Colonel Ivan Liprandi, one of Pushkin's closest friends in Kishinev:

At the end of October, 1820, Colonel Fyodor Orlov, who had lost a leg under Bautzen or Herlitz, arrived for a few days in Kishinev. One day after dinner, he came up to me and Colonel Alexeyev [Alexey Alexeyev, a retired colonel, whose brother-in-law was later to marry Pushkin's sister Olga, was the Kishinev postmaster], and said that he'd rather go anywhere than listen to his brother, the General, and his

aide-de-camp Okhotnikov discussing political economy. We gladly
accepted his proposal. He said that it would be a good idea to get
someone else to come with us and, going into the drawing room, came
out with Pushkin arm in arm. We went to Golda's billiards saloon.
There was not a soul there. We ordered some beer and Orlov and
Alexeyev began playing billiards for small stakes. After the third game,
the loser ordered a jug of punch, which we all drank in turn. The first
jug did not seem to have any effect on any of us, but the second did,
and particularly on Pushkin. He grew merry and began walking up to
the billiard table and interfering with the game. Orlov called him a
schoolboy and Alexeyev added that schoolboys had to be taught a
lesson. Pushkin dashed away from me and, disarranging the balls,
began telling the two officers what he thought of them. It ended by his
challenging both of them to a duel and inviting me to be his second.
We had all to meet at my place at ten o'clock next morning. It was
almost midnight. I invited Pushkin to stay the night with me. On the
way to my lodgings he came to his senses and began to abuse himself . . .
When I pointed out to him that what was so awful was that the reason
for the duel was not a very creditable one and that it must not therefore
take place, Pushkin stopped short, and said, 'Never! I'll show them
that I am not a schoolboy!'

'That's all very well,' I replied, 'but people will all the same soon
find out that punch was the real reason for the duel and, besides, the
fight is not evenly matched.'

'How do you mean not evenly matched?' Pushkin asked me, stopping
short a second time.

I tried to appeal to his vanity.

'It is not evenly matched,' I said, 'because it doesn't matter so much
if there are two less out of thousands of colonels but you are unique:
only twenty-two and already famous.'

He made no reply. On approaching my house, he said:

'The whole thing is rotten and disgusting, I agree, but how are we to
settle it?'

'Very easily,' I replied. 'You were the first to interfere with their
game. They said something to you. You said twice as much to them and,
finally, it was not they but you who issued the challenge. If, therefore,
they were to come with a proposal to make it up with you, your honour
will not be in question.'

He was silent for a long time and at last said in French:

'You're making it all up. They will never agree. Alexeyev will, perhaps, because he is a family man, but Orlov never: he has made up his mind to die a natural death, but I am sure he'd prefer to kill me or die by a bullet fired by Pushkin.'

I did not despair of success. After having had something to eat, I put Pushkin to bed. I did not go to bed myself but waited till morning and at eight o'clock went to see Orlov. I was told that he had just left. That worried me a little, for I was afraid that he might have gone to see me. I hurried to see Alexeyev. Driving past my house, I saw that there was no carriage at my doors. When I arrived at Alexeyev's I was overjoyed to see it outside his house. I began to feel more pleased when, as I entered the room, both of them declared in one voice that they were about to go to see me in order to ask my advice how best to bring last night's stupid affair to a satisfactory end.

'That can be done easily,' I replied. 'Come and see me at ten o'clock as arranged. Pushkin will be there and you can tell him that both he and you ought to forget last night's punch.'

They readily agreed, though Orlov doubted whether Pushkin would agree. On returning home, I found Pushkin already dressed and trying to make up his mind what to do about last night's quarrel. When I told him about the result of my meeting with the two colonels, he took me by the hand and asked me to tell him frankly whether his honour would be in any way impugned if he agreed to make it up. I merely repeated that it was not they but he who had challenged them and that they were eager for a peaceful settlement. 'What more do you want?' I asked him. He agreed, but I could not help feeling that he did not trust Orlov to give up such a wonderful opportunity for a fight. However, when I told him that the colonel did not want to do anything that might displease his brother, Pushkin seemed to calm down. It was obvious that what he disliked was that their quarrel should have occurred in a billiard saloon after they had had too much to drink. 'Otherwise,' he declared, 'it would have been lovely to have a fight! Yes, lovely!' Half an hour later, Orlov and Alexeyev arrived. Everything was settled as arranged. All three of them looked very satisfied, though no one was more pleased than I that the matter did not have a tragic sequel: I always hated the role of a second and preferred to act myself. At dinner that day at Alexeyev's, Pushkin was very cheerful and, on the way home, thanked me, saying that if something like that happened again, he would gladly seek my advice.

Duelling was forbidden in Russia, but no Russian nobleman would refuse to fight a duel on the slightest provocation. Pushkin summed up the duelling code of his time in his unfinished story, beginning with the line, 'We spent the evening at a Country House' (1835): 'Some stupid oaf, whom I despise, says something that cannot possibly harm me and yet I find myself in a position where he can blow my brains out. I have no right to refuse that pleasure to the first fire-eater who may take it into his head to test my sang-froid.'

Such an irresponsible fire-eater was Colonel Starov with whom Pushkin was forced to fight a duel in January, 1822. Pushkin had arranged to meet some friends at the so-called Casino in the city park, where balls and parties were usually held. It was the custom for a visitor to ask the band to play the dance he fancied. Pushkin asked the band to play a mazurka, while a newly arrived officer of Colonel Starov's regiment wanted it to play a French quadrille. Pushkin repeated his order, the officer repeated his. Pushkin shouted laughingly for a third time 'Mazurka!' and the band, Vladimir Gorchakov writes, 'in spite of the fact that they were military men themselves and Pushkin was a civilian,' obeyed his order and struck up a mazurka. Colonel Starov, who was present at the Casino, took it as a slight on the honour of his regiment.

'You were uncivil to one of my officers,' he said to Pushkin after the dance. 'Unless you apologise to him you'll have to deal with me personally.'

'I don't know what to apologise for, Colonel,' Pushkin replied. 'As for you, I am at your service.'

'Very well, till tomorrow then,' said Starov.

'Very well, Colonel.'

They shook hands and parted.

The duel was to take place at nine o'clock next morning. The duelling ground was situated in a very picturesque spot among vineyards on top of a hill at the end of a twisting path. But when the duellists and their seconds arrived at the appointed hour, a blizzard blotted out the landscape and prevented them from taking aim. Both fired and missed. Pushkin and the colonel demanded the right to exchange more shots, but missed again.

They then decided to meet another time, but Liprandi again intervened and succeeded in effecting a reconciliation.

In the spring of the same year Pushkin fought another duel with an army officer by the name of Zubov, with whom he had had a quarrel after a game of cards. Pushkin, who, according to Liprandi, appeared on the duelling ground 'looking as cold as ice', is said on this occasion to have filled his cap with cherries and to have been calmly eating them and spitting out the stones in his opponent's direction. This seems to have distracted Zubov who fired first and missed. Pushkin refused to fire and that was the end of the duel. On his way back home mortally wounded after his duel with d'Anthes, Pushkin mentioned his duel with Zubov to Danzas, one of his Lycée classmates who acted as his second. Unfortunately, Danzas did not record what exactly Pushkin had said about it or why he should have mentioned it.

A duel that did not come off and a plot to disgrace Pushkin that misfired followed a quarrel between Pushkin and an elderly official at dinner at Inzov's on January 28, 1822. The official, Ivan Lanov, was, according to Liprandi, a sixty-five-year-old State Councillor and a senior member of the Southern Colonial Office. Liprandi described him as of medium height, heavily built, with a large paunch, bald-headed, with a wide red face, which invariably wore an expression of self-satisfaction. Lanov always had dinner at General Inzov's and met Pushkin at table daily. (On November 5, 1821, Inzov's house was damaged by an earthquake and Inzov moved out, while Pushkin remained there till May, 1822. Pushkin, however, was expected to dine at Inzov's every day as before, the old General making sure that the poet had at least one good meal a day.) Lanov disliked Pushkin's free-and-easy behaviour in the presence of his superiors. As a rule, Lanov paid no attention to Pushkin's conversation, but one day he felt so provoked that he called Pushkin a milksop. Pushkin replied by calling Lanov a winesop. Inzov smiled, got up and retired to his study. Lanov challenged Pushkin to a duel. At first Pushkin only laughed, but in the end he accepted the challenge. According to Prince Pavel Dolgorukov, a reactionary official attached to Inzov's office who was certainly in Lanov's confidence, Lanov asked Pushkin to call on him to discuss the arrangements for the duel. Lanov intended to lay a trap for him by having a number of soldiers concealed in his lodgings, who were to seize Pushkin and flog him. In fact, Inzov, hearing the laughter in the dining room and informed of what had happened, came back and forced them to make it up. Inzov also took steps to see that Pushkin and Lanov never met at dinner again. Pushkin, however, found out that Lanov had intended to flog him and wrote an epigram in which he told Lanov that even if he went on abusing him, he would never provoke him (Pushkin) to slap his (Lanov's) face. 'Your solemn mug,' Pushkin went on, 'is so like an old peasant woman's arse that all it asks for is to be kicked.' The epigram was soon widely circulated in Kishinev and Inzov threatened to put Pushkin under arrest. 'You can do so,' Pushkin replied, 'but I shall insist on being respected even then.'

3

A challenge that to Pushkin's extreme annoyance was rejected, was the upshot of Pushkin's lighthearted affair with Maria Balsh, the wife of a Moldavian grandee. Maria became more than a nuisance when Pushkin's affections were momentarily bestowed on another Moldavian lady. To punish her, Pushkin began to flirt with her twelve-year-old daughter Anka. Maria interpreted this to mean that he wanted to show her that she was too old for him. He wrote her a poem (*To a Coquette*) in which he pointed out that she was thirty and he over twenty, that both of them knew that 'eternal love lasts at most three weeks', that they were good friends at first, but

> boredom, opportunity, a jealous husband – I pretended to be madly in love, you pretended to be shy, we vowed to be true – then – alas! we forgot our vows . . . we parted . . . We could once more have lived without quarrelling, in peace and amity, but no! This morning you suddenly resurrected the ancient past in a tragic scene – once more you preach the love of the dead knights-errant, courteous ardour, sadness, jealousy – good heavens! I am not a child, although a poet. In our declining years, we ought to give up the youthful ardour of passions – you to your older daughter, I to my younger brother: they can still enjoy life and be ready to shed tears; it becomes them to kiss, while it is time for us to start talking scandal.

Such a poem was not likely to appease the scorned Maria: to talk of their 'declining years' was adding insult to injury. Pushkin liked women to be as free in conversation with him as he was with them. This time, however, Maria went too far in telling Pushkin what she thought of him. His 'unlimited vanity', Liprandi commented, was hurt and, as he could not very well challenge a woman, he rushed quixotically to her husband, waving a pistol and demanding satisfaction. Her husband not unnaturally refused. Pushkin met him again at the house of a mutual friend, this time armed with an iron stick. While it was impossible to demand satisfaction from a woman, he said, there was nothing to prevent him slapping the face of her husband. This he did, but it seemed that Moldavian nobles did not share the acute sense of honour of their Russian counterparts. Balsh simply lodged a complaint with General Inzov, who promptly put Pushkin under house arrest from March 8 to March 22, 1822. In a fragment of a poem, written while under arrest, Pushkin described Balsh in uncomplimentary terms as 'a coward and a coarse fellow'.

The only real trouble Pushkin had with one of his more serious love affairs in Kishinev occurred when he *was* challenged by the husband, a local landowner by the name of Inglesi, and 'meek Ivan', (as General Inzov was known among his subordinates), again put him under arrest, this time for ten days. The Inglesis were ordered to leave Kishinev. They went abroad, where Lyudmila Inglesi developed consumption and died 'cursing, both Pushkin and her husband', as the story current in Kishinev went.

In *Recollection*, one of his most powerful lyrical poems, written on May 19, 1828, Pushkin recalls (in the second unpublished part of the poem), 'two dear shades', who both 'revenge themselves' on him and both speak to him 'in a dead tongue of the mysteries of eternity and the grave'. Only two young women with whom Pushkin had been passionately in love died in Italy, one was Amalia Riznich, with whom he had fallen in love in Odessa and to whom he had dedicated many poems, and the other may well have been Lyudmila Inglesi, about whom very little is known.

Much more is known of Pushkin's brief affair with Calypso Polychroni, whom he met in the spring of 1822. Calypso had fled from Constantinople to her mother in Kishinev on the outbreak of the Greek insurrection. She boasted of having been Lord Byron's mistress at the age of fifteen. Pushkin loved to listen to her singing the passionate, mournful Turkish songs, accompanying herself on the guitar, rolling her eyes and gesticulating. She was very tall and thin and had a very long, hawk-like nose, but that did not seem to lessen the attraction of what Pushkin described in *To a Greek Girl*, a poem dedicated to her, as 'the glitter of her mirror-like eyes' or her 'immodest little foot'. Indeed, in this poem he went so far as to declare that she was born 'to set ablaze the imagination of poets' and to ask her whether Byron did not draw her when 'drawing his immutable ideal in heavenly dreams'. Pushkin ends his poem by declaring that he had long been a stranger to happiness and the enjoyment of it was new to him for, 'overcome by a secret sadness, I fear that everything dear is untrue . . .' In Calypso's case Pushkin's fear was fully justified, for the girl was not only free with her favours, but demanded payment for them. Writing to Vyazemsky on April 5, 1823, Pushkin promised, as an inducement to meet him in Kishinev, to introduce him to 'a Greek girl whom Byron kissed'.

Pushkin was very fond of another Kishinev girl, Pulcheria Varfolomey, the eighteen-year-old daughter of a Moldavian grandee. Pulcheria, though, frustrated the poet's blandishments by her usual reply: *Ah, quel vous êtes, M. Pouchkine!* Pushkin is thought to have written several poems to her, but none of them has been preserved.

Much earlier, during his visit to the Davydov estate of Kamenka, Pushkin had one of his characteristic whirlwind affairs. On December 4, 1820, he described his visit to Nikolai Gnedich in one laconic sentence: 'Few women, much champagne, many witticisms, many books, few poems.' Among the 'few women', however, was Alexander Davydov's ravishing French wife Aglaya, the daughter of the Duc de Gramon, who was thirty at the time. Good-looking, flirtatious, and constantly in search of all sorts of distractions in 'barbarous Russia', she attracted men 'like a magnet', from the Commander-in-Chief to the last ensign. 'Everything,' a visitor to Kamenka writes, 'lived, but especially died at the feet of charming Aglaya.' She must have dropped Pushkin a little too unceremoniously, for in two poems *On A. A. Davydov*, he did not spare her. In one, enclosed in a letter to his brother on January 24, 1822, he wrote: 'One man had my Aglaya for his uniform and black moustache, another for money – that I understand, a third because he was a Frenchman, Cleon scaring her by his intellect, Damis by his tender singing. Tell me, dear Aglaya, what did your husband have you for?' In another, a more outspoken one, he described her as 'a living victim of the furies', who loved the male sex since childhood.

Disgruntled by Aglaya's cavalier treatment, Pushkin turned his attentions to her pretty twelve-year-old daughter Adèle. Once at dinner he glared so terribly at the young girl that she did not know what to do and was ready to burst into tears. 'I want to punish the little flirt,' Pushkin said to one of the diners. 'She was very nice to me before, but now she pretends to be cruel and doesn't want even to look at me.'

Pushkin wrote a little poem to Adèle in which he told her that she was born 'for delight' and advised her to devote her young years to love and especially to love his 'reed in the turmoil of the world'. Poor Adèle! Thirteen years later she was forced to enter a convent by her mother, who had returned to France after Alexander Davydov's death and married a French general.

4

In Kamenka, only a few weeks after his arrival in Kishinev, Pushkin found himself in the thick of the political conspiracy that was to erupt in the Decembrist uprising five years later. He was invited to the birthday party of Yekaterina Davydov, the mother of General Raevsky and, by her second marriage, of the retired General Alexander Davydov and Vasily Davydov, at her Kamenka estate in the Kiev province. General Inzov readily gave Pushkin leave of absence for a few more months. Pushkin arrived in Kamenka in the middle of November, 1820, and stayed there till the beginning of March, 1821. He shared one of the rooms in Vasily Davydov's little cottage in the great park. Vasily Davydov was an active member of the Union of Welfare and it was at his mother's birthday parties that many of his fellow conspirators met.

Ivan Yakushkin, one of the leaders of the Union of Welfare, whom Pushkin had met in Petersburg, was also in Kamenka. Apart from the members of the Raevsky family, the other visitors included General Orlov, whose engagement to Katerina Raevsky was to be officially announced, and his aide-de-camp, Okhotnikov, both prominent members of the Union of Welfare.

Yakushkin writes in his memoirs:

Every day we dined downstairs in the apartment of the Davydovs' old mother. The evenings we spent in Vasily Davydov's room. General Raevsky suspected the existence of our secret society and watched with intense interest everything that was going on around him. On the last evening Orlov, Vasily Davydov, Okhotnikov and I agreed to make it impossible for the General to find out that we were members of the secret society. We elected the General chairman of our meeting. After we had debated all sorts of matters, Orlov proposed to discuss the question whether the foundation of a secret society in Russia would be beneficial or not and gave his reasons for and against such a secret society... Pushkin argued warmly that a secret society would bring great benefits to Russia. I, on the contrary, tried to prove that the existence of a secret society in Russia was quite impossible. General Raevsky enumerated all the cases in which a secret society could act with success and be of benefit. In reply, I said to him: 'I can easily prove to you that you are joking. I shall put this question to you: If such a society already existed, would you or would you not have joined it?'

'I should most certainly have joined it,' he replied.

'In that case, give me your hand,' I said to him.

He offered me his hand, after which I burst out laughing and said that the whole thing was a joke. The others also laughed, except Alexander Davydov, the husband of the beautiful Aglaya whom Pushkin had nicknamed 'the majestic cuckold', who was dozing. Pushkin, who was very excited, did not laugh either. He had been convinced that the secret society was already in existence or would be founded that very evening and that he would be one of its members. Seeing, however, that the whole thing was a joke, he got up, blushing, and exclaimed, with tears in his eyes: 'I have never been so unhappy as I am now. I was ready to see my life ennobled and a lofty aim before me, but now it seems it is only a bad joke.'

At that moment [Yakushkin concludes] he was truly beautiful.

Beautiful or not, the fact remained that none of the members of the secret revolutionary society would trust Pushkin not to reveal its existence in one of his uncontrolled outbursts. And they were right. For Pushkin never made a secret of his political views and, as can be gleaned from the following entries in the diary of Prince Pavel Dolgorukov, the civil servant attached to Inzov's chancellery, he expressed them fearlessly at Inzov's dinner table:

January 11, 1822: Had dinner at Inzov's. Listened to Pushkin at table . . . Instead of realising how little the principles he advocates can be tolerated in society, Pushkin tries to convince everybody he meets at the General's house and in the streets and squares that only a scoundrel would not wish a change of government in Russia. His favourite conversation is based on abuse and sarcasm and even when he tries to be polite there is a sardonic smile on his lips . . .

April 30: Pushkin had a heated discussion at dinner about the slavery of our peasants. He maintained heatedly that he would never have serfs because he could not guarantee their welfare and . . . went on to denounce the Russian landowners, speaking with great conviction.

May 27: Pushkin's words: 'Before, nations rose one against another, but now the Neopolitan king fights against his own people and the Spanish king also. It is not difficult to guess which side will get the better of which.' Dead silence greeted these words. It lasted a few minutes, Inzov finally interrupting it by changing the subject.

July 20: The General having gone out hunting this morning with gun and dog, the table in his absence was laid for the people who usually dined at his house, including myself and Pushkin. Feeling completely unrestrained, Pushkin began with his favourite text about the Russian government. Smirnov, our interpreter, began arguing with him, but the more he contradicted him, the more excited did Pushkin grow, the more he raged and the more he got exasperated. At last he began to pour abuse on all classes of the population. Civil servants were scoundrels and thieves, generals were swine, most of them at any rate, only the class of the tillers of the soil was spared. Pushkin especially attacked the Russian noblemen. They ought all to be hanged, he declared, and if they were, he would tighten the noose round their necks with pleasure.

Secret agents reported to the authorities in Petersburg that 'in public and even in coffee houses Pushkin abuses not only the military authorities but even the government'. Inzov took a great deal of trouble to counteract these reports by denying that the poet put under his 'supervision' was disloyal to the government. Whenever he got a direct enquiry from Petersburg, he replied: 'Mr Pushkin, who is attached to my office, conducts himself excellently,' or: 'Living with me in the same house, Mr Pushkin behaves well and in the present unquiet times takes no part in these affairs.'

Pushkin's remarks about the kings of Naples and Spain referred to the aggravation of the struggle between the progressive and the reactionary forces in Europe. The government of Alexander I quite openly embarked on the path of reaction. A characteristic feature of this reactionary policy was the dismissal of a large number of university professors and the abolition of certain university courses as subversive to the Greek Orthodox religion. The censorship, especially, went to ludicrous lengths in its attempt to carry out these reactionary policies. For instance, it prohibited the description of a woman's smile as 'heavenly'. Alexander I increased his reactionary measures when he learnt of the formation of secret political societies. These new measures led to the dissolution of the Union of Welfare in January, 1821, and the formation of two underground revolutionary societies, the Southern and the Northern Unions, which were now actively preparing a revolutionary *coup*.

Pushkin was a close friend of the members of the Southern Society. 'In Kishinev,' Pushkin wrote to Zhukovsky after the arrest of the Decembrists in January, 1826, 'I was friendly with Major Raevsky and Generals Pushchin and Orlov. I was a member of the Kishinev Masonic Lodge, that is, the lodge which was responsible for the abolition of all masonic lodges in Russia. Finally, I was in close touch with the greater part of the present conspirators . . . People spoke about the conspiracy everywhere.' Pushkin made the acquaintance of Major Vladimir Raevsky, a fellow poet and a leading member of the revolutionary Southern Society, in March, 1821. He became a member of the Kishinev Masonic Lodge 'Ovid' on May 4, 1821. After the closing down of the Lodge, Pushkin kept its ledgers bound in black morocco and used them for writing down his works in. It was Pushkin who, on February 5, 1822, informed Raevsky of his impending arrest and thus enabled him to destroy all incriminating documents in his possession.

After Major Raevsky's arrest, General Orlov, who had put Raevsky in charge of the soldiers' school in his division, was forced to resign his command of the Second Division.

Pushkin was a frequent visitor at General Orlov's. 'Pushkin,' Katerina wrote to her brother Alexander Raevsky in November, 1821, 'no longer pretends to be cruel. He comes to see us frequently, smokes his pipe and chatters very pleasantly. He has just finished his ode to Napoleon which, in my humble opinion, is very good.' A week later she wrote: 'There are incessant noisy debates at our house on philosophic, political, literary and other subjects. I can hear them arguing from my distant room . . . We often see Pushkin who comes to discuss all sorts of subjects with my husband. He is now obsessed with the idea of perpetual peace of the Abbé de Saint Pierre. He is convinced that, as they become more and more perfect, governments will gradually introduce perpetual and general peace into the world.'

Among Pushkin's papers were found notes in French about Abbé de Saint Pierre's *Projet de Paix perpetuelle* made in 1821. 'It is impossible that in time people would not come to recognise the ridiculous cruelty of war, in the same way as they have come to recognise the true nature of slavery, of Tsarist power, etc. They will realise that our destiny is to eat, drink and be free.' After observing that democratic reforms must lead to the gradual disarmament of all armed forces, Pushkin wrote:

> Since a constitution is already a great step in human consciousness and since this step will not be the only one, it is bound to arouse a desire for a decrease in the numbers of armies in states, for the principle of armed force is directly opposed to any constitutional idea. It is therefore possible that in less than a hundred years from now there will be no more regular armies.

Pushkin then quoted Rousseau who argued that the ideal of world peace could be realised only through revolutionary measures for 'what is useful to society is introduced into life only by force because private interests are almost always against it. Therefore, this can be achieved only by cruel and terrible means'. Pushkin concluded by saying that it was 'obvious that these terrible means about which Rousseau spoke are revolution and now the time for them has come'. A note in French in Pushkin's diary reads: 'O . . . [probably Orlov] said: a revolution in Spain, a revolution in Italy, a revolution in Portugal, constitutions here, constitutions there . . . Emperors, you have made a stupid mistake in overthrowing Napoleon.'

The revolutions in southern Europe in the 'twenties made a great impression on Pushkin. Discussing these events in the Tenth Canto of *Eugene Onegin* (1830), Pushkin wrote: 'The Pyrenees shook menacingly, Naples' volcano blazed . . .' Pushkin also welcomed with enthusiasm the news of the Greek revolution. He believed that it was bound to involve Russia and, as can be gathered from his poem *War*, was contemplating joining in the fray: 'War! At last the banners of warlike honour are raised! I shall see blood, I shall see the festival of vengeance; and how many strong impressions for my thirsting soul!'

Pushkin met the Greek revolutionary leaders, including the brothers Ypsilanti, at Orlov's. On April 2, 1821, he wrote in his diary: .

> Spent the evening at H.G.'s – a delightful Greek woman. We spoke about Alexander Ypsilanti; among the five Greeks I alone spoke like a Greek: they all despaired of success of the enterprise of the Hetaeria [the Greek secret political organisation]. I am firmly convinced that Greece will be triumphant and that the twenty-five million Turks will

leave the flourishing country of Hellas to the legal heirs of Homer and Themistocles.

To Vasily Davydov Pushkin wrote enthusiastically: 'Greece has arisen and proclaimed her freedom,' and after describing the arrival of Prince Alexander Ypsilanti in Jassy from Kishinev and the execution by Ypsilanti of seven Turks, 'a strange piece of news on the part of a European general,' and several atrocities committed by the Turks, Pushkin went on: 'The enthusiasm has reached the highest pitch. All thoughts are directed to one thing – the independence of the ancient fatherland.' He ends his letter by posing 'an important question', namely, what was Russia going to do. 'Shall we seize Moldavia and Valakhia under the guise of peace-loving mediators or shall we cross beyond the Danube as the allies of the Greeks and enemies of their enemies?'

But, characteristically, Pushkin's enthusiasm quickly waned after the Greek defeats and Ypsilanti's flight to Austria. 'We have seen these new Leonidases in the streets of Kishinev and Odessa,' he wrote to Vasily Davydov in June, 1823. 'Many of them we know personally and we can vouch for their complete worthlessness – they have no idea of the art of war, no concept of honour, no enthusiasm . . . I am neither a barbarian nor an apostle of the Koran, I am greatly interested in the cause of Greece and it is just because of that that I am indignant when I see these poor wretches entrusted with the sacred office of defenders of liberty . . .' In a second letter to Vasily Davydov, Pushkin wrote a few days later:

I am surprised to hear that you regard me as an enemy of the liberation of Greece and as an advocate of Turkish slavery. My words must have been strangely misinterpreted to you, but whatever people say, you must not believe that my heart would at any time feel any ill-will towards the noble efforts of a rising people. . . .

Pushkin was no less disillusioned with the suppression of the revolutions in Italy, Spain and Portugal. He felt so bitter about it that in his letter to Alexander Turgenev on December 1, 1823, he bade farewell to his 'liberal delirium':

The other day I wrote an imitation of the parable of the moderate democrat Jesus Christ (behold, a sower went forth to sow): 'A hermit sower of freedom, I went out early, before the stars; with a pure and innocent hand I threw the life-giving seed into the enslaved furrows –

but I only wasted my time, my good intentions and my labour . . .
Graze, peaceful peoples! The call of honour will not awaken you.
What are gifts of freedom to flocks? They should be slaughtered or
shorn. From generation to generation, their heritage has been a yoke
with rattles and a whip.

But while disillusioned with the national revolutions in Europe, Pushkin
never ceased believing in the coming revolution in Russia, although the
leaders of the different revolutionary secret societies, whose company he
cultivated, were still too mistrustful of his enthusiasm to confide their
secret plans to him. On April 8, 1821, Pushkin met Peter Pestel, one of the
chief leaders of the Southern Society and one of the five men executed in
1826 after the collapse of the Decembrist insurrection. 'I spent the morning with Pestel,' he wrote in his diary. 'An intelligent man in every sense
of the word. I had a metaphysical, political and moral conversation with
him. He has one of the most original minds.' Pushkin met Pestel three
more times, but nothing is known of the subjects they discussed, or,
indeed, whether Pushkin was aware of Pestel's leading part in planning the
uprising of 1825.

5

Duels, love affairs, gay parties and political plots were not the only, nor indeed the chief, occupation of Pushkin in Kishinev. It was a time of intensive creative activity, during which he wrote more than a hundred poems, including three long narrative poems: *The Caucasian Captive*, *The Fountain of Bakhchisaray* and *The Gabriliade*.

In Bessarabia Pushkin was faced with a financial crisis that could only be resolved by his income from literary work. His nominal civil service job provided a salary of only seven hundred and fifty roubles. Pushkin's appeals for money to his father fell on deaf ears. He had therefore to rely entirely on his pen for a living. He was, in fact, the first Russian professional writer. 'Aristocratic prejudices are all very well so far as you are concerned,' he wrote to Vyazemsky in March, 1823, 'but they do not suit me. I look upon a finished poem of mine as a shoemaker looks upon a pair of his boots: I sell for profit.'

But while Pushkin had a large public only too eager to buy his works, he also had constantly to fight the censorship which did its utmost to mutilate them. The chief censor was a certain Alexander Birukov to whom Pushkin addressed his *Epistle to the Censor* in 1822. In this epistle Pushkin dismissed Birukov as 'a fool and coward', who regarded 'poetry as depravity', 'the voice of truth as rebellion', and Pushkin's old Lycée master Kunitsyn, whose book *Natural Law* had been banned in 1821, as 'a second Marat'. On the other hand, Pushkin freely admitted that 'what London needs is too early for Moscow' and proceeded to define his idea of a censor as a citizen who, conscious of his 'sacred office', 'does not suppress opinions, does not grovel before the aristocracy, is sensible, firm, free and just'.

In Pushkin's letters from Kishinev the subject of the censorship is raised again and again. On February 6, 1823, he wrote to Vyazemsky:

Thank you for tweaking the nose of our censorship . . . It is shameful that the most noble class in the nation, the class, which, say what you like, is doing some thinking, is subjected to the arbitrary reprisal of some cowardly fool. We laugh, but it would seem to be much more sensible that the Birukovs should be taken in hand; it is time that due weight was given to our opinion and the government forced to respect our voice, for its contempt for Russian writers is intolerable . . .

In March, 1823, he again wrote to Vyazemsky:

Do me a favour and write to me in greater detail about your complaint against the censorship. [Vyazemsky had lodged a complaint against one of the censors in 1822 for re-writing an article of his.] This concerns all our orthodox crowd. But your proposal that we should all unite and lodge a complaint against the Birukovs could have dire consequences. According to the military code, if more than two officers send in a report at the same time, such an action will be considered an act of mutiny. I do not know whether writers are subject to military law, but a joint complaint on our part could draw terrible suspicion upon us and cause a lot of trouble . . . In fact, to act singly seems to me to be much more the proper way.

Pushkin's repeated attempts 'to act singly' were of no avail as was clearly demonstrated by the cavalier treatment of *The Caucasian Captive* by the censors, who distorted some passages and excised others. The poem, in which Pushkin tried to express not only his own feelings, but the general feelings of his generation, was written at a time when Pushkin, as he himself admitted, was 'mad about Byron'. 'There are lines in it,' Pushkin wrote to Gnedich on April 29, 1822, 'that came straight out of my own heart. I wanted to depict in it the indifference to life and its joys, the premature senility of the soul, which is so characteristic of our younger generation.' Pushkin later ascribed his failure to provide a convincing portrait of the disillusioned young man of his own time to his attempt to give too subjective a description of himself in the portrayal of the hero of *The Caucasian Captive*. 'The character of the Captive,' he wrote to Vladimir Gorchakov in November, 1822, 'is unsuccessful, which proves that I am not cut out to be the hero of a romantic poem.' Indeed, while endowing the Captive with all the characteristics of a hero of 'the gloomy and powerful poetry' associated with the poetry of Byron, Pushkin was too much of a realist even at the age of twenty-two. He makes his hero commit the quite un-Byronic act of refusing to save 'the maid of the mountain', that is, the Circassian girl when she throws herself into a mountain stream. Pushkin wrote to Vyazemsky on February 6, 1823:

> One more word about *The Caucasian Captive*. You say, my dear fellow, that he is a son of a bitch because he does not grieve for the Circassian girl, but what do you want him to say? *He understood everything* expresses everything; the thought of her had to take possession of his soul and fuse with all his thoughts – that is self-understood, it could not be otherwise; but is it not necessary to state everything – that is the secret of entertainment. Some people may be vexed that the *captive* did not dive into the river to pull out my Circassian girl. Well, you just try it! I have swum in Caucasian streams. You can easily drown without finding a damn thing! My captive is an intelligent and sensible fellow. He is not in love with the Circassian girl, he did right not to drown himself.

In his essay on *The Refutation of Criticism*, Pushkin has this to say about his un-Byronic attitude towards *The Caucasian Captive* even during his Byronic period: '*The Caucasian Captive* is my first successful attempt at characterisation which I mastered with difficulty; it was received better than anything else I had written thanks to certain elegiac and descriptive lines, but, on the other hand, Nikolai and Alexander Raevsky and myself have had a good laugh over it.'

Pushkin first planned *The Caucasian Captive* during his stay in the Caucasus. He worked on it in Gurzuf and kept revising it in Kishinev, Kamenka and Kiev. Its final version is dated: 'February 23, 1821, Kamenka.' Its epilogue is dated: 'Odessa 1821, May 15.' Pushkin dedicated the poem to Nikolai Raevsky: 'You will find here,' he wrote, 'memories of days dear to my heart: the contradictions of passions, familiar dreams, familiar sufferings and the secret voice of my heart.'

The descriptive passages are further evidence of the realistic trends dormant in the poem. In the introduction to the second edition of the poem in 1828, he wrote: 'This poem, which was received indulgently by the public, owes its success to the truthful, though only lightly-sketched, descriptions of the Caucasus and the customs of its mountaineers.' Pushkin, in fact, was quite astonished at the truthfulness of his descriptive passages. 'I can't understand myself,' he wrote in his *Journey to Erzerum* (1830), 'how I could have portrayed so truthfully, though a little weakly, the customs of the people and nature which I had seen only from a distance.'

Pushkin began writing *The Fountain of Bakhchisaray* in the spring of 1821 and wrote most of it during 1822. He finally revised it in 1823. In his letter to his brother of August 25, 1823, from Odessa, Pushkin mentions that he told a fellow poet, Vasily Tumansky, that he would not like to publish the poem because 'many passages in it relate to a certain woman with whom I was for a very long time stupidly in love and that the role of Petrarch is not to my liking'. Pushkin also referred to the poem on February 8, 1824, in a letter to Bestuzhev. The lack of plan in the poem, he wrote, was not his fault. 'I superstitiously put into verse the story of a young woman.

> *Aux douces loix des vers je pliais les accents*
> *De sa bouche aimable et naive.*

[To the sweet laws of verse I adapted the accents of her lovable and innocent lips.] However, I wrote it solely for myself, but am publishing it because I need money.' In revising the poem, Pushkin removed from the text his 'love delirium', that is to say, the passages containing the poet's intimate confessions.

The Fountain of Bakhchisaray most closely approaches the generally accepted idea of a 'Byronic' poem. It is based on Pushkin's impressions of the Crimea. The two heroines of the poem, the chaste Maria and the passionate Zarema, are purely romantic figures, as is the hero Khan Girey. The reader finds himself in a world of extravagant passions, dark characters, murders, executions, and all sorts of highly dramatic events. The entertainment value of the poem is much greater than that of *The Caucasian Captive*, which explains its much greater success. The death of both heroines is surrounded by an aura of mystery. The characteristic features of romanticism in its 'pure' form can also be detected in the heightened anguish of Zarema's monologue during her meeting with Maria, in the description of Zarema's eyes, which are 'brighter than the day and blacker than the night', and the exaggerated portrayal of Girey's passion. Pushkin has this to say about the poem in his article on *The Refutation of Criticism*:

> *The Fountain of Bakhchisaray* is weaker than the *Captive* and, like the *Captive*, shows signs of my reading of Byron about whom I was mad

at the time. The scene between Zarema and Maria is dramatically
effective. I don't believe it has been criticised. Alexander Raevsky used
to laugh at the following lines: 'He often in fateful battles raised his
sabre and, as he swung it, suddenly became motionless, looked round
him madly, went pale,' etc. Young writers, in general, do not know how
to depict the physical expressions of passion. Their heroes always
shudder, laugh wildly, gnash their teeth and so on. All this is as ridiculous as melodrama.

The Gabriliade was written during Holy Week as a protest against the
growing mysticism of Alexander I and his court. It was this that Pushkin
had in mind when he wrote to Vyazemsky on September 1, 1822: 'I am
sending you a poem of a mystical nature – I have become a courtier.'
Pushkin wrote his 'blasphemous' poem shortly after he had finished *The
Caucasian Captive*. He dedicated *The Gabriliade* to his friend Alexeyev,
whose lodgings he shared in Kishinev. Not far from Alexeyev's house was
the Church of the Annunciation where Pushkin had the idea of writing
the poem.

Pushkin probably finished the poem in April or during the first half of
May, 1821. He wrote to Alexander Turgenev on May 7, 1821 on com-
pleting it:

> . . . I wish I were able to spend two weeks in that disgusting Peters-
> burg of yours . . . Father, into thy hands I commit my spirit. Could
> you, who are so near to the inhabitants of Stone Island [Alexander I
> was living in the Stone Island, *Kamenny Ostrov*, Palace], summon me
> for a few days (no more) from my Island of Patmos [where St John was
> supposed to have written the Apocalypse]? I could bring you in return
> a work in the manner of the Apocalypse and dedicate it to you, Christ-
> loving shepherd of our poetic flock; but first ask the fleeting friends of
> my fleeting youth to send me some money with which they will greatly
> oblige the *seeker of new impressions*.

Nothing, incidentally, came of this proposed journey to Petersburg.
'The inhabitants of the Stone Island,' that is to say, Alexander I and his
court, were certainly not thinking of letting the troublesome Pushkin into
their capital. Neither were Pushkin's 'fleeting friends' more forthcoming.

In 1821 the Feast of the Annunciation was celebrated on March 25 and
the service may have suggested to Pushkin the subject of *The Gabriliade*.

Pushkin was not particularly keen on going to church. In his *Epistle to Vasily Davydov*, written at the beginning of April, 1821, he refers to the death of the local archbishop, whose funeral took place on April 3:

The other day our archbishop, a grey-haired glutton, accidentally gave up the ghost before dinner and went to paradise with the Son of the Bird and Mary to exchange kisses on the occasion of the Resurrection. [Pushkin went on:] I have grown intelligent. I have become a hypocrite – I fast, I pray, and I believe firmly that God will forgive me my sins just as the Emperor will forgive me my poems. Inzov fasts and attends Divine Service and the other day I exchanged my Parnassian ravings and my lyre, the sinful gift of fate, for the Book of Hours, the Mass and dried mushrooms.

The Gabriliade is a parody of the two basic dogmas of the Christian religion, the fall of Adam and Eve and the Virgin birth. The narrative is based on the gospel version, and its central episode turns on an erotic interpretation of the Annunciation. The episode of Adam and Eve is related in a long interpolation in Satan's monologue. In one of his digressions, Pushkin seems to have admitted authorship of the poem by referring to his Lycée years with revealing accuracy: 'Do you remember, my friends the meadow where in the old days in the spring we ran about freely and amused ourselves in brave single combats . . .' The poem is written in colloquial language except for the dialogues of the biblical figures in which Pushkin used all sorts of biblical expressions. It could not be published for obvious reasons. It circulated in manuscript copies and by 1825 became widely known. In 1826 it attracted the notice of the police. On March 8 General Bibikov, the Head of the Gendarmerie, reported to Count Alexander Benkendorf, the Chief of the Secret Police, that 'a rebellious poem which carries the torch of revolt among all the classes of the population and attacks the sanctity of faith, the indispensable bridle for all peoples and, especially, for Russians, with the dangerous and treacherous weapon of sarcasm,' was widely circulated among young people.

It was only in 1828, however, that the attention of the government was drawn to the poem after some house-serfs reported to the church authorities that a copy of *The Gabriliade* was to be found in the house of their master. In May, 1828, an official enquiry was ordered. A special commission of three men was set up. At his interrogation, Pushkin denied authorship. He asserted that he had come across it for the first time at the Lycée in 1815 or 1816 and had copied it out, but had never seen it since and did not remember where he had put it. Interrogated again 'at the order of the Tsar' in the middle of August, Pushkin declared, in a written statement, that manuscript copies of the poem had been circulating at Tsarskoye Selo among Hussar officers and that he had been given a copy of it, but could not remember by whom. He had burnt his copy in 1820. 'I venture to add,' he wrote, 'that in none of my works, not even in those I regret most, is there any trace of the spirit of disbelief or blasphemy. I can only express my regret that such a shameful and miserable work should be ascribed to me.' To wriggle out of a situation which might have been very dangerous for him, Pushkin even tried to father the authorship of the poem on to 'the late poet, Prince Dmitry Gorchakov'. 'You invite me to come to see you in Penza,' he wrote to Vyazemsky on September 1, 1828, 'but for all I know I shall have to go much farther than that. Indeed, straight to the East. The most idiotic joke has been played on me. *The Gabriliade* has at last come to the notice of the government and they think that I must be the author of it. Information has been laid against me and I shall most probably have to answer for someone else's pranks, if Prince Dmitry Gorchakov does not come from the other world to claim the rights of his property.' Vyazemsky realised what was happening and replied on September 25: 'I am very sorry to hear of your trouble in connection with *The Gabriliade*. I hope there will be no evil consequences and that Von Fok [an officer of the Secret Police] will say to your Muse: Maiden, mother of poetry, rejoice, thou art blessed among women, etc.'

Pushkin was again interrogated on October 2 and, according to the official report:

> after a long silence and careful thought, asked whether he would be permitted to write directly to the Emperor and, having received a satisfactory answer, immediately wrote a letter to his Majesty and, sealing it, handed it over. The Commission decided not to open the letter, but to forward it to his Majesty.

The text of Pushkin's letter is unknown. Nicholas I's answer, which Pushkin received on October 16, is also not known. On December 31, 1828, Nicholas I announced his decision: 'I know all the details of this affair and it is now closed.'

6

Pushkin was not only 'mad about' Byron during his southern exile. In Bessarabia Ovid, too, greatly exercised Pushkin's mind and left a mark on some of his finest poetry.

'Pushkin was very interested in Ovid,' Liprandi records. 'I don't know whether or not he had read him before, but I do know that the first book he borrowed from me in 1820 was Ovid in a French translation and that he kept it till 1823.'

Pushkin paid his tribute to Ovid, exiled by Augustus to the shores of the Black Sea, in a poem of one hundred and four thirteen-foot rhyming iambic lines which he wrote on December 26, 1821. He thought so highly of it that in a letter to his brother on January 20, 1823, he declared that *Ruslan* and *The Captive* were 'trash' compared to it. It is the first historic work by Pushkin. Its basic theme is a poet's exile, a theme that was naturally near to his heart. After describing Ovid's complaints and his pleas for forgiveness, Pushkin says of himself: 'A stern Slav, I have never shed any tears, but I understand them; an unwarranted exile, dissatisfied with the world, myself and life, I now visited the country in which you had dragged out a melancholy existence . . . and, Ovid, repeated your poems . . .' Ovid's appeal to his friends to carry his supplication to Augustus and with their tears to deflect 'his chastising hand' merely put in different words Pushkin's own appeal to Alexander Turgenev to intercede on his behalf with 'the inhabitants of Stone Island'. Pushkin draws the parallel between Ovid and himself even closer in the last lines of his poem *To Ovid*:

Like you, submissive to hostile fate,
Not in fame, but in suffering the same fate,
I am your equal.
Here, filling the air of the northern desert with the sound of my lyre
I wandered during the days when, on the banks of the Danube,

The magnanimous Greek called for freedom,
And not a single friend in the world listened to me,
But the alien hills, fields and sleepy woods,
And the peaceful Muses were kind to me.

Pushkin's poem *Napoleon*, written in May, 1821, shortly after he had received the news of Napoleon's death, shows the change in the attitude of the Russian radicals towards Napoleon after the suppression of the European revolutionary movements by the Holy Alliance. Napoleon is no longer the ogre of Pushkin's earlier poems. He is 'a great man', 'the mighty minion of victories', on his urn 'the ray of immortality' shines, from 'the darkness of exile' on 'the torrid isle' he bequeathed 'perpetual peace to the world'. In his letter to Alexander Turgenev from Odessa on December 1, 1823, Pushkin described the poem as his 'last liberal delirium'. It was published in the collection of Pushkin's poems in 1826 with the excision by the censorship of four stanzas describing Napoleon's betrayal of 'the bright day of liberty' that had dawned on 'the great, inevitable day' when 'on the rebellious square the king's dead body lay in dust'. A little earlier that year Pushkin wrote *The Dagger*, a much more revolutionary poem in which he hailed the murder by the German student Sand of the reactionary playwright Kotzebue. He described the dagger with which the murder was committed as 'the secret guardian of freedom'. The poem was widely circulated in manuscript copies and was first published in a French translation in 1827.

In Bessarabia Pushkin wrote two poems based on events mentioned in the Russian chronicles. One of them, *The Song of Prophetic Oleg*, a school recitation piece, describes the fulfilment of the prophecy by an old soothsayer that the Russian prince would die, the victim of his favourite horse. In a way, this expresses Pushkin's own belief in the occult powers that speak through the mouths of fortune-tellers. The other is an unfinished fragment *Vadim*. Vadim is mentioned in the Chronicles as having challenged the autocratic rule of the Varangian Prince Ryurik. The Russian writers of the eighteenth and the beginning of the nineteenth centuries regarded Vadim as the defender of the ancient Slav liberties. Only a few hundred lines of Pushkin's poem have been preserved. Pushkin began writing it in 1821. He also planned to write a tragedy on the same subject.

The Brigand Brothers is another narrative poem which Pushkin left unfinished. According to Pushkin's original 'Byronic' plan, the poem was to deal with the two mistresses of a brigand chief. The brigands board a merchant ship and their chief gets the merchant's daughter as part of his booty. His first mistress is jealous and goes mad. The second does not love him and dies. The brigand chief thereupon commits all sorts of atrocities, but is betrayed by one of his fellow brigands. Only a small fragment of this part of the poem has been preserved. According to another version, the poem begins with the story of two brothers which corresponds to the extant version of the poem. The date of the poem is June–July, 1821. It is thought that originally Pushkin intended to write two different poems: one about brigands and another in the form of a ballad about two convict brothers. Pushkin, however, changed his mind and included the story of the brothers in the first poem. This version he finally revised and completed in April, 1822.

On November 11, 1823, Pushkin wrote to Vyazemsky: 'The poem owes its theme to an event from actual life: while I was in Yekaterinoslav in 1820, two brigands who were chained together swam across the Dnieper and regained their freedom. Their rest on an island and the drowning of one of the warders was not invented by me.' The theme of brigands, no doubt, occurred to Pushkin also because of the great many acts of brigandage that took place in Bessarabia and throughout southern Russia. These were mainly a result of poverty. In his poem, too, Pushkin emphasises that the reason why the two brothers became robbers was poverty. 'Life was no joy to us children,' one of the brigands observes, 'for even then we knew the meaning of want.' An interesting facet of the poem is the great number of colloquialisms which were later to become an organic part of Pushkin's poetic style. Nikolai Raevsky wrote to Pushkin on May 10, 1825: 'Your introduction of simple and natural speech which our readers are not yet ready for in spite of the beautiful models of your *Brigands* and *Gipsies* will finally make it generally accepted.' Simplicity of vocabulary corresponds also with simplicity of construction. It is written in short sentences which assist the uninterrupted unfolding of the story. In his letter to Vyazemsky of October 14, 1823, Pushkin wrote: 'As for the style [of *The Brigand Brothers*], I have written nothing better.'

A confirmed gambler, Pushkin attempted at the end of June, 1821, to write a comedy about the conversion of a card player. Only a brief synopsis of several scenes and a rough sketch of the first scene have been preserved. One of Pushkin's notes states: 'The game starts, Sosnitsky [the hero to whom Pushkin has given the name of one of the leading Petersburg

actors] loses all. He is in despair.' Another note introduces a rather
dramatic theme and reads: 'Time to go to the theatre. Our friend eats his
last luncheon. He is going to shoot himself.' The play appears to deal with
an aristocratic widow who wishes to save her brother from his passion for
gambling. She consults her lover, who is also a gambler. The lover
promises his help and persuades a cardsharper to play with the widow's
brother and win all his money. At the end of the game the widow's
brother loses all his money and is persuaded to stake his old servant. The
heart-rending scene which follows ends with exhortations and admonish-
ments on the evil of gambling.

A survey of the works Pushkin wrote in Kishinev would be incomplete
without a quick glance at his 'immodest' fairy tale *Tsar Nikita and his
Forty Daughters*. Pushkin had most decided views on obscenity:

> An obscene work is one whose aim or action leads to the undermining
> of the rules upon which social happiness or human dignity is based.
> Poems whose aim is to inflame the imagination by lascivious descrip-
> tions degrade poetry, transforming its divine nectar into an inflammable
> substance and the Muse into a revolting Canidia [a Neopolitan cour-
> tesan, the mistress of Horace, who held her up to contempt as an old
> sorceress when she deserted him]. But a jest inspired by heartfelt gaiety
> and a momentary play of imagination can appear immoral only to those
> who have a childish or obscure idea of immorality confusing it with
> didacticism and who see in literature only a pedagogic occupation.

Tsar Nikita and his Forty Daughters is an inspired jest. Tsar Nikita once
upon a time lived an idle, gay and luxurious life 'doing neither good nor
ill', eating, drinking and saying his prayers. He had forty daughters by
different mothers, 'forty lovely girls, forty heavenly angels, endowed with
charming hearts and souls'. Everything about them was fascinating, but
'between their legs the princesses . . . no, that is too clear and dangerous
to modesty – let me put it another way: in Venus I love her bosom, her
lips and, especially, her little feet, but the fiery spark of love, the aim of all
my desires . . . that the young princesses did not possess . . .' An old
councillor advised the grief-stricken Tsar to seek the help of a witch who
'cured all maladies and knew how to put everything right and, if necessary,
how to put something back'. The witch made the devil bring her 'a casket
full of the sinful things we all adore. There were all sorts there, all sizes,
all colours, of the best quality and with curls . . .' The witch counted forty

of the best, wrapped them in a napkin, locked them up in a casket, and gave it to the Tsar's courier, who could not, however, control his curiosity and on his way back opened the casket. The moment the casket was opened 'the little birds gave a flutter, flew away and sat down in a circle on the branches, twirling their tails'. Fortunately, the witch, who was following him, told him that all he had to do was to 'show them . . . and then they will all fly down to you for sure'. He 'showed' them and the birds at once flew down to him and took possession of his quarters. 'Without any further ado' the courier put them all back into the casket and as soon as the princesses received them they put them at once into their cages . . .' Pushkin mentions his delightful, light-hearted *fairy* tale only once in a joint letter to his brother and the poet Pletnyov in March, 1825. After discussing the poems to be included in the first volume of his works, Pushkin added jestingly: 'Sixty poems! Will it be enough for one volume? Should I not also send you my *Tsar Nikita and his Forty Daughters* for good measure?'

But however 'immodest', its humour, gaiety and *style* make this fairy tale a worthy precursor of the great fairy tales Pushkin was to write towards the end of his life.

7

I should like to write you a whole novel: the last three months of my life. This is what happened: my state of health having long been in need of sea bathing, it took me a great deal of trouble to persuade Inzov to let me go to Odessa. I left my Moldavia and made my appearance in Europe. The restaurants and Italian opera reminded me of old times and, my goodness, how they have restored my spirits! Meanwhile, Vorontsov arrived. He received me very amicably and told me that I am being transferred to his office and that I am to remain in Odessa. It would seem that nothing could be better, but then I felt depressed again – I was sorry for the ties I had left behind. I went back to Kishinev for a few days, spent them in an unutterably elegiac way, and having left it forever, I heaved a sigh for Kishinev. Now I am in Odessa again and I still cannot accustom myself to the European way of life. I still do not go anywhere except to the theatre . . . Explain to my father that I cannot live without some money from him. It is impossible for me to live by my pen because of the present censorship. I am afraid I have not learned cabinet-making and am not fit to be a teacher, though I do know the Scriptures and the first four rules of arithmetic. I am in the service not of my own free will and it is impossible for me to offer my resignation. Everybody and everything tries to deceive me and who am I to rely on except my nearest and dearest. I am not going to sponge on Vorontsov. I don't want to and that's that. One extremity could lead to another – it hurts to see my father's indifference to my situation, though his letters are very amiable

Pushkin wrote this to his younger brother Lev from Odessa on August, 25, 1823, about a month after he had left Bessarabia.

The letter is typical of the way Pushkin never mentions any of the real important events of his life in his letters. His transference to Odessa had nothing to do with the state of his health or his need for sea bathing.

It was due entirely to the efforts of Vyazemsky and Alexander Turgenev. On April 30, 1823, Vyazemsky wrote to Alexander Turgenev:

The other day I received a letter from Bes-Arabian [bes – devil, arabsky – obviously refers to Pushkin's Negro ancestors: arap – Negro, a pun Vyazemsky must have chuckled over] Pushkin. He is depressed by his hopeless situation, but, according to a man who has just arrived from there, he is writing a new poem *Harem* about a Potocki girl abducted by some Khan, an historical event [a reference to *The Fountain of Bakhchisaray*]. But what is better still, I am told that he has sobered down considerably and has become quite sensible.

On May 31, 1823, Vyazemsky again wrote to Turgenev: 'Have you spoken to Vorontsov about Pushkin? He must get him a job in his office. Do what you can, particularly as Pushkin really does want to sober down and boredom and vexation are bad counsellors.' Alexander Turgenev's efforts were successful as, indeed, Pushkin himself acknowledged in his letter to Turgenev on December 1, 1823. 'I fully appreciate,' Pushkin wrote from Odessa, 'your remembering me and your friendly solicitude to which I owe the change in my fortunes.' In July, 1823, Pushkin received permission to leave for Odessa.

Meantime, Count Vorontsov was appointed vice-regent of the Bessarabian region with headquarters in Odessa. Vorontsov enjoyed the reputation of an enlightened administrator. As commander of the Russian expeditionary corps in France, he was one of the first Russian generals to abolish corporal punishment in the army. In 1820 he was even in danger of forfeiting his favour at court for supporting a project for the gradual abolition of serfdom. By 1823, however, he had given up his liberal ideas and he interpreted his appointment as vice-regent as an act of 'forgiveness' on the part of Alexander I. Vorontsov was educated in England. He was a rabid Anglophile.

Vorontsov treated Pushkin as an insignificant, low-grade civil servant. One day he said to Vigel, recently appointed vice-governor of Bessarabia: 'I believe you like Pushkin. Can't you persuade him to do something worth while?' 'Why,' Vigel replied, 'such men as Pushkin can only be great poets!' 'What are they good for then?' the Count remarked drily. To begin with, Vorontsov hoped to ingratiate himself even more in the Emperor's favour by turning the rebellious poet into a loyal servant of the crown. He may also have hoped that by exercising some control over

Pushkin he would obtain a reputation as 'a patron of the Muses'. But Pushkin had his own views about 'patrons of the Muses' and his relations with the powerful vice-regent gradually worsened and became strained to breaking point when he became Countess Vorontsov's lover.

Pushkin did not take long to get used to 'the European way of life' in Odessa. The restaurants and the Italian opera reminded him only too well 'of old times'. It was true Odessa had its drawbacks. One of its terrible scourges was the light soil which, in summer, covered the few spindly trees, the roofs of houses and the clothes of passers-by with a thick layer of sand, while in the autumn and winter, it turned into thick mud. 'For five or six weeks a year,' Pushkin recalls in *Onegin's Journey*. 'Odessa is submerged in thick mud, all houses are buried in it for some two feet and the pedestrian can ford the streets only on stilts.' Another drawback was the lack of water which, Pushkin declared in *Onegin's Journey*, 'was no great loss, since wine is imported free of duty.' At first Pushkin lodged not far from the Odessa theatre at the Hotel Reno. According to Liprandi, Pushkin also lived at 'the club-house of Automne', an excellent, small hotel, where the drinking parties did much to restore Pushkin's spirits. One of these Pushkin described in *Onegin's Journey*: 'Noise, arguments, light wine is fetched from the cellars by obliging Automne. The hours slide by, while the terrible bill invisibly grows.' Pushkin gives a much more realistic description of such a party in a letter to Vigel at the end of October, 1823: 'Here it is cold and muddy. We dine gloriously. I drink like Lot of Sodom and my only regret is that I have not a single daughter with me. Not long ago we had a glorious day here. I was president at a drinking party. Everyone got drunk and then we all made the rounds of the brothels.' Liprandi, who used to visit Odessa regularly on official business, went to see Pushkin one evening. He found him in a very cheerful mood, sitting in his shirt-sleeves on the knees of the moor Ali, a native of Tunis and captain of a merchant ship. Pushkin nicknamed Ali 'the Corsair'. 'My arrival,' Liprandi writes, 'did not make Pushkin change his position. Pushkin said: "I like him very much. Who knows, perhaps his forebears and my grandfather were near relations." He then began tickling Ali, which the moor could not bear. That seemed to amuse Pushkin.' Pushkin told Liprandi that he had felt much happier in Kishinev. Ali, he declared, was the only distraction he found in Odessa. In *Eugene Onegin* Pushkin refers to Ali as 'the son of Egyptian soil, a corsair in retirement, Morali'. On another visit to Odessa, Liprandi found Pushkin asleep in the afternoon after returning at five o'clock in the morning from a masked ball at Count Vorontsov's. At one o'clock in the afternoon, Liprandi found Pushkin writing in bed, his legs, as usual, tucked up under him. He kept abusing Vorontsov, referring to him and his wife as 'milord and his spouse'. It would seem that Pushkin was irritated by the strict etiquette observed at the ball and the way Vorontsov's subordinates had treated him. One of Vorontsov's secretaries, for instance, described Pushkin to Liprandi as 'our immortal bard, who in spite of his great talent, is an extremely vain, bad-tempered man, spoilt by the admiration of his contemporaries'. The general hostility of his colleagues provoked Pushkin into writing epigrams on many of them, which further irritated everybody and led to all sorts of uncomplimentary stories about him.

Pushkin was still more exasperated by his straitened circumstances. He received no money from his parents, while life in Odessa was much more expensive than in Kishinev. His small salary was quite inadequate to cover his most ordinary needs, let alone pay his gambling debts. On November 29, 1823, Alexander Turgenev wrote to Vyazemsky: 'Although Pushkin may be happier in Odessa, he finds life much more difficult, for everything is expensive there and he has no free board and lodgings as he used to have with Inzov.'

The hotels in which Pushkin lived, and the restaurants where he had his meals, were situated in the aristocratic quarter of Odessa near the Maritime Boulevard. The descent to the sea from the Maritime Boulevard was very steep. At the end of one of the two piers was a small terrace reserved for the Odessa nobility who came to enjoy the sea air in the evenings. Near by were the bathing huts which Pushkin often used. 'No sooner did the sunrise gun roar out from the ship,' he wrote in *Onegin's Journey*, 'than, running down the steep shore, I would be on my way to the sea. Then, sitting with a glowing pipe and revived by the salt waves, like a Muslim in his paradise, I drank coffee with oriental grounds.' Pushkin was a regular visitor of the Odessa theatre. Its repertoire included plays as well as operas. In *Onegin's Journey* Pushkin mentions the operas of 'the entrancing Rossini, the darling of Europe', who is 'always the same, always new, he pours out melodies – they effervesce, they flow, they burn like young kisses, everything is sunk in voluptuousness, in the flames of love, like the stream and golden bubbles of hissing Ay'. Among the other 'enchantments' of the theatre, Pushkin mentions 'the exploratory lorgnette, the assignations in the wings, the prima donna and the ballet', and 'the box where, radiantly beautiful, the proud and languorous wife of a businessman is surrounded by a crowd of admirers. She seems to listen and not to listen to the cavatina, the entreaties, and the flattery half concealed in a witticism, while her husband is dozing behind her in a corner and, half awake, cries: Fuora! then yawns and snores again'. After the show 'the people leave noisily and in haste' running into the square 'by the gleam of street lamps and stars, the sons of happy Ausonia humming a playful tune . . . while we roar the recitative'.

8

Pushkin's first acquaintances in Odessa were connected with the theatre. One of these was Ivan Riznich, a rich Dalmatian grain merchant. Pushkin had a violent love affair with his wife in the summer and autumn of 1823.

There were three women in Pushkin's life in Odessa and all of them left their mark on his writings. One of them, Carolina Sobansky, a famous beauty, Pushkin had met in Kiev in February, 1821. She was six years older than Pushkin. At the time of Pushkin's arrival in Odessa Carolina was in Kishinev, and it was she to whom he referred in his letter to his brother as 'the ties he had left behind' which made him rush back there 'for a few days' and spend them 'in an unutterably elegiac way'. Carolina Sobansky was the elder sister of Evva (Evelina) Hansky, who was to marry Balzac. In Odessa Carolina's salon (she was the mistress of Count de Witt at the time and lived in his palatial establishment on top of a cliff overlooking the harbour) was visited by 'the choicest male society', as Vigel expressed it. Vigel, incidentally, was the first to suggest that Carolina and de Witt were in the pay of the Russian secret police and that Carolina, in particular, encouraged her radical guests to express their views freely so as to be able to betray them more easily to the authorities later. There was no danger of that so far as Pushkin was concerned, for the authorities were well aware of his views. In Odessa Pushkin seemed to have spent his time with Carolina reading Benjamin Constant's novel *Adolphe* to her. The novel had so impressed Pushkin that in a note announcing the forthcoming publication of Vyazemsky's translation, he wrote that it belonged 'to one or three novels in which the spirit of the age is reflected and modern man . . . is represented with his selfish, immoral and arid soul'.

It was as 'dear Ellénore', the heroine of *Adolphe*, that Pushkin addressed Carolina in one of the two letters he wrote to her in French in Petersburg on February 2, 1830:

on the ninth anniversary of the day I saw you for the first time.

Permit me to call you by this name which reminds me of the ardent
readings of my youthful years and the sweet phantom which then
fascinated me, and your own life, so violent, so stormy and so different
from what it ought to have been. Dear Ellénore, . . . it is to you that I
owe having known everything that is most convulsive and painful
in the intoxication of love as well as everything that is most stupid . . .

After declaring that she was still as beautiful as on the day she laid her
fingers on his forehead, 'an impression which still remains with me –
cool, moist,' Pushkin went on to repay her for 'making fun' of him and
not having taken his passion seriously in the past by telling her that her
beauty would soon fade and 'fall like an avalanche'.

In the same year Pushkin wrote two lyrical poems to Carolina, one
beginning with the lines 'I loved you and perhaps my love has not yet
faded from my soul', and the other, beginning with the line, 'What care
you about my name?', which Pushkin wrote in Carolina's album on
January 5, 1830.

In fact, Pushkin definitely broke with Carolina by the middle of
October, 1823. His passion for Carolina, he wrote on October 15, 1823, to
Alexander Raevsky, 'his unfailing mentor in matters of morality,' had
cooled considerably 'since in the meantime I have had occasion to fall in
love with somebody else'. Pushkin had fallen in love with Amalia Riznich.
According to the conventions of those days, it was much safer to fall in
love with a married woman since, apart from the trifling matter of having
to fight a duel, there were no other obligations incurred in affairs of this
kind, particularly as the husbands usually had mistresses of their own. It
was rarely that one came across a recalcitrant husband like Count Vorontsov, a well-known womaniser, who because of his exalted position held
firmly to the view that Caesar's wife ought to be above suspicion. Amalia
was the daughter of an Austrian banker. She married Riznich in Vienna in
1822. She was an extraordinarily beautiful young woman, tall and slender,
with sparkling eyes, a neck of remarkable whiteness and a black plait of
hair that reached to her waist. Pushkin's affair with her began in the
summer of 1823 and lasted into the autumn. It would seem that a Polish
landowner, Alexander Sobansky (possibly a relation of Carolina), succeeded in supplanting Amalia's affections for the poet. She ran away with
him to Italy in the spring of 1824. He soon left her and, abandoned by
everybody, she died of consumption in Genoa in June, 1825. Pushkin

wrote some of his most moving and heartrending poems to Amalia Riznich. In *Night*, written on October 26, 1823, he describes how in the darkness her eyes 'shine before me and smile at me – and I hear sounds: My friend, my dear friend . . . I love . . . I'm yours . . . yours.' The next poem written on November 11, 1823, gives a still more intimate picture of their relationship. It begins with the lines, 'Will you forgive me my jealous dreams, the insane agitation of my love?' Pushkin does not seem to have been sure whether her protestations of love were genuine or not.

Tell me why, finding me alone with you, my constant rival greets you slyly? What is he to you? Tell me, what right has he to turn pale and be jealous? In the immodest hour between night and day . . . alone, half-dressed, why must you receive him? But I am loved . . . Alone with me, you are so tender. Your kisses are so fiery! Your words of love are so sincerely full of your soul! You are amused by my sufferings; but I am loved. I understand you. My dear friend, I implore you, do not torment me; you do not know how much I love, you do not know how terribly I suffer.

Pushkin learnt of the death of Amalia Riznich on July 25, 1826. On the manuscript of his next famous poem to her, beginning with the line: 'Beneath the blue sky of her native land,' he wrote four days later the dates of the death of Riznich as well as the death of the five Decembrists executed on July 13, 1826. 'From indifferent lips I heard the news of death and, indifferent, listened to it,' Pushkin writes in this poem. 'So this is whom I loved with . . . such poignant intensity, with such tender and painful longing, with such madness and suffering! . . . Alas, in my soul I find neither tears nor reproach for the poor, fickle shade, for the sweet memory of irrevocable days.'

In the same year in two excised stanzas of the Sixth Canto of *Eugene Onegin* Pushkin described more minutely 'the madness and suffering' caused by his fits of jealousy in the summer and autumn of 1823. In Stanza XV he describes these 'fits of jealousy' as 'an illness just like the plague, like black spleen, like a fever, like a derangement of the mind'. And more directly in Stanza XVI:

I do not wish to disturb your tomb's peace with empty reproach; you are no more. Oh, in the storm of my young life, I owed a terrible experience and voluptuous moments of paradise to you. As one who teaches a weak child, you taught my tender soul deep sorrow . . . You agitated my blood . . . you kindled love in it and the flame of cruel jealousy; but that distressful day has passed: sleep now tormenting shade.

Almost on the eve of his marriage, Pushkin wrote his posthumously published 'invocation' to Amalia Riznich:

> Oh, if it is true that at night when the living rest and when the moonlight glides from the sky over the tombstones, Oh, if it is true, that the quiet graves are empty then – I call your shade, I wait for Leila: to me, my friend, come here . . . here! Appear, beloved shade, as you were before our parting, pale, cold, like a winter's day, deformed by your last torment. Come, like a distant star, like a faint sound or a puff of air or like a terrible vision, I do not care, come here, come here! . . . Longing, I want to say that I still love you, that I am still yours: come here, come here!

The third woman with whom Pushkin fell passionately in love in Odessa, who left an even greater mark on his works, was the Countess Eliza Vorontsov, who joined her husband in Odessa on September 6, 1823. Eliza was the daughter of a Polish magnate and a niece of Potemkin. Though in her early thirties, she was, according to Vigel, 'young at heart and in looks', she did not possess, Vigel explains, what is generally called beauty, but 'the darting looks of her small but charming eyes seemed to go through people'. Vigel found Eliza's smile particularly enchanting. It seemed 'to invite kisses'. Eliza was ten years younger than her husband. Vigel claims that Alexander Raevsky persuaded Eliza, who was his mistress at the time, 'how wonderful it would be to have the famous poet at her feet.' Raevsky had fallen in love with the Countess as early as 1820. He resigned from the army to follow her to Odessa. 'I will not enter into the secret of his [A. Raevsky's] love affair with the Countess,' Vigel writes, 'but I am quite sure he influenced her mind more than her heart and feelings.' If it is true that Raevsky had tried to involve Pushkin in an affair with the Countess in order to amuse himself at his expense, he was soon to be disillusioned. Indeed, it would seem that Pushkin became Eliza's lover almost at once. 'Already in winter,' Vigel writes, 'I felt that Pushkin had got himself into a very dangerous stituation, but I dared not give him any advice, though once I did say to him jokingly that I could not help comparing him to Othello and Raevsky to Iago, but Pushkin only laughed.' At the beginning of March, the Vorontsovs left for their Ukrainian estate where they stayed till the end of the month. Pushkin had just received three thousand roubles from Vyazemsky (the proceeds of the sale of *The Fountain of Bakhchisaray* to a Moscow bookseller) and he immediately sent Inzov the three hundred and sixty roubles he had borrowed from him to defray the expense of his removal to Odessa, and left for Kishinev where he stayed till the end of March.

On returning to Odessa Vorontsov, who had made up his mind to get rid of Pushkin at any cost, wrote to General Kiselev:

I talked here to people who wished Pushkin well and, as a result, I am going to write to Nesselrode to ask him to transfer Pushkin to another place. There are too many people here who flatter his vanity and encourage his stupidities, causing him a great deal of harm. In summer there will be more of them and, instead of learning and working, Pushkin will go astray even more. Since I have nothing to reproach him with except idleness, I shall give Nesselrode a good account of him. I believe it will be much better for Pushkin himself not to remain in Odessa.

Count Karl Nesselrode, Minister for Foreign Affairs, was Pushkin's chief, for Pushkin was still officially a member of the Foreign Office staff. In his letter to Nesselrode Vorontsov asked that Pushkin should be recalled from Odessa before the summer because, he wrote, 'during the bathing season Pushkin will attract even more people who are enthusiastic admirers of his poetry and who turn his head and support his conviction that he is a remarkable writer, while he is only a weak imitator of a little respected model [Lord Byron].' Claiming that he was acting in the interests of the poet himself, Vorontsov proposed that Pushkin should be transferred to 'some other province' where 'he would find a less dangerous environment and more leisure for his work'. On May 2, 1824, in another letter to Nesselrode, Vorontsov again stressed the undesirability of Pushkin's stay in Odessa in view of 'the dangerous environment' and 'the bad society which surrounds him there'. Receiving no satisfactory reply from Petersburg, Vorontsov tried another expedient to make Pushkin's stay in Odessa intolerable: in May he sent Pushkin together with a number of other low-grade civil servants to inspect the measures taken by several provincial

governments to combat an invasion of locusts in the South of Russia.
Vigel writes in his memoirs:

> A few days after my arrival in Odessa, Pushkin, looking alarmed,
> ran into my room and said that a terrible unpleasantness was being pre-
> pared for him. At the time several civil servants of the lowest grade
> were despatched to organise the destruction of the locusts which were
> invading the steppes. Among them was Pushkin. Nothing could have
> been more humiliating to him . . . Kaznacheyev, secretary of the vice-
> regent's chancellery, tried to postpone the date of Pushkin's departure,
> but Vorontsov refused to rescind his order. I, too, tried to put in a
> word for Pushkin, but Vorontsov turned pale, his lips trembled and he
> said to me: 'My dear Vigel, if you want to remain on the same friendly
> terms with me as before, never mention the name of that blackguard
> to me,' and, a moment later, added: 'And this goes also for his worthy
> friend Raevsky.' There was so much evil and baseness in all this that I
> don't think Vorontsov was responsible for it. Indeed, as I learned later,
> it had been suggested to him by Raevsky himself.

Before leaving for the affected districts, Pushkin wrote a letter to
Alexander Kaznacheyev, in which he pointed out that for the past seven
years he had done nothing in the Service, that he had never written a
single official document and never had any dealings with a single depart-
mental chief. As for his salary, he accepted it 'not as a salary of a civil
servant, but as a ration doled out to an exiled prisoner'. He would be ready
to give up his salary, if he were allowed to dispose of his time as he pleased:

> I repeat here what the Count knows already, namely, that if I wished
> to carry out my official duties, I should never have chosen any other
> chief than His Excellency. But being aware of my complete incapacity,
> I am anxious to give up all the advantages of the Service and every
> hope of any future success in it. I realise that this letter is enough, as
> they say, to destroy me. If the Count orders me to send in my resigna-
> tion I am ready to do so, though I cannot help feeling that by changing
> one chief I may lose a great deal without any hope of gaining anything.
> One more word, I wonder if you know that I am suffering from an
> aneurism. For eight years now I have been carrying death within me.
> I can present a certificate from any doctor you please. Can I not be left
> in peace for the remainder of my life, which probably will not last long?

Pushkin's 'aneurism' was a varicose vein in one of his legs, which he again later used as an excuse for obtaining permission to leave Mikhailovskoye for Moscow or Petersburg. The letter to Kaznacheyev did not produce any result. Pushkin had to leave for the affected districts, but returned a few days later and immediately sent in his resignation. In another letter to Kaznacheyev at the beginning of June, 1824 (only a rough draft of it in French has been preserved), Pushkin wrote that he did not think Kaznacheyev's fear of the consequences of his resignation was well-founded:

What should I regret? My ruined career? I have had plenty of time to resign myself to that. My salary? Considering that my literary work could procure me more money, it is only natural to sacrifice my job in the Service to it. You speak of patronage and friendship. The two things are incompatible: I neither can nor wish to depend on the friendship of Count Vorontsov and still less on his patronage: nothing degrades a man more than patronage and I have too high an opinion of Count Vorontsov to wish to abase myself before him. So far as this is concerned, I have democratic prejudices which are quite as valid as the prejudices and the pride of the aristocracy. I am, besides, tired of depending on the good or bad digestion of one or another of my chiefs and of being treated in my native country with less regard than the first young Englishman who comes here to parade his dullness and his slang. The only thing I desire is independence . . . I have overcome my repugnance to writing and selling my poems for a living – the greatest step has been taken. Though. I still only write under the sporadic influence of inspiration, I regard my poems, once written, just as merchandise to be sold at so much a piece . . . I have no doubt that Count Vorontsov, who is an intelligent man, may well be able to put me in the wrong so far as public opinion is concerned, but I am quite willing to let him enjoy that triumph to his heart's content, for I am as little worried by public opinion as by the disapprobation or admiration of our journals.

In his letter to Vyazemsky written about the same time (on June 7, 1824), Pushkin reiterates his view that patronage was dead:

None of us would wish for the magnanimous patronage of an enlightened grandee . . . Modern literature is and must be nobly independent. We alone must apply ourselves to this business and unite. The trouble is that we are all damn lazy – we have the materials, we have the materialists, but *où est le cul de plomb qui poussera ça?* ... Nothing would be easier if we were united ...

In his next letter to Vyazemsky, Pushkin still seems to be in doubt about the result of his resignation. 'What the authorities will do is still unknown,' he writes. 'Tiberius [Alexander I] will be glad of an excuse to find fault with me and the European way of thinking of Count Sejanus [Vorontsov] will put the whole blame on me. For the time being I do not speak with anyone about this. My head is in a whirl.' On July 14, 1824, Pushkin wrote to Alexander Turgenev:

> I expect you know that I sent in my resignation and I am now waiting patiently for a decision, which will determine my future ... Isn't it strange that I should have got on well with Inzov and could not get on at all with Vorontsov? What happened was that Vorontsov began treating me with indecent disrespect and, expecting great unpleasantness, I tried to anticipate his wishes by my letter of resignation. Vorontsov is a vandal, a court boor and a petty egoist. All he saw in me was a collegiate secretary [a civil servant of the lowest grade] and I confess I had quite a different opinion of myself. Old Inzov, it is true, used to put me under arrest every time I happened to give a Moldavian noble a thrashing, but, on the other hand, he used to come and discuss the Spanish revolution with me. I do not know whether Vorontsov would put me under arrest, but I am quite certain that he would never come to discuss the constitution of the Cortes with me.

In his *Imaginary Conversation with Alexander I*, written later in the same year, Pushkin makes the Emperor ask him how it was that he could live amicably with Inzov but not with Vorontsov. Pushkin replied:

> Your Majesty, General Inzov is a kind and worthy old man, a Russian at heart; he does not prefer the first English charlatan he comes across to well-known or not so well-known fellow-citizens of his own. He is not chasing after women, he is not an eighteen-year-old adolescent, and if the passions ever had any sway over him, they have long died away. He trusted nobleness of feelings because he had noble feelings himself; he was not afraid of gibes because he was above them, and he never could have become the victim of well deserved sarcasm because he was

courteous to everybody and did not believe in slanderous stories spread by enemies.

As it turned out, it was not Count Vorontsov, but Pushkin himself who brought about his dismissal from the Service and his exile to Mikhailovskoye. As early as December 20, 1823, Pushkin wrote to Vyazemsky: 'I wonder if we could not somehow avoid the post office in our correspondence. I'd like to send you something too weighty for it.' Vyazemsky understood him to mean that he could not afford the postage for a large parcel, but three months later Pushkin explained that what he meant was that he preferred to send his letters not through the post but through private hands. 'The postmaster will trust me with credit,' Pushkin wrote, 'but I don't trust him.' A few weeks later Pushkin forgot his own misgivings and wrote a letter to Kuechelbecker which was opened in the post, forwarded to the police and resulted in his dismissal and exile.

. . . Reading Shakespeare and the Bible [Pushkin wrote], the Holy Spirit is sometimes to my liking, but I prefer Goethe and Shakespeare. You want to know what I am doing. I am writing miscellaneous stanzas of a romantic poem and taking lessons in pure atheism. An Englishman, an obscure philosopher, lives here. He is the only intelligent atheist I have met. He has written about a thousand pages to prove *qu'il ne peut exister d'être intelligent Créateur et régulateur* and, in passing, destroyed the flimsy evidence of the immortality of the soul. His philosophic system is not so consoling as it is usually thought to be, but unhappily it is more than plausible.

The doctor mentioned in the letter is Dr William Hutchinson, personal physician to the Vorontsovs. It is certainly curious that Pushkin, who abominated Vorontsov's English ways, should have been so impressed by 'milord's' English physician as to ignore the obvious precautions in writing such an incriminating letter.

9

Pushkin's position in Odessa was becoming so desperate that all sorts of rumours began to reach Petersburg. It had even been reported that he had committed suicide. On July 21, 1824, Vyazemsky wrote to Alexander Turgenev: 'They write to me from Petersburg that our Odessa Pushkin shot himself. I am so sure that this rumour is completely unfounded that it does not worry me. *J'espère que Pouchkine ne sera jamais suicidé, que par une bête.*'

Princess Vyazemsky arrived in Odessa on June 7, 1824, bringing Pushkin the news of Lord Byron's tragic death. Pushkin wrote to Vyazemsky on June 24, 1814:

To judge from what Princess Vera [Vyazemsky] tells me, you are sad about Byron, but I am glad of his death as a lofty theme for poetry. Byron's genius paled with his youth. In his tragedies, not excluding *Cain*, he is no longer the fiery demon who created *The Giaour* and *Childe Harold..* The first two cantos of *Don Juan* are superior to the following ones. His poetry has obviously changed. He was all created inside out. There was no gradualness in him. He suddenly matured and grew up – sang his song and fell silent, and his first sounds did not return to him. After the Fourth Canto of *Childe Harold* we no longer heard Byron, but some other poet wrote with great, human talent. Your idea of paying tribute to his death in a fifth canto of his *Hero* [i.e. *Childe Harold*] is delightful, but I am afraid it is not in my power. Greece has spoilt it for me. One may think of the fate of the Greeks just as of the fate of my brothers the Negroes and one may wish both freedom from unendurable slavery, but it is unforgivable childishness for civilised European nations to be raving about Greece. The Jesuits have talked to us so long about Themistocles and Pericles that we imagine that a disgusting people made up of bandits and shopkeepers are their legitimate descendants and heirs. You will say that I have changed my opinion. If you'd come to us in Odessa and have a look at the fellow countrymen of Miltiades, you would agree with me. Why, just see what Byron himself wrote a few years ago in one of his notes to *Childe Harold* – I am referring to the passage where he quotes the opinion of Monsieur Fauvel, the French consul in Smyrna, if I am not mistaken. However, I promise you some verses on His Excellency's death.

(Pushkin was doubly wrong: Fauvel was the French consul in Athens and Byron's note reads: 'Monsieur Fauvel has frequently declared in my hearing that the Greeks do not deserve to be emancipated, reasoning on grounds of their national and individual depravity, but he forgot that such depravity is to be attributed to causes which can only be removed by the measures he reprobates.')

Princess Vyazemsky took a house near Eliza Vorontsov's seaside residence which was surrounded by high cliffs, with a bathing pavilion in the shape of a large shell clinging to the rocks. In a letter to her husband, Princess Vyazemsky wrote that she loved 'to sit on the rocks by the sea and watch the waves breaking at my feet. At times I experience a pang of fear before the onrush of the ninth wave . . . Yesterday I stayed for an hour on the seashore in pouring rain. With Pushkin and Countess Vorontsov we watched a ship tossed by the storm and we were all soaked to the skin by the ninth wave'. Pushkin told the Countess and the Princess of his plans for fleeing from Russia, but, as he wrote in his poem *To the Sea*: 'I did not succeed in leaving for good your motionless shore . . . and steering my poetic flight along the crests of your waves! You waited, you called . . . I was chained; in vain did my soul long to run away: I was bewitched by a powerful passion, I remained on your shores. . . .'

The impatience with which Vorontsov tried to expedite Pushkin's departure from Odessa was increased in June and July when he learned that, with the help of his wife and Princess Vyazemsky, Pushkin was trying to acquire a boat for a flight abroad. On June 15, 1824, the Vorontsovs left Odessa for their new house in Gurzuf. 'Three days ago the Count left for the Crimea with his wife, leaving us here to feed on the dust,' an official of Vorontsov's chancellery wrote to Liprandi on June 18. The Vorontsovs invited a number of people to a house-warming party in Gurzuf. Pushkin, who had counted on being invited, was not included.

The official order for Pushkin's dismissal and exile to Mikhailovskoye, where he was to be put under constant civil and church surveillance, was

signed on July 8, 1824. On July 2 Pushkin's uncle, Vasily, wrote to
Nikolai Krivtsov, a former member of Arzamas and at the time governor
of Tula province:

> Yesterday I received news which grieved me greatly, and I must tell
> you about it for I know how much you care for us all. Alexander, my
> nephew, having fallen into the bad books of Count Vorontsov, has just
> been dismissed the Service. This is a sad blow to his parents and real
> grief to me. My brother, who is at present in Mikhailovskoye, still does
> not know about this. I learnt about it from Alexander Bulgakov
> [the Moscow Postmaster] who had heard about it only a few days
> ago.

Count Vorontsov suddenly returned to Odessa on July 14, followed by
the Countess on July 24. 'When his deportation from Odessa was announced,' Vyazemsky wrote in his memoirs, 'Pushkin came running from
the Vorontsovs' summer residence, looking completely lost, without a hat
and without gloves, which were sent up to him by one of Vorontsov's
servants. Princess Vyazemsky asked him where he had been. "On board
ship," he replied. "We drank and made merry for three whole days." '
Pushkin said goodbye to Eliza at night in the garden of her seaside villa.
He left Odessa on July 31, taking with him the first draft of *The Gipsies*
and the first two cantos of *Eugene Onegin*.

No other woman is mentioned in so many of Pushkin's poems as is the
Countess Vorontsov. Pushkin drew her picture on the manuscripts of
Eugene Onegin and several other poems. He referred to her in his *Conversa-
tion of the Bookseller with the Poet* and his elegy beginning with the line,
The rainy day has come to an end. In the *Conversation* occur the lines

> Where was she whose eyes smiled at me like the sky? Is not one's
> whole life – one night or two? . . . With whom can I share my inspira-
> tion? There was one . . . before her alone I breathed with the wondrous
> ecstasy of love and sacred poetry. There, there where the shadow, where
> the wondrous leaf, where the eternal streams flow, I found the heavenly
> language, burning with the desire of love. Oh, the thought of her who
> could have revived the youth of my wilted soul and again stirred up in
> swarms the dreams of former poetry! She alone would have lit the lamp
> of pure love in my heart, she alone would have understood my obscure
> verses. Alas, vain desires! She has rejected my supplications, my

prayers, the anguish of my soul: the effusions of earthly raptures, as to a goddess, are of no use to her.

In the elegy, too, after describing the contrast between the wintry days in Mikhailovskoye and the southern skies of Odessa, Pushkin conjures up a picture of Eliza sitting on the rocks 'alone . . . no one weeps, no one pines for her; no one kisses her knees in a trance; alone . . . she does not offer her shoulders or moist lips or snow-white breasts to anyone's lips . . . no one is worthy of her heavenly love. Is it not true? You alone, you weep . . .'

The elegy was written in 1824, but Pushkin published it under the date of 1823 as he did his *Conversation*, to conceal the identity of the woman. In the autumn of 1824, Pushkin finished the Third Canto of *Eugene Onegin* and began the Fourth. One of the first stanzas of the Fourth Canto contains lines reminiscent of those in the *Conversation*:

There was one among their throng. I was long enraptured by one, but was I loved and loved by whom, and where and for how long? Why should you know? That is not what matters: what was is past, it is of no account. What matters is that ever since my heart has grown cold in me; it is closed to love; and everything in it is empty and dark.

In the autumn of 1824, Eliza Vorontsov was 'the only one' that lived in Pushkin's poetic imagination. Other poems, which quite certainly hark back to his affair with her, include *The Talisman*, *The Burned Letter* and *The Angel*. Pushkin believed in the magic power of rings. Eliza gave him an old ring bearing a 'mystical' inscription in Hebrew, which he wore as a talisman against unhappy love. So attached was he to the ring that his wife was jealous of the woman who had given it to him. After his death, she gave it to Dr Dahl, a perfect stranger, who attended Pushkin after his last duel and whom she had only met on that occasion. In *The Talisman* the ring is supposed to preserve its wearer when 'perfidious eyes' suddenly bewitch him, or from 'lips that kiss him without loving in the darkness of the night'. *The Burned Letter* refers to the receipt by Pushkin of a letter from Eliza, which she asked him to burn. It begins with the lines: 'Farewell, letter of love, farewell: she gave the order. How long did I hesitate! How long did my hand refuse to consign all my joys to the fire, but the hour has come. Burn, letter of love!'

It was only in October, 1824, that Pushkin discovered to his horror that Alexander Raevsky had all along been the lover of the Countess Vorontsov. On October 18, 1824, he wrote his poem *Perfidy*, in which he declared that if his 'friend' had made use of 'the sacred power of friend-ship' for 'malicious persecution', if he had found 'proud amusement' in his 'anguished sobs and humiliation', if he had been 'the invisible echo' of contemptible slander, if he had thrown a chain over him while he was asleep and 'betrayed him with laughter' to an enemy – then 'go, do not waste empty words, for you have been condemned to the supreme penalty'.

In a long letter from Alexandria where he was staying with the Countess at the time, Alexander Raevsky wrote to Pushkin:

> You were unjust, my dear friend, not to give me your address. Quite apart from your great and beautiful talent, I have for a long time felt a brotherly friendship for you . . . If you won't answer my letter, I shall continue to write and bore you until I force you to reply. Now let me say a few words about Tatyana [that is, Eliza, whom both Pushkin and Alexander had christened with the unlikely name of the heroine of *Eugene Onegin*]. She was very sorry for the misfortunes that befell you. Her enchanting daughter also remembers you and often talks of you, about mad Pushkin, and plays with the head of the dog which you gave her as a present.

Eliza gave birth to another daughter after Pushkin's forced departure from Odessa. It is a mooted point whether the child's father was Pushkin, or Alexander Raevsky or, indeed, the Count himself. Alexander Raevsky certainly considered himself to be the father of the child, for some years later after the end of his affair with the Countess, he stopped her carriage in the streets of Odessa and, shaking his riding crop at her, shouted: 'Take good care of our daughter!' Vorontsov tried to have him arrested and in the end got the authorities to deport him to his father in Poltava.

When Alexander Raevsky was arrested on suspicion of being involved in the Decembrist plot (he was soon released and given a decoration as a reward for his wrongful arrest), Pushkin felt a twinge of regret for his treacherous friend. He wrote to Delvig on January 20, 1826: 'I have been told that A. Raevsky is under arrest. I have no doubt at all of his political innocence. But he has bad legs and the dampness of the casemates [in the Peter and Paul Fortress] would be the death of him. Find out where he is and reassure me.' In the 1830's they met again in Moscow, but their friendship had not survived this crisis. Pushkin mentions him only twice in his correspondence. In a letter to his wife on May 11, 1836, he wrote: 'Raevsky [Alexander], who seemed last time I saw him to have gone a little stupid, has, I believe, livened up again and has become more intelligent.' In a letter to Chaadaev on October 19, 1836, he mentions Raevsky in passing merely to ask to be 'kindly remembered' to him.

PART FOUR

1824-1826
Mikhailovskoye

I

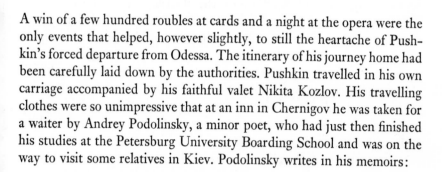

A win of a few hundred roubles at cards and a night at the opera were the only events that helped, however slightly, to still the heartache of Pushkin's forced departure from Odessa. The itinerary of his journey home had been carefully laid down by the authorities. Pushkin travelled in his own carriage accompanied by his faithful valet Nikita Kozlov. His travelling clothes were so unimpressive that at an inn in Chernigov he was taken for a waiter by Andrey Podolinsky, a minor poet, who had just then finished his studies at the Petersburg University Boarding School and was on the way to visit some relatives in Kiev. Podolinsky writes in his memoirs:

> On entering the dining room in the morning, I saw a young man in the next room who kept walking up and down by the buffet counter. He wore a pair of yellow nankeen trousers and a red, crumpled Russian shirt tied round the waist with a threadbare black sash. His rather long, thick, curly hair flew about in disorder. Suddenly the man, whom I took for a waiter, walked up to me rapidly.
>
> 'Are you from the Tsarskoye Selo Lycée?' he asked.
>
> My uniform was the same as the Lycée uniform. I thought the curiosity of a waiter out of place and not wishing to start a conversation with him, I replied rather curtly.
>
> 'Oh, so you must know my brother!' the man said.
>
> This puzzled me and this time I asked him courteously what his name was.
>
> 'I am Pushkin,' he replied. 'My brother Lev was a student at your school.'
>
> Pushkin's fame was at its height at the time. Young men venerated his name and one can easily imagine how glad a seventeen-year-old schoolboy like myself was at this unexpected meeting and how confused I was by my lack of consideration.
>
> In spite of it, Pushkin and I were soon talking freely to one another.

He told me that he was travelling from Odessa to his country estate, but that he had not been entirely suppressed as yet. He laughed and showed me his order for posthorses where all the towns he had to pass through on the way were carefully written down.

The authorities were particularly anxious to isolate Pushkin from his old friends, and the strict order for the posthorses made it quite certain that he would not stop at Kiev where the Raevskys lived. Pushkin gave Podolinsky a note for General Raevsky to inform him and his sons of this latest 'spiteful trick', as he was to write later in his epistle to the poet Yazykov, dame fortune had played on him, forcing him to wander 'without a roof over my head wherever the autocracy is pleased to blow'.

Pushkin had another unexpected meeting in Mogilev, where a nephew of his former headmaster Engelhardt, a young army officer, invited a group of his fellow officers to a party in honour of the poet and spent a whole night with him, drinking, arguing and reading poetry.

It was not long before Pushkin was in his native province of Pskov: peasants in bast shoes and homespun coats, doffing their caps as he drove past, thatched cottages, palings, broken wooden bridges . . . A turning from the highway to a rough country road, another ten miles or so along fields and wooded hills and soon the tall belfry of the Svyatogorsk Monastery came into sight and, to the left of it, after another mile and a half, there lay his mother's Mikhailovskoye surrounded by pine forests. That was where autocracy had 'blown' him in order to 'drag along' his 'fettered days', to quote his epistle to Yazykov again, 'in the village where Peter's nursling, the favourite slave of emperors and empresses . . . my great-grandfather had hid himself . . . and where . . . beneath the canopy of linden avenues he thought in his chill years of his distant Africa. . . .'

Pushkin found his entire family – father, mother, brother and sister – at Mikhailovskoye. His father certainly did not slaughter a fatted calf (if such a beast existed on the Mikhailovskoye estate) to celebrate the return of his prodigal son, but neither did he show any hostility towards him. He was a worried man: his favourite son Lev had just been expelled from school 'for failure to show progress in his studies'. It was rumoured that the real reason for Lev's expulsion was that he had been the leader of a 'mutiny' in defence of their Russian master, the eccentric idealist poet and rebel, Pushkin's classmate, Wilhelm Kuechelbecker.

It was necessary to find a government job for Pushkin and his latest disgrace complicated matters. Pushkin had been put under the double surveillance of the church, in the person of Father Jonah, abbot of the Svyatogorsk Monastery (an inquisitive though innocuous old monk with a pronounced weakness for rum), and the civil authorities, in the person of Boris Aderkas, Governor of Pskov province. The governor delegated his powers to Alexey Peshchurov, the local Marshal of Nobility, who, in turn, enrolled as his assistant Ivan Rokotov, a rather dim personage who amused the young ladies of the neighbourhood by his constant repetition of *Pardonnez ma franchise* or *Je tiens beaucoup à votre opinion*. But even these two gentlemen could not always be on the spot to uncover some dastardly plot by the rebellious poet. Peshchurov therefore decided to ask Sergey Pushkin to supervise his son, the 'dangerous freethinker', by opening his correspondence, eavesdropping on his conversation – in short acting as a police informer on his own son. The old man agreed. Pushkin would not perhaps have minded his father's eavesdropping, but he drew the line at opening letters. He was still obsessed by Countess Vorontsov and, according to his sister Olga, 'every time a letter arrived from Odessa with a seal bearing the same cabalistic signs as were on my brother's ring, he used to lock himself up in his room, did not go out anywhere and did not let anyone in.' After Stanza XXXII of the Third Canto of *Eugene Onegin*, Pushkin added the note: '5 September, 1824: *Une lettre de Elisa Worontsoff.*'

Pushkin wrote to Zhukovsky on October 31, 1824:

When I arrived here, I was met by all as well as could be, but soon everything changed: frightened by my exile, my father kept repeating over and over again that he was expecting the same thing to happen to him; Peshchurov, appointed to keep an eye on me, had the effrontery to saddle my father with the duty of opening my letters, in short, of being my spy; my father's hot temper and morbid sensitivity made it impossible for me to talk to him; I decided to be silent. My father began to reproach my brother for allowing me to preach atheism to him. I still kept silent . . . Finally, wishing to put an end to this painful situation, I went to my father and asked permission to speak frankly to him . . . My father flew into a temper. I bowed, mounted a horse and rode off. My father called my brother and ordered him to have nothing to do *avec ce monstre, ce fils dénaturé* (think of my position, Zhukovsky, and judge for yourself). I seethed with rage. I went to my father, found

him with my mother and told him all I had been keeping back for the
last three months. I concluded by saying that I was talking to him for
the last time. Taking advantage of the absence of witnesses, my father
rushed out of the room and declared to the whole household that *I had
struck him, that I wanted to strike him. that I raised my hand to him,
that I could have thrashed him* . . . I am not justifying myself to you,
but what does he want to achieve by his accusation of a criminal
assault? Siberian mines or deprivation of honour? Save me. Let it be a
fortress or the Solovetsky Monastery! I needn't tell you what my
brother and my sister have to put up with on my account. Once more,
save me. A.P.

Hurry: my father's accusation is known to the whole household.
Nobody believes it, but everybody repeats it. Our neighbours know. I
do not want to offer any explanations to them. You can imagine what
would happen if it were to reach the government. To try to disprove my
father's slanderous allegations in a court of law would be too horrible
for me, but there is no court of law for me. I am *hors de loi.*

P.S. I think you ought to know that I have already written to the
governor of our province requesting him to confine me to a fortress,
but without mentioning my reasons. Mrs Osipov, at whose house I am
writing these lines, has persuaded me to take you into my confidence
about this, too. I confess I am a little vexed at myself and, my dear
fellow, my head is just whirling round and round.

The letter brings home vividly the heated atmosphere of unreason that
led to the final rupture between father and son. It was written at Trigorskoye on the advice of Praskovya Osipov. She also sent off one of her
servants to Pskov with Pushkin's absurd letter to Aderkas with instructions
not to deliver the letter, but to return to Trigorskoye with it a few days
later. By that time, she guessed rightly, Pushkin would have cooled off.

The only other person besides Zhukovsky Pushkin informed about his
'stupid existence' was Princess Vera Vyazemsky to whom he wrote in
October:

What I foresaw has come to pass. My presence in the bosom of my
family has merely redoubled my distress . . . My father has had the
weakness to accept an employment which places him in a false position
with regard to me; as a result I spend all the time I am not in bed on
horseback and in the open country. Everything that reminds me of the

sea saddens me: the faint sound of a running brook makes me feel literally ill. A beautiful sky would make me weep with rage but, thank God, our sky is grey and the moon is just like a turnip . . . I am in the best possible position to finish my novel in verse, but boredom is a frigid Muse and my poem isn't progressing very much.

He ends his letter with the pathetic cry: 'In heaven's name, a word about Odessa. . . .'

By mid-November Pushkin's parents left for Petersburg (Pushkin's brother and sister had left earlier). The whole thing seemed to have been a storm in a teacup.

Pushkin wrote to Zhukovsky on November 29:

I am sorry, my dear honoured friend, to have raised this alarm, but what was I to do? I was exiled for one line of a stupid letter, what would have happened if the government learnt of my father's accusation? That smells of the public hangman and Siberia. Father told me afterwards: 'What a fool! What an excuse to make! Why, if he just dared to strike me, I'd have him bound' – Then, why accuse his son of an act that could never have happened?

A fortnight later he wrote to Dmitry Schwartz, an Odessa friend:

The storm, it seems, has abated and I venture to peep out of my nest and speak to you. I have been in this god-forsaken hole for four months now – I am terribly bored, but I'm afraid nothing can be done about it. There is neither sea, nor southern sky, nor Italian opera here. On the other hand, there aren't any locusts nor milords Vorontsovs, either. My solitude is complete – idleness triumphant . . . I spend all day on horseback and in the evening listen to the fairy tales of my old nurse, the prototype of Tatyana's nurse. She is my only girl friend and with her alone I am not bored. No news from Odessa. My heart craves for news. For a long time I have not dared to engage in correspondence with the colleagues I left behind. I restrained myself a long time, but I cannot restrain myself any longer. For God's sake send me a word about Odessa. Tell me what's going on there. . . .

Pushkin's manuscripts of the Odessa period are covered in drawings of a severe profile with a bowed head, in which his contemporaries recognised Countess Vorontsov. His poem *The Desire for Fame* describes his feelings when he learnt at last of his mistress's treachery and his friend's perfidy: 'Tears, suffering, treachery, calumny – all fell upon my head suddenly . . .' But his amazing resilience came to his rescue again. 'Do you know how I spend my time?' Pushkin wrote to his brother in November, 1824. 'I write my memoirs until dinner, dine late, ride on horseback after dinner, listen to fairy tales in the evening – making good the shortcomings of my accursed education! How wonderful these fairy tales are! Each of them is a poem.' He also described his life in detail (as he wrote to Vyazemsky on May 27, 1826) in the Fourth Canto of *Onegin*:

> Onegin lived like an anchorite. In summer he got up before seven o'clock and, lightly clad, went to the river at the foot of the hill; imitating the poet of Gulnare [Lord Byron], he swum across this Hellespont, then drank his coffee, while leafing through some wretched journal, and dressed . . . country walks, reading and some sleep, the sylvan shade, the purl of streams, sometimes the young and fresh kiss of a white-skinned, dark-eyed girl, a mettlesome horse obedient to the bridle, a fastidious dinner, a bottle of light wine, solitude, quiet . . .

In winter, when he could not go for walks and when 'galloping on horseback' entailed the danger that his horse might catch 'with a blunted shoe the treacherous ice and fall down' (as, indeed, happened to Pushkin), he stayed 'under the lonely roof' and read Walter Scott or the French political writer Dominic de Pradt, and – wrote.

Pushkin was as neglectful as his father of his duties as a landlord. According to his coachman Peter Parfenov, he never did anything about the estate:

> He did not care whether a peasant slept or drank. When at home he used to read books and he read them even at night . . . He was very attached to Arina Rodiodnovna. On getting up in the morning, he would run to see her and ask her: 'Are you all right, Mother?' He always called her mother. When she asked him why he called her mother, he would say, 'Of course, you are my mother: a mother is not one who gives birth to a child, but one who feeds him on her milk' . . .

Arina ruled the Mikhailovskoye roost with a rod of iron. When Rosa Grigoryevna, the housekeeper engaged by Pushkin's mother, fell out with her, she was immediately dismissed. Pushkin wrote to his brother at the end of February, 1825, not without a certain humorous panache:

'. . . There has been a change in my Ministry. I am sorry to say, I had to sack Rosa Grigoryevna . . . otherwise she would have been the death of our nurse who had begun to lose weight on her account . . . She is a rogue and a thief. For the time being, I have taken over the reins of government.'

A much more intimate glimpse into the Mikhailovskoye ménage is provided by Ivan Pushchin in his memoirs. He visited 'the little house of the poet in disgrace' on January 11, 1825. Pushkin, awakened by the sound of sleigh-bells, rushed out on the front steps to see who his visitor was. Pushchin writes:

I looked round and saw Pushkin barefoot, in his nightdress, with raised arms. I jumped out of the sledge, took him in my arms and dragged him into the house. We kept looking at one another, exchanging kisses and standing there without uttering a word. He forgot that he should have covered his nakedness and I forgot to think of my snow-covered fur coat and hat.

It was about eight o'clock in the morning. Pushkin's old nurse ran into the room, found us still in each other's arms . . . I at once realised that it was his kind old nurse whom he had mentioned so many times in his poems and almost strangled her in my arms.

Pushkin's small room was next to the hall, with a window looking out into the yard. Its furniture consisted of a writing desk, a bookcase, etc. Everything was in poetic disorder, everywhere lay sheets of paper covered in writing, the floor was strewn with bitten off bits of quills (in the Lycée, too, he used to write with bitten off bits of quill pens which were so small that he could hardly hold them in his fingers).

Pushkin struck his friend as being 'a little more serious than before'. Otherwise he had changed very little except that he had let his side-whiskers grow. He ascribed his exile to the machinations of Count Vorontsov 'from jealousy', an inadvertent admission of his unhappy love affair with the Countess. Pushkin seemed anxious to find out how the Decembrist conspiracy, in which his friend was deeply involved, was progressing, but Pushchin refused to be drawn. 'Perhaps,' Pushkin commented, 'you are quite right in not trusting me. I suppose I do not deserve your trust because of the many stupid things I have been guilty of.'

They then went round the house. In Arina Rodiodnovna's room, where the seamstresses had by that time gathered, Pushchin immediately noticed

a small figure of a girl who was quite different from the others; I did not, however, tell Pushkin my conclusions. I could not help glancing at him with a kind of a new feeling, aroused by this singular situation: it raised him very high in my eyes and I was afraid to offend him by some inappropriate remark. However, he immediately guessed my playful thought and smiled significantly. That was all that I needed; I winked at him in turn and everything was understood without any words.

This is the first mention of the intimate relationship between Pushkin and one of his serf girls (Olga Kalashnikov, daughter of the steward of Boldino, Sergey Pushkin's estate in the Nizhny–Novgorod province). Why a relationship, which was common enough in those days, should have raised Pushkin 'very high' in Pushchin's eyes is a mystery. Pushchin did not really think that Pushkin would marry the girl!

Pushchin had brought three bottles of champagne with him and, at dinner, they 'drank toasts to Russia, the Lycée, our absent friends, and to *her*'. Once more, as earlier in his mention of Vorontsov's 'jealousy', Pushchin is deliberately vague. Was it the countess or the serf-girl they toasted? It seems more likely to have been the first. They then offered a glass of champagne to the nurse (no mention of the serf-girl!) and 'glasses of home-made brandy' to the other domestics, who 'became very jolly and noisy'. 'They were all,' Pushchin writes with unconscious humour, 'celebrating our reunion.'

The general jollification was interrupted by the unexpected arrival of Father Jonah. The abbot had been informed of Pushkin's visitor and came at once to investigate.

Pushchin had brought Pushkin a present of Griboyedov's great comedy *The Misfortune of Being Clever* (*Gore ot uma*), which Pushkin did not seem to know, and Pushkin began to read it as they were having coffee when someone drove up to the house. Pushkin glanced through the window, looked embarrassed and hastily opened the *Lives of the Saints* which was lying on the table. Pushchin describes what happened:

Noticing his embarrassment and not suspecting its cause, I asked him what it meant, but before he had time to answer, a very short monk with ginger hair entered the room and was introduced to me as the abbot of the neighbouring monastery. I went up to him for his blessing. Pushkin followed me and then asked him to be seated. The monk began by apologising for intruding and then said that, having been told my name, he expected to find an acquaintance of his of the same name whom he had not seen for a long time. It was clear that the abbot had been informed of my arrival and that he was not being quite frank. Although his visit was not altogether opportune, I wanted to *faire bonne mine à mauvais jeu* and did my best to persuade him that he had made a mistake, that I was a Lycée classmate of our host and that General Pushchin, his friend, was in command of a brigade in Kishinev where I had met him in 1820. We talked of all sorts of things and in the meantime tea was served. Pushkin asked for rum which the monk was apparently rather fond of. He drank two glasses of tea, not forgetting to add some rum to them, and after that got up to take his leave, apologising again for interrupting our conversation.

I was glad to get rid of our visitor [Pushchin concludes his description of this characteristic episode], but I could not help feeling embarrassed for Pushkin. At the appearance of the abbot he had grown quiet like a schoolboy. I told him that I was sorry to have been the cause of the visit. 'Don't apologise, my dear fellow,' said Pushkin, 'he often visits me. You see, I am under his surveillance. Why talk about such trifles?'

Pushkin then went on reading Griboyedov's comedy as well as some of his own works. The reading was interrupted by the strong smell of charcoal fumes: it seems that the nurse, thinking that Pushchin would stay the night, had given orders to heat the stoves of the other rooms, unheated since the beginning of winter. By the time the charcoal fumes had been cleared and the house was habitable again, it was almost midnight. Pushchin concludes his account of his visit:

We were offered some snacks and opened the last bottle of champagne at our parting. We embraced warmly in the hope that we might perhaps soon meet in Moscow. It was a faint hope, but it made our parting much easier after a day that had passed so quickly and so happily. By the time my carriage was at the door and the sleighbells were ringing, the clock struck *three*. We clinked glasses for the last time, but we drained them sadly; we seemed to feel that we were drinking together for the last time and that we should never meet again. I threw my fur coat over my shoulders in silence and ran out into the hall. Pushkin said something, but I did not hear. I looked back: he was standing on the front steps with a lighted candle in his hand. The horses started with a jerk. I heard Pushkin cry: 'Goodbye, friend!' The gates closed with a creaking noise behind me.

Three months later, in the middle of April, 1825, Pushkin's other Lycée classmate, Anton Delvig, spent a few days at Mikhailovskoye. The two poets read their poems to each other, discussed literature and politics, and visited Pushkin's Trigorskoye neighbours. At the end of August Pushkin met his third Lycée classmate, Prince Vladimir Gorchakov, the future Minister of Foreign Affairs. His meeting with Gorchakov was something of an anti-climax. 'We met and parted rather coldly, at least on my part. He has dried up terribly,' Pushkin wrote to Vyazemsky at the end of September, 1825, 'but that's to be expected: we do not mature in the North: we either dry up or we rot: the first, all the same, is preferable. Having nothing better to do, I read him a few scenes from my play [*Boris Godunov*] . . .' Pushkin met Gorchakov at the estate of Alexey Peshchurov, Gorchakov's uncle and Pushkin's 'lay' supervisor.

2

Pushkin was obsessed by one thought during the two years in Mikhailov-skoye: flight from Russia! He had tried to escape abroad while in Odessa but, as he wrote in *To the Sea*, he was 'fettered' there. In Mikhailovskoye there was no 'powerful passion' to keep him back. He had discussed the plans for his escape with his brother before Lev had left for Petersburg. 'My brother,' he wrote in an unfinished poem written at the end of 1824, 'in the dangerous hour of parting all my heart's thoughts go out to you. For the last time let us clasp hands and resign ourselves to our fate. Bless the poet's flight . . . Contemning the voice of reproach and the calls of sweet hopes, I go to a foreign land to shake the dust of my native land from my travelling clothes . . .' Two years later (on May 26, 1826), at the beginning of a new reign, he wrote to Vyazemsky:

> I, of course, despise my country from head to foot . . . If the Tsar grants me freedom, I shall not remain here for one month. We live in a sad age, and when I think of London, railways, steamships, English journals or Paris theatres and brothels, my God-forsaken Mikhailov-skoye bores me to death and drives me to distraction. In the Fourth Canto of *Onegin* I have described my life. Should you read it sometimes and ask with your charming smile: And where is my poet? . . . You will hear in reply: he has run off to Paris and will never return to accursed Russia – the clever fellow!'

Pushkin tried two ways of escape: the direct one of obtaining an exit permit from the Tsar and the indirect, melodramatic one of fleeing abroad disguised as a servant of Alexey Vulf, the nineteen-year-old son of Mrs Osipov. Needless to say, nothing came of his second plan. All that is known about it is contained in some 'coded' letters to his brother and Vulf, which were as puerile as the plan itself. To obtain the Emperor's permission to go abroad, Pushkin enrolled the aid of Zhukovsky. To make his request more plausible he mentioned his old complaint, a varicose vein in his right leg, which he elavated to the status of an 'aneurism'. This, he declared in a letter to Alexander I on April 24, 1825, required 'an immediate operation, which could only be satisfactorily performed abroad'. He sent the letter to Zhukovsky who was to deliver it to 'the White Tsar' himself. But Zhukovsky and Pushkin's Petersburg friends became really worried about the poet's 'aneurism' and decided to take what seemed to them the much more effective step of asking Pushkin's mother to petition the Tsar to permit her son to go to Riga 'or some other place' for treatment. The request was promptly refused, but Pushkin was given permission to go to Pskov. He was furious. 'Why was it necessary,' he wrote to Delvig on July 23, 1825, 'to replace my sensible and reasonable letter by my mother's letter? Did they think it would be more touching? A grave mistake. In the former case, I should have been acting straightforwardly, in the latter, they could only suspect me of cunning and obduracy.' And he concluded with a story from Tacitus:

A certain Vibius Serenus, on being denounced by his own son, was sentenced by the Roman Senate to be confined on some waterless island. Tiberius opposed this decision, saying that a man to whom life had been granted must not be deprived of the means for sustaining life. Words worthy of a lucid and humane mind. The more I read Tacitus the more reconciled do I become to Tiberius. He was one of the greatest statesmen of antiquity.

In his letter to Zhukovsky in July he allowed himself to be openly sarcastic:

His Majesty's unexpected favour has touched me deeply, particularly as our provincial governor has already proposed that I should move my domicile to Pskov . . . I have made enquiries about the Pskov surgeons; a certain man was pointed out to me as a very skilful specialist in veterinary work and well known in the scientific world for his book on the treatment of horses.

Deeply conscious as I am of the fatherly indulgence of his Majesty, I have, nevertheless, made up my mind to remain in Mikhailovskoye . . .

Having given little thought to my aneurism for ten years, I see no reason why I should suddenly make a fuss about it. I am still expecting that the Emperor may with time give me permission to seek a place I fancy and a physician that my own reason and not the command of the highest authorities may persuade me to trust.

But Zhukovsky was not to be put off so easily when, for all he knew, the very life of a poet of Pushkin's genius was at stake. He, therefore, approached a well-known surgeon, Dr Ivan Moyer, and asked him to go to Pskov to operate on Pushkin. That would have exposed Pushkin's plot, for it would not have taken the surgeon long to discover that Pushkin's 'aneurism' was just a pretext for getting out of Russia. Pushkin at once rushed off a letter to Dr Moyer imploring him not to trouble to come to Pskov. 'The operation my aneurism requires,' he wrote on July 29, 1825, 'is too unimportant to take a famous man away from his duties and his domicile.' Meanwhile, Pushkin's friends were planning to send another petition to Alexander I. 'My friends,' Pushkin complained bitterly to Mrs Osipov on July 25, 'are taking up my cause so enthusiastically that in the end I shall be incarcerated in the Schluesselburg Fortress.' To his sister Olga he wrote on August 25:

My friends have done exactly what I implored them not to do. They are merely exacerbating his Majesty and prolonging my exile . . . My state of health requires a change of climate and not a word was said to his Majesty about it. Is it his fault if he knows nothing of it? I am told that the public is indignant; so am I too because of the thoughtlessness and carelessness of the people who interfere in my affairs. Lord, deliver me from my friends!'

He echoed the cry in the eighteenth stanza of the Fourth Canto of *Eugene Onegin* he had just then been writing: 'Everyone has enemies in the world, but preserve us from our friends, O Lord! Some friends, my friends!' He even made a bad pun on his wretched vein: 'My dear fellow,' he wrote to Vyazemsky on September 13, 1825, 'here is a pun on my aneurism: My friends are fussing about my vein [*zhile*], but what about my domicile [*zhilyo*]?' But his fury with his friends (and, perhaps, even more with himself for having misjudged the situation so badly) had now reached its apogee:

It is very natural [he wrote in the same letter] that the Tsar's favour has upset me, for . . . Pskov is worse than the country, where at least I am not under the surveillance of the police. It is easy for you to reproach me with ingratitude at your leisure, but if you were in my place (which God forbid), you would perhaps have been even more enraged than I. My friends keep interceding on my behalf and my position is getting worse and worse . . . I have nurtured my aneurism for five years as a last resort for my deliverance, my *ultima ratio libertatis*, and suddenly my last hope is shattered . . . They are worrying about my life. Thank you very much, but what the devil of a life is it? I'd much rather die in Mikhailovskoye for lack of treatment, for then my grave would at least be a living reproach and you could write an agreeable and useful epitaph on it. No, friendship is entering into a conspiracy with tyranny and is taking upon itself to justify it . . . They send for Moyer, who, of course, could perform such an operation even in a Siberian mine; they deprive me of my right to complain (not in verse, but in prose, a devil of a difference!), and then they tell me not to get worked up . . . Why am I unwilling to agree to the arrival of Moyer in Mikhailovskoye? I am not wealthy enough to send for celebrated specialists and pay them for treating me. Moyer is Zhukovsky's friend, not Zhukovsky. I want no charity from him.

He once again tried to appeal direct to Alexander I and even drafted a letter in French, in which he spoke of his 'aneurism' which 'necessitated a prompt operation' and besought the Emperor to permit him to reside in Moscow or Petersburg or to 'specify some locality in Europe' where he could look after his health. The letter was probably drafted in September. In November Alexander I died suddenly in Taganrog. The news of his death reached Mikhailovskoye about December 10. Pushkin had long been anxious to meet his Petersburg friends. He made up his mind to leave for Petersburg, believing that the authorities would pay little attention to his disobedience in view of such important events. He decided first to see Ryleyev who could give him the latest news. He ordered his carriage and drove off to say goodbye to his Trigorskoye neighbours. On the way to Trigorskoye a hare ran across the road. On his return another hare ran across the road. Pushkin returned home, feeling upset by what he took to be a bad omen for his journey. At home he found his coachman in bed with a violent attack of the d.t.'s. At length, his carriage was ready to leave. As it was driving through the gates, a priest happened to walk past along the road. This third unlucky omen finally decided Pushkin to give up his idea of going to Petersburg. Pushkin told Mrs Osipov later:

These would have been the results of my voyage. I calculated to arrive in Petersburg late at night. To prevent my arrival from being discovered too soon, I would have gone straight to the meeting of the conspirators at Ryleyev's flat on December 13, that is, on the eve of the armed uprising. They would have received me with open arms and I would most probably have joined the others in Senate Square and would not have been sitting with you today.

But the news of the ascension to the throne of Nicholas I and the widely shared views of the young Emperor's supposedly 'liberal' policies revived Pushkin's hopes of obtaining permission to go abroad. 'For God's sake, do not ask the Tsar for permission for me to live in Opochka or in Riga,' he wrote to Pletnyov on December 6, 1826. 'What the hell do I want to live there for? Ask for permission for me to enter the capitals or to go abroad . . . It would be much more sensible to go abroad. What is there for me to do in Russia? Show this letter to Zhukovsky who is perhaps angry with me. He may be able to arrange something.' A month later when rumours of the Decembrist insurrection reached him, he wrote to Pletnyov:

I hope the Tsar will be merciful to me. Incidentally, could not Zhukovsky find out if I may hope for the indulgence of his Majesty? For the last six years I have been in disfavour and, say what you like, I am only twenty-six. The late Emperor exiled me to my country estate in 1824 for two irreligious lines – I do not know of any other artistic misdemeanours on my part. Won't our young Tsar permit me to take myself off to some warmer clime, if indeed it is quite impossible for me to show myself in Petersburg – eh?'

Between mid-May and mid-June, 1826, when it had become evident that the authorities did not think that he was involved in the Decembrist plot, he decided (on the advice of Vyazemsky) to write to Nicholas I, renewing his request for permission to go abroad. 'My health,' he wrote, 'shattered in my early youth, and a kind of aneurism, have for a long time now been in need of constant treatment, in support of which I present a medical certificate. I venture to request most humbly for permission for this purpose to go to Moscow or to Petersburg or abroad.' On a separate sheet of paper, he added the following 'pledge': 'I, the undersigned, pledge myself in future not to belong to any secret societies under whatever name they may exist. I hereby certify that I have never belonged and do not belong to any secret society and that I have never had any knowledge of them.

'Civil Servant of the tenth class, Alexander Pushkin [that is, collegiate secretary, the same rank in which Pushkin entered the Government Service in 1817]. May 11, 1826.'

This certificate was signed by the Pskov inspector of the Medical Council, testifying that Pushkin actually had *varicositus totius cruris dextris*. He wrote to Vyazemsky on July 10, 1826:

I have already written to the Tsar at the completion of the investigation and I concluded my petition in your exact words. I am waiting for an answer, but my hopes are not bright. It is true I have never liked mutiny and revolution, but I was in close touch with almost all, and in correspondence with, many of the conspirators. All the subversive manuscripts are ascribed to me, as all the obscene ones are attributed to Barkov. If I had been summoned by the Commission, I should, of course, have cleared myself, but I have been left in peace and that does not seem to bode any good.

The authorities did not forget Pushkin. At the end of July Boshnyak, a government secret agent disguised as a 'botanist', arrived in Pskov to study the flora of the Pskov province. He paid visits to the estates near Mikhailovskoye and made discreet enquiries about Pushkin. No one suspected that the 'botanist' was really a government secret agent who had been ordered to 'carry out a secret and detailed investigation into the conduct of the well-known poet Pushkin, suspected of actions directed towards the liberation of the peasants' and to arrest him 'if he happened to be really guilty'. Boshnyak, however, could find nothing reprehensible about Pushkin's way of life. His report to the government contained no mention of Pushkin's 'revolutionary activities'. It did mention a number of highly interesting facts about the poet's life in the country:

. . . I have discovered that Pushkin appeared at the fair of the Svyatogorsk Monastery wearing a shirt with a pink sash and a wide-brimmed straw hat and carrying an iron stick in his hand; that he was modest and circumspect, that he never spoke about the government and that, generally, there are no rumours current about him among the common people . . . I also learned that Pushkin treats the peasants in a friendly fashion, shaking hands with those he knows, that sometimes he goes riding on horseback and on arriving at his destination tells his servant to let the horse graze freely, saying that every animal has a right to freedom . . . Pushkin is reputed to be an excellent and kindly master who conducts himself very simply and does not offend anyone; he has very few acquaintances and leads a very secluded life. The only information about him I gathered was from his own servants who spoke of him in the highest terms of praise . . . From the Abbot Jonah I learned the following: Pushkin sometimes visits the Abbot Jonah, drinks home-made brandy with him and discusses all sorts of things with him. To my question whether Pushkin was sowing dissension among the peasants, Abbot Jonah replied: 'He does not interfere in anything and lives as innocently as a young girl.'

Pushkin visited the Svyatogorsk fair on May 19, 1825, the ninth Friday after Easter, and scandalised the local gentry by his unconventional attire. A local shopkeeper left the following note in his diary about that memorable occasion:

On May 19 there was a fair at the Svyatogorsk Monastery and there I had the good fortune to see Alexander Pushkin, who surprised me by the strange clothes he wore. For instance, he wore a straw hat, a red cotton shirt with a blue [?] sash round his waist and carried an iron stick in his hand. He had very long sidewhiskers, which looked more like a beard, and very long fingernails with which he peeled oranges, eating them with great relish, half a dozen of them.

Pushkin's coachman Parfenov gives the additional information about a crowd of beggars and blind men who gathered round Pushkin at the fair and 'sang him songs'. Pushkin himself refers to his 'Russian shirt' in an expunged stanza of the Fourth Canto of *Eugene Onegin*, mentioning the fact that a Pskov lady was greatly distressed by his 'immoral and reckless attire'.

The authorities found nothing incriminating or particularly shocking in Boshnyak's report and shortly after the arrival of Nicholas I in Moscow for his coronation, Pushkin was unexpectedly summoned to Pskov and from there sent off posthaste to Moscow accompanied by a government courier. Maria, one of Mrs Osipov's youngest daughters, records the occasion:

On the first or the second of September, Pushkin came to see us. The weather was glorious and we went for a long walk. Pushkin was particularly cheerful. At eleven o'clock at night we saw him off to

Mikhailovskoye. Early next morning his old nurse, Arina Rodiodnovna, came to see us. She had run all the way from Mikhailovskoye, she was out of breath, her white hair fell in disorder over her face and shoulders, she was sobbing bitterly. She told us that between three and four o'clock in the morning an officer had arrived and taken Pushkin away. 'After he had gone,' Arina added, 'I too destroyed something.' When asked what it was, she said it was 'the horrid cheese which Pushkin liked to eat and I could not bear. It has such an awful smell, that foreign cheese has!'

In a letter, written as usual in French, to Mrs Osipov from Pskov on September 4, Pushkin wrote:

I suppose my sudden departure with a courier must have surprised you as much as it did me. But then in our country one can do nothing without a courier. I have been given one for greater safety. According to a very pleasant letter from Count Ivan Dibich [informing Pushkin that he was summoned to Moscow to see Nicholas I, but was not under arrest], I should be proud of it. I am going straight to Moscow where I expect to be on the eighth of the present month. As soon as I am free, I shall return in all haste to Trigorskoye where from now on my heart is forever fixed.

3

Pushkin was very fond of the picturesque road which led from Mikhailovskoye to Trigorskoye, where he spent most of his leisure hours during his exile. When revisiting Mikhailovskoye in the autumn of 1835, in his famous nostalgic poem beginning with the line: 'Once again I visit you,' Pushkin wrote:

Here is the little house of the exile where I lived with my poor nurse. The old woman is no longer alive, and no longer do I hear her steps behind the wall . . . Beyond the house there is a hill covered with old pines, spruce and birches . . . on which I often used to sit motionless, looking at the lake and remembering with a feeling of sadness other shores and other waves . . . Villages are scattered along the steep banks and in the distance a windmill is turning its sails laboriously in the wind.

Skirting the lake, the road rose steeply half-way between Mikhailovskoye and Trigorskoye, where, Pushkin recalls in the poem, 'three pine trees stood, one apart and the others close together – when I rode past them on horseback in the moonlight the familiar rustle of their tops welcomed me . . .' From the place of the three pines the meandering river Sorot and the three hills rising over it could be clearly seen. The first was the village of Voronich, the second an ancient ruined fortress and the third the Trigorskoye estate with its park, ponds, avenues, flowerbeds and orchard. The Trigorskoye country house was a long, one-storied, wooden building (formerly a canvas mill). Mrs Praskovya Osipov (Vulf by her first marriage) was eighteen years older than Pushkin, but still of the right age to appeal to his yearning for motherly love which he had lacked as a child. She was below medium size, plump, with a longish face, a beautifully shaped nose, soft and silky chestnut hair, brown eyes and a mouth that was neither too large, nor unpleasant, except that her lower lip protruded a little. A very masterful woman, she had brought up her children very strictly. She was one of the few women Pushkin really respected. She helped him with her advice during his exile, tried to protect him from his more foolish entanglements and supervised his burial. The eldest of her five daughters, Anna (Annette) Vulf, was of the same age as Pushkin. She was a sentimental, not particularly beautiful nor very intelligent girl. Her sister Euphraxie (Zizi) was the life and soul of the Trigorskoye society. Born in 1810, she was the first to attract Pushkin's attention. In the neighbourhood there was even talk about an impending marriage of Pushkin and Zizi Vulf. 'The other day,' Pushkin wrote to his brother in November, 1824, 'I compared measurements with Euphraxie and our waists turned out to be the same. One of two things: either I have the waist of a fifteen-year-old girl or she has the waist of a twenty-five-year-old man.' Pushkin refers to her slender waist in *Eugene Onegin* (Canto Five, Stanza XXXIII), comparing it to a long narrow wineglass and describing Zizi herself as 'the crystal of my soul, the object of my innocent rhymes, love's alluring phial, you with whom I used to be infatuated'. At one time or another Pushkin had more or less intimate affairs with the mother and her two elder daughters. Of her other daughters, Maria was a child of five or six during Pushkin's exile in Mikhailovskoye and Yeka-terina was three years younger than Maria. There were, besides, Anna (Netty) Vulf, a niece of Mrs Osipov's, and Alexandra Osipov, Mrs Osipov's stepdaughter, to whom Pushkin wrote his poem *Confession*, beginning with the line: 'I love you, though it makes me mad' (1826), a poem full of elegiac sighs, which it is difficult to take seriously. Of Mrs Osipov's three sons, the eldest Alexey Vulf, a student of Dorpat University, was five years younger than Pushkin at the time of Pushkin's exile. Maria Osipov writes in her memoirs:

All my sisters were at the time marriageable young women and Euphraxie was particularly beautiful. Every day after two o'clock in the afternoon, Pushkin used to appear at our house from Mikhailovskoye. He usually came riding on a beautiful hunter or, more rarely, on an old peasant mare. We all, my sisters and I, would run out to meet him. One day (I remember that very clearly), when he came riding on an old peasant mare, his feet almost dragging on the ground, I burst out laugh-ing at him. He ran after me, shaking his long fingernails at me. Often he would come on foot and steal up to our house and, in summer, when all the windows were open, he would climb through a window. We would all be busy, but the moment he arrived everything turned topsy-turvy: laughter, jokes, loud talk in all the rooms. Pushkin was always bursting with life, he never sat still. In Petersburg, before his marriage, he was sitting in our drawing room, laughing and cracking jokes, when suddenly he got up from the sofa and jumped over the table, overturning the burning candles. We said to him, 'Pushkin, it's about time you sobered down,' but he only laughed. I always used to tease him. In the 'twenties it was the fashion to cut out figures and paste them on paper. I would cut out a monkey and tease Pushkin with it. He would get terribly angry at first, but remembering that he was only dealing with a child, he would say: You are as young as April . . . Pushkin often recited impromptu poems to us, but very seldom any of his longer poems.

Pushkin was not particularly enamoured of the young ladies of the Pskov province, among whom, he wrote to Vera Vyazemsky, he enjoyed 'the reputation of an Onegin'. He dismissed them rather cavalierly in one of the expunged stanzas of the Fourth Canto of *Eugene Onegin* as lacking both 'the refined courtesy of the aristocracy' and 'the frivolity of charming trollops'. He would gladly forgive them 'their gossip, their self-conceit, their family jokes and, at times, even the uncleanness of their teeth', let alone 'their rudeness and affectation', but could never forgive them 'their mad obsession with fashions' and 'their clumsy etiquette'. As for the Trigorskoye girls, Pushkin described them a little uncharitably in his letter to Princess Vyazemsky at the end of October 1824 as '*assez mauvaises sous tous les rapports* who play for me some Rossini whose music I sent for'. Sometimes he could not disguise his contempt for them. 'Your Trigorskoye friends,' he wrote his sister Olga in December, 1824, 'are unendurable fools, except for the mother.'

The only emotional upheaval Pushkin experienced in Trigorskoye was connected with the visit of Anna Kern, Mrs Osipov's niece, who had made such a deep impression on him at the Olenins' in 1819. Pushkin met her again in June, 1825. But already on December 8, 1824, he wrote to Arkady Rodzyanko, whose mistress, he knew, Anna Kern happened to be at the time: '. . . Explain to me, my dear fellow, what sort of person is Anna Kern, who wrote so many nice things about me to her cousin. They tell me she is very lovely . . . Anyway, knowing how easily you fall in love and your *unusual talents* in every respect, I assume that your business is done or half done. I congratulate you, my dear fellow.'

Anna Kern was twenty-seven and Pushkin had not seen her for six years. But he could never forget 'the wondrous moment' when she had first appeared before him 'like a fleeting phantom, like a genius of pure beauty' – a description of the real Anna Kern he knew very well, when he met her again, to be false. But whether real or not, the memory was potent enough to inspire one of his loveliest lyrical poems. This is Anna Kern's description of their meeting which resulted in the almost instantaneous birth of a masterpiece:

We were all sitting at dinner . . . when suddenly Pushkin came in with a big stick in his hand. Afterwards he very often appeared at dinner like that, but he never sat down at table: he dined at home much earlier and he ate very little. He always arrived accompanied by two large wolf hounds. My aunt introduced me to him and he bowed very low, but never uttered a word; all his movements betrayed shyness. I did not know what to say to him, either, and it took us some time to get used to one another and talk freely. Besides, it was difficult to become friendly with him all of a sudden. He was very uneven in his behaviour: one moment he would be noisily gay, another he would be sad or shy or impudent or infinitely polite or wearisomely bored. It was quite impossible to guess what his mood would be one moment later. On one occasion he was so discourteous that he admitted it himself to my cousin by saying: '*Ai-je été assez vulgaire aujourd'hui!*' Generally, he did not know how to conceal his feelings. He expressed them always sincerely and was indescribably charming when excited by some pleasant occurrence . . . When he made up his mind to be nice to someone, nothing could compare with the brilliance, the wit and the sheer fascination of his speech . . . One day he arrived in Trigorskoye with a large black book, on the margins of which were drawn lots of female heads and feet. He said that he had brought it for me. Soon we all sat down in a circle round him and he read us his *Gipsies* . . . A few days after this reading my aunt proposed that we should all go to Mikhailovskoye after supper. Pushkin accepted the proposal with glee and we drove off. The weather was glorious, the moonlight June night was cool and redolent of the fragrance of the fields. We drove in two carriages, my aunt and her son in one and my cousin, Pushkin and I in the other. Neither before nor since have I seen him so good-humouredly cheerful and courteous. He joked without sarcasm, said nice things about the moon, did not call it stupid, but said, *J'aime la lune, quand elle éclaire un beau visage* . . . On arriving in Mikhailovskoye, we did not enter the house, but went straight to the old neglected park, 'the shelter of pensive dryads', with its long avenues of ancient trees whose intertwining roots ran over the paths. I tripped over them and Pushkin gave a start. My aunt who was walking behind us said: *Mon cher Pouchkine, faites les honneurs de votre jardin à Madame.* He quickly offered me his arm and ran fast, fast, like a schoolboy who had suddenly received permission to go for a walk. I do not remember the details of our conversation; he reminded me of our first meeting at the Olenins' and spoke of it excitedly and rapturously, adding at the end of our conversation: '*Vous aviez un air si virginale: n'est ce pas que vous aviez quelque chose comme une croix?*'

The impression Anna Kern made on Pushkin did not escape Mrs Osipov, who had no illusions about her niece and certainly saw nothing 'virginal' or anything resembling a cross about her. She was much too fond of Pushkin herself not to feel jealous. Besides, she was certainly not going to let Pushkin make a fool of himself over a woman who was notorious for her promiscuity. Next morning, therefore, she packed Anna Kern and her own daughter Annette off to Riga where Pushkin could not follow them. She, too, went with them. Anna Kern goes on with her tale, omitting, characteristically, every significant fact:

Next day I had to go to Riga together with my cousin Anna Vulf. Pushkin came to see us off in the morning and, as a parting gift, brought me a copy of his second [it was actually the first] canto of *Onegin*. Between its uncut pages I found a page of note-paper folded in four with the poem beginning with the line, *I remember a wondrous moment*, etc., etc. When I was about to put his poetic gift away in a box, he gazed long at me, then snatched it convulsively out of my hands and refused to give it back to me; it was with great difficulty that I made him return it to me. What had flashed through his head at that moment I do not know. I sent the poem to Baron Delvig, who published it in his *Northern Flowers*. Mikhail Glinka set it to beautiful music and kept it.

What a give-away scene! Suddenly realising how little his 'genius of pure beauty' resembles the real Anna Kern, Pushkin snatches his poem 'convulsively' out of her hand and refuses to give it back; Anna Kern gets it back 'with great difficulty' and, as Pushkin quite certainly suspected, sends it off immediately to be published. And yet the enchantment of an old memory persisted. Not that Pushkin deceived himself. In his first letter to Riga meant for Anna Kern's eyes, though written to Anna Vulf, he is quite outspoken about it. He wrote on July 21, 1825, in French, of course:

Every night I take a walk in the garden and I keep repeating to myself: She was here – the stone she tripped over lies on my table. ['There was no stone in the garden,' Anna Kern comments, 'I tripped over the intertwined roots of the trees.'] Beside it is the spray of faded heliotrope. ['A spray of heliotrope he did indeed beg me to give him,' Anna Kern again comments.] I write many poems – all this if you like bears a strong resemblance to love, but I swear to you that it has nothing to do with love. Had I been in love, I'd have had spasms on Sunday from rage and jealousy, while all I felt was vexation, – and yet the thought that I mean nothing to her, that, having awakened and interested her imagination, I merely amused her curiosity, that the memory of me does not make her more pensive for a single moment amid her conquests, nor more sad during her melancholy, that her beautiful eyes will be fixed upon some Riga fop with the same piercing feeling and voluptuous expression – this thought I find unbearable; tell her that I shall die of it, no, don't tell her that, she will only laugh at me, the entrancing creature. But tell her that, if she has no hidden feeling of tenderness for me in her heart, no mysterious and melancholy attraction to me, then I despise her – do you hear? Yes, despise her, in spite of all the astonishment such an unaccustomed feeling may arouse in her.

'The thought that I mean nothing to her' – that was, of course, the situation in a nutshell and that was why he kept writing those frantic letters to her from July 25 to December 8, full of amorous clichés and entreaties that concealed his wounded *amour-propre*. Only once did a genuine note of anger break through the thin film of false sentiment. On the return to Trigorskoye of Mrs Osipov, who had quarrelled with Anna

Kern because she was having an affair with her son, Pushkin wrote to her on August 21: 'I would very much like to know why your cousin left Riga only on the 15th of this month and why his name slipped from the point of your pen three times in your letter to me. May I know, if it isn't too rude to ask?' A month later, on September 22, Pushkin revealed himself, surprisingly, as a stickler for the proprieties:

Incidentally, you swear to me by all that is holy that you are not flirting with anyone and yet you are on intimate terms with your cousin: *Vous tutoyez votre cousin, vous dites: je m'éprise ta mère. C'est affreux: il fallait dire; votre mère!* It would have been much better to have said nothing at all because that sentence has had a most devilish effect. Jealousy apart, I advise you, as a friend who is truly devoted to you, to break off that correspondence. I can't understand why you are flirting with a young student (who is not a poet) at such a respectable distance.

On May 7, 1826, in a letter to 'the student', that is, Alexey Vulf himself, Pushkin no longer disguised his opinion of the 'enchantress' he had been bombarding with letters with so little effect. 'Are you receiving letters from Anna [Vulf],' he inquired, 'and what is the Whore of Babylon, Anna Petrovna [Kern] doing?'

When Pushkin met Anna Kern again in 1827 in Petersburg, she seemed for a time to resist his advances. In her memoirs she claimed that in January, 1828, she had been only once alone with Pushkin for a few minutes. Unfortunately for her, Pushkin, to whom the possession of Anna Kern had by then become a matter of personal prestige, wrote to his friend Sobolevsky in February, 1828: '. . . You keep writing to me about Anna Kern whom with the help of God I fucked the other day . . .' They had, in fact, by that time gone through the ritual of an exchange of rings, but whatever there was left of Pushkin's passion had been spent much earlier and their relationship assumed the rather prosaic nature of a casual affair between old friends. In her memoirs, Anna Kern gives this shrewd appraisal of Pushkin's character:

Pushkin often said: 'Only fools and children are malicious.' In spite, however, of this view he was often malicious himself, though he always regretted it . . . I find that Pushkin was often inconsiderate and presumptuous, that in spite of his genius, he was not always sensible and sometimes not even intelligent . . . I believe that he was more capable of being carried away by brilliance and by a vain desire to be liked rather than by a truly deep feeling of love. If I am not mistaken, that was his tribute to the spirit of the age: I can find no other explanation. He always liked *un bon mot, la répartie vive*. He told me once – it was after I had told him that it was not nice to be unkind to me – *moi, qui suis si inoffensive:* I don't mind having a quarrel with you, but your cousin is quite a different matter.

Her cousin Anna Vulf was, indeed, quite a different matter. Pushkin had known her ever since he had first visited Trigorskoye after leaving the Lycée and he always had a warm spot for her in his heart. The trouble was that not only was Annette exasperatingly in love with him, but that she seemed resigned to his indifference. '*Rien de plus insipide,*' Pushkin told Anna Kern in a reference to Anna Vulf, '*que la patience et la résignation!*' But in January and February, 1826, he gave in to her dumb entreaties and became her lover for a short time. Was Anna his 'victim', as some Pushkin biographers maintain? Did he really 'debauch' her, a grown-up woman of twenty-seven, as others assert? Are her letters to Pushkin, after she had been whisked off by her mother to her aunt's estate of Malinniki, as 'heart-rending' as they are said to be? In her very first letter to Pushkin from Malinniki at the beginning of March, 1826, Annette boasts of having found 'an enchanting cousin who is passionately in love with me and who does not wish anything better than to prove it to me, following your example. I have only to wish . . . He cannot reconcile himself to the idea that I spent some time with a terrible rake like you, but, alas, I feel nothing at his approach; his presence does not evoke any emotions in me.' She ends her letter petulantly: 'Goodbye, I hate you!' She wrote to Pushkin again after 'a terrible scene' with her mother a few days later: 'I really believe that, like Anna Kern, Mother wants to be the only one to possess you and leaves me here because she is jealous of me . . . I am furious with mother. What a woman! After all, you are to blame for this too. Mother found that you looked sad at the time of our departure. "*He seems to be sorry for you to go,*" she said. My wish to return fills her with suspicion and I am afraid to insist too much.'

Pushkin, as was to be expected, was by then thoroughly sorry and ashamed of having given in to poor Annette and was in no hurry to answer her letter. On March 15, she wrote to him again in the same lachrymose vein, announcing her mother's departure for Trigorskoye the next day and imploring him not to 'compromise' her. She, naturally, blamed him for everything and excused herself for being 'under a horrible spell'. 'For God's sake,' she wrote, 'tear up my first letter and break the cup I bought you as a present in Pskov. It's a bad omen to give cups as presents. I am very superstitious and to reward you for that loss I promise to make you a present of sealing wax for your letters on my return.'

Pushkin's reply has not been preserved, but it naturally provoked another storm, this time because she suddenly became jealous of her cousin Anna (Netty) Vulf. She was going through a terrible time, she told Pushkin, which, however, did not prevent her from telling him about another conquest she had made. On April 20 she wrote:

> Another man, a very handsome and interesting person, is paying court to me and I had the honour and the happiness of conquering him. His ways are even more superior than yours, something I could believe to be hardly possible. He goes towards the goal with gigantic steps; I believe that he excels even you in impudence . . . He repeated several of your own phrases, for instance, that I am much too intelligent to have any prejudices . . . He follows me around everywhere . . . However, do not be afraid, I do not feel anything towards him. He does not produce any *effect* on me, while one memory of you excites me . . . I am very much afraid that you do not love me at all. All you feel is a passing desire . . .

On June 2, she wrote to Pushkin again threatening to come to Trigorskoye just to see the reception her mother would give her. On learning about Pushkin's forced departure for Moscow, she wrote to him from Petersburg hoping that the Emperor would forgive him, for 'what a terrible thing it would be to be in love with a convict!' A week later she learned the truth, but her joy was short-lived, for Pushkin was lost to her forever. She wrote to him: 'Tell me why have you stopped writing to me? What is it? Indifference or forgetfulness? What a horrible man you are! You do not deserve to be loved. Goodbye, never in my life did anyone force me to experience the same feelings and the same emotions that I experienced with you.'

While all these passionate exchanges were hurtling through the post from Riga, Malinniki and Petersburg to Mikhailovskoye, Pushkin was

faced with a real crisis, for Olga Kalashnikov, the serf girl he was living
with, the daughter of his father's steward, became pregnant and he had to
decide what to do with her. He turned for help to Vyazemsky. He wrote
to him at the beginning of May, 1826:

This letter will be handed to you by a sweet and good girl whom one
of your friends has been careless enough to get with child. I rely on
your humanity and friendship. Give refuge to her in Moscow, give her
as much money as she may need and then send her off to Boldino (my
father's estate where there are hens, cockerels and bears). You see, there
is something here about which one could write a whole epistle in the
style of Zhukovsky, but posterity need not know anything about our
humane exploits. In addition, I beg you with true paternal tenderness
to take good care of the future baby, if it should be a boy. I would not
like to send him to the Foundling Home. Can't he be sent to Ostafyevo
[Vyazemsky's estate]? My dear fellow, I really am ashamed but . . . it's
a little late now.

But Vyazemsky refused to take Olga Kalashnikov under his protection
because she was legally the property of Pushkin's father. He wrote to
Pushkin:

I should have been glad to be the adopted father of your illegitimate
Fountain of Bakhchisaray, but the fear of being the cause of a new
classical-romantic conflict with your father or the author of Buyanov
[i.e. Pushkin's uncle who was co-owner of what remained of their family
estates] prevents me and I am afraid that your request cannot be fulfilled or satisfied. You had better write a semi-polite and semi-penitent
letter to your father-in-law [i.e. Olga's father], confess everything to
him and put his daughter in his charge, reminding him that one day
you will, with God's help, be his master and then you will square
accounts with him.

To which Pushkin replied on May 27: 'You are right, favourite of the
Muses, I shall take advantage of my rights as prodigal son-in-law and
future master and try to settle the whole affair with a letter.'
On July 1, 1826, Olga gave birth to a son at Boldino. He was registered
as the son of the local sexton Yakov Ivanov and christened Pavel. Nothing

is known of him. Olga herself was married in Boldino to a small landowner, Pavel Klyuchnikov, a notorious drunkard. Her marriage was, needless to say, unhappy and in 1833 she appealed to Pushkin for help. Pushkin was in Boldino in 1830, 1833 and 1834, but whether he did anything to alleviate Olga's circumstances is not known This, too, was, in Anna Kern's words, Pushkin's 'tribute' to the spirit of his age.

4

'The spirit of our literature depends on the [aristocratic] status of the writer,' Pushkin wrote to Ryleyev in the summer of 1825. The fact that most Russian writers belonged to the upper classes led Pushkin to the further assumption that, as he wrote to Bestuzhev in June, 1825:

> in them aristocratic pride is inseparable from the author's self-esteem. We do not want to be patronised by our equals. That is what that scoundrel Vorontsov does not understand. He imagines that a Russian poet will come to his ante-chamber with a dedication or an ode, but instead the poet comes with a demand for respect as a noble-man of six hundred years standing – a devilish difference.

At the beginning of July, 1825, he wrote to Vyazemsky: '. . . I have always been inclined to play the aristocrat and since the plague has descended upon the Pushkins [a reference to the recent deaths of several of Pushkin's relatives, including an aunt, an uncle and a great-aunt] I have begun to put on airs even more: I am trading in poems wholesale and am shutting up my retail shop.'

This obsession with the idea of his aristocratic status as a writer ('You are angry that I should be bragging about my six-hundred-year-old nobility – N.B. My nobility is more ancient,' he wrote in his letter to Ryleyev) was soon to bring him into conflict with the representatives of the 'new' aristocracy and gradually lead to his undoing. But it is significant that this obsession did not deter him from realising that literature was a profession that must provide a decent living for the writer. He was furious with his brother for reading his poems in public and thus reducing his income from them. In his *Conversation of a Bookseller with a Poet* (published as an introduction to the First Canto of *Eugene Onegin*), he summed up his attitude to literature as a profession in the bookseller's two lines:

Inspiration cannot be sold
But one can sell a manuscript.

Pushkin arrived in Mikhailovskoye with three cantos of *Eugene Onegin*, ending with Tatyana's letter. He completed the third canto and wrote three more, incorporating in them a great deal of his personal experiences of country life and, particularly, the scenery and gentry round Mikhailovskoye and Trigorskoye (though hardly, as Alexey Vulf claims, all the members of the Osipov family).

On October 10, 1824, Pushkin finished *The Gipsies*, the fourth and finest long poem written in his exile. He begun it in Odessa in January, 1824. It was published in Moscow in May, 1827. It is based on a personal experience among the Bessarabian gipsies, in one of whose encampments he spent three weeks from July 27 to August 21, 1821. There he met the gipsy girl Zemfira, the prototype of the heroine of his poem. Zemfira's song in the poem is a translation of a popular Moldavian folk song: 'Cut me, burn me.' In a letter to Vyazemsky in the second part of September, 1825, Pushkin wrote: 'I am glad of the fate of my song *Cut me*. It is a very faithful translation and I am sending you the wild refrain of the original. Show it to [Count Mikhail] Vyelgorsky [well-known Petersburg cellist and composer]. I think the tune is an extremely happy one.'

In *The Gipsies* Pushkin abandons his romantic past. Aleko, the hero of the poem, is not at all like the anonymous hero of *The Captive*. A weak and inept figure, he is 'vengeful', 'vicious' and 'bold'. His disappointment with civilised life is not based, as in the case of the Captive, on personal motives. 'If you knew,' he tells Zemfira, 'the bondage of suffocating towns! In crowds behind walls men there do not breathe the cool of the morning or the spring fragrance of meadows; they are ashamed of love, persecute ideas, bargain with their freedom, bow their heads before idols and beg for money and chains.' In Aleko's monologue over the cradle of his son, written in January, 1825, and later excised, Aleko's protest against civilisation is expressed even more strongly. He tells his son not to exchange 'simple vices for civilised depravity', for then he would be satisfied with life and not perpetually crave for new 'needs!' Throughout the poem the contrast is stressed between Aleko and the 'primitive' gipsy community, their freedom characterised by 'meekness and kindness', ideas which demand unquestionable respect for the freedom of another individual. Aleko, however, does not accept these ideas. He demands freedom only for himself. He murders Zemfira and her young lover, not in a moment of blind jealousy, but because of his innate egoism. He cannot find peace among the gipsies, for, as Pushkin declares in the Epilogue, there is no happiness even among those 'poor sons of nature'. 'Tormenting dreams' live even under their 'ragged tents', and their 'nomadic homes' are not saved from trouble, for there are 'fateful passions everywhere' and there is no 'protection from fate'.

The poem consists of eleven short scenes and a lyrical epilogue. The dramatic element is more in evidence here than in *The Fountain*; it is more in the nature of a stage dialogue. In one instance Pushkin even adds a stage direction: 'She goes out and sings: Old Husband, etc.' All the climaxes in the poem are expressed in dramatic form. The whole poem assumes the character of a lyrical drama. Replying to the criticisms of his friends, who seemed to believe that he had discredited his romantic hero by making him into a wandering gipsy, Pushkin wrote: 'Ryleyev was indignant because I made Aleko lead a bear and collect money from the public. Vyazemsky repeated the same remark. Ryleyev asked me to make Aleko a blacksmith, which he thought would be a much nobler occupation for him. I suppose I should really have made him into a civil servant of the eighth grade, or a landowner, and not a gipsy.'

Pushkin wrote his humorous narrative poem *Count Nulin* in two days (December 13 and 14, 1825). In his unfinished article *Refutation of Criticism* (1830) he declared that the poem had given him a great deal of trouble because critics condemned it as 'obscene':

> A young man dares to enter the bedroom of a young married woman at night and has his face slapped by her! What horror! . . . The critics [Pushkin continued], discovered a strange way of judging the degree of morality of a poem. One of them has a fifteen-year-old niece, another a fifteen-year-old acquaintance, and everything their parents do not allow them to read is proclaimed to be indecent, immoral, obscene, etc. As though literature existed only for fifteen-year-old girls! . . . But the public is not a fifteen-year-old girl or a thirteen-year-old boy! . . .

A note by Pushkin, written in the same year, gives the following explanation of the genesis of *Count Nulin*:

> At the end of 1825 I lived in the country. Re-reading *The Rape of Lucrece*, Shakespeare's rather weak poem, I thought to myself: What

if Lucrece had taken it into her head to slap Tarquin's face? That might have cooled off his enterprising spirit and he might have beaten a shame-faced retreat. Lucrece would not have stabbed herself, Publicola would not have got into a rage, Brutus would not have exiled the kings, and the history of the world would not have been the same. So that we owe the republic, the consuls, the dictators, the Catos, the Caesars, to a titillating incident such as occurred recently in my neighbourhood [a reference to Alexey Vulf's unfortunate experience with a priest's young wife]. The idea occurred to me to parody history and Shake-speare. I could not resist the double temptation and wrote this poem in two mornings.

In the *Conversation* Pushkin defines the poet's aims as an appeal to man's conscience, a view he succinctly expressed in the poem he wrote shortly before his forced departure from Moscow, *The Prophet*, in the line: 'Burn the hearts of men with your word.' In other poems written in Mikhailovskoye he emphasised this claim of the poet's duty again and again. In his cycle of nine poems *In Imitation of the Koran*, dedicated to Mrs Osipov and written in November, 1824, Pushkin chooses those passages in the Koran which stress the powerful influence of the word on people. In *André Chénier*, one of the most powerful poems of this period, which he dedicated to Nikolai Raevsky ('Judge it as a Jesuit – in accordance with its intention,' Pushkin warned Vyazemsky in his letter of July 13, 1825). Pushkin depicted himself in exile under the guise of André Chénier in prison on the eve of his execution. The 'ferocious wild beast', the 'worthless pigmy', the 'tyrant',· whose fall from power 'is not far' is quite obviously meant to be Alexander I. André Chénier's monologue is much more than a discussion of whether a poet should confine himself to the portrayal of the peaceful joys of life or stand in the front rank of the fighters for freedom. In casting his mind over the events of the French Revolution, Pushkin seems to gain a deeper insight into the cataclysmic events of history, and to forecast a similar fate for Russia barely a hundred years after:

Where is freedom and law?
Over us
The axe alone holds sway.
We have overthrown the Tsars. A murderer with hangmen
We have chosen for our Tsar. Oh, horror! Oh, shame!

The first part of André Chénier's monologue, cut by the censors, was circulated in 1826 in manuscript under the title of *On December Fourteenth* and led to the decision of the State Council in July, 1828, to put Pushkin under police surveillance.

In contrast to Pushkin's great lyric poem beginning with the line: *I remember a wondrous moment*, his *Scene from Faust* shows him not only as a great expert of the human heart, but also as a detached observer of humanity. To the echo of the first poem contained in Faust's comments on Gretchen: 'O, wondrous dream, O, flame of pure love,' Mephistopheles replies drily: 'When your beautiful love was in a state of ecstatic rapture, you were already plunged in meditation (and we have proved, you and I, that meditation is the seed of boredom).' Pushkin sums up Faust's and, surely, also his own feelings in the lines:

> On the victim of my infatuation
> I look, having had my fill of pleasure,
> With uncontrollable disgust . . .

Pushkin's Mikhailovskoye exile also produced two folk poems, *The Bridegroom* (July, 1825) and *Songs About Stenka Razin*, the seventeenth-century Cossack rebel ('the only poetic figure in Russian history,' as Pushkin described him in November, 1824, in a letter to his brother). Also of this period are *A Winter Evening*, addressed to his old nurse, and *Cleopatra* written in October, 1824, and based on an incident related by Aurelius Victor in his history *On Famous Men*, which fascinated Pushkin: Cleopatra's offer to sell herself to anybody who would buy her night at the price of his life, a theme he first touched on in his *Conversation of a Bookseller and a Poet*: 'Is not one's whole life one night or two?' and which he was to elaborate ten years later in his short stories *Egyptian Nights* and *We Spent the Evening at a Country House*.

Pushkin's major work written in Mikhailovskoye was his historical play *Boris Godunov*. He began it in November, 1824, and finished it a year later. '. . . My tragedy is finished,' he wrote to Vyazemsky on November 7, 1825. 'I re-read it aloud and clapped my hands and cried: You're a fine fellow, Pushkin, you're a fine fellow, you son-of-a-bitch! . . . Zhukovsky says the Tsar will forgive me for my tragedy. Hardly, my dear fellow. Though written in a good spirit, I could not quite hide all my ears under my holy fool's cap. They stick out . . .'

The historical events of the play are largely based on Karamzin's

History of the Russian State, but the analogy with contemporary political events did certainly 'stick out'. In it Pushkin challenged the conventional dramatic canons of the Russian stage. He did not divide it into acts, he made a final break with the three unities, he used unrhymed pentameters instead of Alexandrines and Tsar Boris, the hero of the play, is a murderer and some of the monks are comic figures.

Pushkin, in reply to his critics, wrote (in one of his introductions to the play): 'I tried to replace the system of art sanctioned by custom by a true representation of the characters of the time, in short, to write a truly romantic tragedy.' According to Pushkin's definition, true romanticism was the truthful representation of people as against the theory of the classicists and sentimentalists that art must be limited to 'the imitation of refined nature'. Hence the coarse language used by certain characters in the play which so offended the 'refined' taste of Nicholas I.

While writing *Boris Godunov* Pushkin had been thinking of the nature of tragedy in general, and he explained his views in a long letter in French to Nikolai Raevsky on July 19, 1825:

[Tragedy] is perhaps the least understood genre of poetry. The classicists and the romanticists have all been basing their rules on *verisimilitude* and yet that is exactly what is excluded by the very nature of a dramatic work. For what kind of verisimilitude can there be in a hall cut into two halves, in one of which are seated two thousand people who are supposed to be unseen by those who are on the stage? . . . The true geniuses of tragedy have never troubled themselves about verisimilitude . . . Verisimilitude of situations and truth of dialogue – that is the true rule of tragedy. I have not read Calderon or Vega, but how amazing is Shakespeare! . . . How paltry is Byron compared to him, Byron the tragedian, Byron who only created one character . . . who divided the different traits of his own character among his heroes: to one he gave his pride, to another his hatred, to a third his anguish, etc., and out of one complete gloomy and energetic character he has in this way created several insignificant ones – this is certainly not tragedy . . .

You will ask me [Pushkin concludes] is your tragedy a tragedy of character or of manners? . . . I shall try to unite both. I am writing and thinking. The greater number of scenes require only reasoning; but when I come to a scene which demands inspiration, I wait for it or leave the scene out – such a method is entirely new to me. I feel that my spiritual powers have reached their fullest development – I can create [*Je sens que mon âme s'est tout-à-fait je développée, puis créer*].

When he announced 'an important piece of news,' – the completion of *Boris Godunov*, to Bestuzhev on November 10, 1825, Pushkin added: 'I am very much afraid to publish it: our timid taste will not swallow true romanticism.' But it was not the timid taste of the reading public, but of no less a person than Nicholas I that prevented the publication of Pushkin's historical play. The Emperor issued the following 'resolutions': 'I consider that Mr Pushkin's aim would be best served if, after the necessary emendations, he would alter his play into an historical tale or a novel similar to Walter Scott's.' Informed of the Emperor's decision by General Benkendorf, Pushkin replied with barely concealed sarcasm on January 5, 1827: 'It is with a feeling of the deepest gratitude that I have received your Excellency's letter informing me of his Majesty's gracious comment as regards my dramatic poem. I agree that it may be more like an historical novel than a tragedy, as the Emperor was pleased to remark. I am sorry I am unable to alter what I have once written.'

The ban on the publication of *Boris Godunov* was only removed in 1830 to help Pushkin with his financial arrangements for his marriage to Natalya Goncharov.

At Mikhailovskoye, Pushkin, in addition to his memoirs, which he later burnt, and his voluminous correspondence, also wrote a number of critical essays, dealing with problems of contemporary literature. Two of these Pushkin published in *The Moscow Telegraph*, owned and edited by the novelist and historian, Nikolai Polevoy.

The death of Byron on April 19, 1824 (April 7, O.S.), is reflected not only in Pushkin's poem *To the Sea* but also in his correspondence. On the first anniversary of Byron's death, Pushkin wrote to Vyazemsky: 'I have ordered a mass to be celebrated this evening for the repose of Byron's soul. My priest was surprised at my piety and gave me part of the host from the mass for the repose of the soul of the servant of God, the boyar Georgy. I am sending it to you.' Pushkin also mentioned his unusual act of piety in his letter to his brother. It was 'a little reminiscent of *la messe de Frédéric II pour le repos de l'âme de M. de Voltaire.*'

Referring to an article by Vyazemsky which mentioned the destruction of Byron's notes by Thomas Moore, Pushkin wrote to Vyazemsky in November, 1825:

> Why do you regret the loss of Byron's notes? To hell with them! He made his confession in his poems in spite of himself. In humdrum prose he would have told lies . . . He would then have been shown up, as Rousseau was shown up, and malice and slander would have triumphed again. Leave curiosity to the crowd and be at one with genius. Moore's action is better than his *Lalla Rookh* (so far as poetry is concerned). We know Byron well enough. We have seen him on the throne of glory, we have seen him in the torments of his great soul, we have seen him in his coffin in the midst of Greece rising from the dead. What do you want to see him on a chamber pot for? The crowd eagerly reads confessions, memoirs, etc., because in its vileness it cannot help rejoicing at the humiliation of the great and the weaknesses of the mighty. It is in raptures at the disclosure of any kind of abomination. He is as small as we are, he is as abominable as we are! You are lying, you scoundrels: he is small and abominable, but not as you are – differently. It is tempting and pleasing to write one's memoirs. You don't love anyone as much as yourself and you don't know anyone as well as yourself. It is an inexhaustible subject, but it is difficult. It is possible not to lie; but to be sincere is a physical impossibility. The pen will sometimes stop as one stops from a running start before a precipice . . . It is not difficult to despise – *braver* – the judgment of people; to despise one's own judgment is impossible.

In the same letter Pushkin bewailed his ignorance of English. 'I must learn English,' he wrote. 'This is one of the disadvantages of my exile: I have the time but I have not the means for studying. It is the fault of my persecutors. Like André Chénier I may tap myself on the head and say: *Il y avait quelque chose là . . .* '

The terrible Petersburg floods of November 7, 1824, provided Pushkin with the plot of one of his masterpieces, his narrative poem *The Bronze Horseman*. It was written in 1833, but banned by Nicholas I and published posthumously. Pushkin's first comment was typical: 'What are you having?' he wrote to his brother at the end of November, 1824. 'A flood? It serves accursed Petersburg right! *Voilà une belle occasion à vos dames de faire bidet.*' But the enormity of the disaster, particularly as it affected the impoverished 'common people', made him change his lighthearted tone to one of real sympathy for the victims. He wrote to his brother on December 4, 1824:

> The closing of the theatre and the prohibition of balls is a sensible measure, decency demanded it. No doubt, the common people take no part in the amusements of the upper classes, but in a time of public calamity one ought not to exasperate it with offensive luxury. Seeing a brightly lit first floor, shopkeepers might break the plate glass windows, and that would be a loss. You see, I am being impartial. I wish I could praise the other measures of the government, but all the papers mention is the distribution of one million roubles. A million is a great thing, but what about salt, bread, oats and vodka? It would not be amiss to think about that in winter, either individually or in committee. I cannot get this flood out of my mind. It is not at all as amusing as it seemed at first. If it should occur to you to help some unfortunate man, help him with the *Onegin* money, but without publicity, oral or written.

It was one of these unfortunates that Pushkin was to make the hero of *The Bronze Horseman* eight years later.

During his country exile Pushkin also for the first time formulated his view on the *aim* of poetry. 'There is a heresy among you,' he wrote to his brother on March 24, 1825. 'They are saying that in verse the verse is not the main thing. What then is the main thing? Prose? That heresy must be eradicated before it is too late, with persecution, the whip, the stake, etc . . .'

To Zhukovsky he wrote at the same time: 'You ask what is the aim of *The Gipsies?* Good Lord! The aim of poetry is poetry.' A couple of years later Pushkin wrote: 'Poetry is higher than morality. Lord Jesus! What does a poet care about virtue or vice – except perhaps their poetic aspect.' In his article on Joseph Delorme (1831) Pushkin declares roundly that

> poetry, according to its free and highest nature, must have no aim except itself and must certainly not demean itself to shape by the power of the word the eternal verities upon which the happiness and majesty of man are founded or transform its divine nectar into an inflamed and sensuous compound. But a description of human weaknesses, delusions and passions is not immoral just as anatomy is not murder. . . .

Finally, in his lecture on *The Opinions of Lobanov on the Spirit of Literature* (published in *The Contemporary* in 1836) he condemns 'the theory, held by ancient rhetoricians, that *utility* is the condition and aim of creative literature', as 'petty and false'.

PART FIVE

1826-1830
Return to Petersburg: Marriage

I

It was raining in Moscow when Pushkin arrived on the morning of September 8, 1826. The streets were gay with bunting and flags in celebration of the coronation of Nicholas I. The courier took Pushkin straight to the Kremlin to the general on duty. At four o'clock in the afternoon Pushkin's interview with Nicholas I took place. According to one version, Nicholas I enquired whether Pushkin was pleased to be back in Moscow, to which the poet replied that he was. The Emperor then asked Pushkin whether he would have taken part in the Decembrist uprising if he had been in Petersburg at the time. 'I most certainly should, Sire,' Pushkin replied. 'All my friends were involved in the conspiracy and I could not possibly have let them down. My absence alone saved me, for which I thank God.' Nicholas I seemed to have been impressed by Pushkin's candour and remarked that he was glad an accident had prevented the poet from sharing the fate of his friends. He next asked Pushkin why he published so little. Pushkin blamed the censorship. The Emperor then offered to be the censor of Pushkin's works himself. 'You have been playing the fool long enough,' he said. 'I hope you will be more sensible in future and that we shall have no more cause to quarrel again.'

Pushkin did not at first realise the full implications of the Emperor's offer. But he was not to be left in ignorance very long. The Emperor's censorship, he was soon to discover, meant that he could not publish anything before sending it to Count Alexander Benkendorf, the head of the Third Department of his Majesty's Personal Office, who was to be the intermediary between Nicholas I and Pushkin. Pushkin was even forbidden to read any of his works to his friends before submitting it for the emperor's approval first. The correspondence between Pushkin and Benkendorf was conducted in French except when, exasperated and humiliated, Pushkin replied to the peremptory demands of the German chief of the secret police in Russian.

The irreconcilable differences of opinion between Pushkin and

Nicholas I became apparent almost immediately after the interview in the Kremlin. On September 30, 1826, Benkendorf informed Pushkin that the Emperor desired that the poet should use his 'excellent abilities' to convey to posterity 'the glory of our native land'. It was therefore his wish that 'you should make a study of the problem of the education of our youth. You are given full and complete freedom when and how to submit your ideas and observations. This subject should offer you, in particular, the widest scope for expressing your views since your own experience has shown you the pernicious consequences of a false system of education', the system of education, that is, of the Lycée at which several active members of the Decembrists were educated. Pushkin went to Mikhailovskoye to write his paper on education. 'When Nicholas asked my opinion about changes in our educational system,' Pushkin later told Alexey Vulf, 'I found myself in a very difficult position. It would have been very easy for me to write what they wanted me to say, but I felt that I ought not to miss such an opportunity to do good.' Pushkin sent his paper on education to Benkendorf at the end of 1826. In it he proposed that all the educational establishments in the country should adopt the curriculum of the Lycée, including the subject of 'higher political sciences'. He advised the Emperor that no attempt should be made to misrepresent 'republican ideas' or 'to defame the murder of Caesar . . . but to show Brutus as the defender of the fundamental laws of his country'. He also sharply criticised the prevalent domestic education of the Russian nobility. 'The child,' he wrote, 'is surrounded only by slaves, he sees only odious examples, he receives no ideas of justice and true honour and is allowed to treat his slaves as he likes.' Finally, Pushkin demanded the abolition of corporal punishment in schools.

Nicholas I, needless to say, was not very pleased with Pushkin's paper. Benkendorf wrote to Pushkin on December 23, 1826:

> His Majesty was so good as to observe that the rule you seem to accept, namely that enlightenment and genius are the only pre-requisites for perfection, is a dangerous rule which has dragged you to the very brink of the abyss and has led to the undoing of a large number of young men. Morality, loyal service and industry must be preferred to enlightenment that is inexperienced, immoral and useless.

Pushkin was no more successful in his attempt to improve the conditions of life of the Decembrists languishing in the Siberian prisons. Ever since he learnt of the execution of the five Decembrist leaders he was haunted by the picture of their bodies hanging from the gallows. He made several drawings of it in his manuscripts. But, as he explained in a letter to Vyazemsky, the dead were dead and it was now his duty to help the living. *Stanzas* (1826), the first poem he wrote after his interview with the Tsar, was meant to do so, first, by justifying the stern measures taken by Nicholas I to put down the revolt and, secondly, by appealing to him to show mercy to the Decembrists. In his poem, therefore, he compares the executions and imprisonment of the Decembrists with Peter the Great's ruthless suppression of the revolt of the Moscow *strieltsy* (the detachments of the regular army). After a poetic characterisation of Peter the Great as one who 'sowed enlightenment boldly' and was 'the first labourer on the throne', Pushkin concludes the poem with the following advice to the young emperor: 'Be, therefore, proud of your family likeness and be like your forebear in everything: like him firm and indefatigable and like him forgiving.'

The poem, published in the *Moscow Herald* on December 22, 1826, did not have the desired effect: Nicholas I remained as unforgiving as ever. What was worse, it shocked Pushkin's admirers and, indeed, was the beginning of the gradual decline in Pushkin's popularity. At first Pushkin had been welcomed with open arms in Moscow. When he appeared at the Bolshoi Theatre the eyes of the entire auditorium turned upon him. Old friends and people he had never met before came up to him to express their pleasure on his return from exile. In the streets crowds of people followed him about everywhere. The publication of *Stanzas* immediately produced a perceptible cooling off in the attitude of the public. Pushkin was accused of renouncing his former convictions and of going out of his way to flatter the monarch. So strong was this revulsion of public opinion that Pushkin thought it necessary a year later to defend himself against these accusations in his poem *To My Friends*, in which he declared that he was no flatterer but merely offered 'free advice to the Tsar'. A flatterer, he pointed out, despised the people and looked upon enlightenment as the expression of a rebellious spirit. 'Woe to the country,' he concluded, 'in which the slave and the flatterer alone are near the throne and the bard, chosen by heaven, is silent, his eyes fixed on the ground.' But his defence never reached the reading public, for Nicholas I, who was not particularly happy about the poem, banned its publication.

A poem which he did not even attempt to submit to Nicholas I,

certainly expressed the views he held not only at the time but throughout
his life. Pushkin sent it directly to the Decembrist prisoners in Siberia by
one of their wives. He wrote it at the beginning of January, 1827. It began
with the lines: 'In the depths of the Siberian mines, preserve your proud
patience,' and foretold that the 'wished for hour' would come and 'freedom' would receive them joyfully 'at the entrance' and their brothers
'would give back the sword' to them. Six months later, in his allegorical
poem *Arion* he depicted himself as the sole survivor from a boat which
sank in a storm: 'I alone, the mysterious poet, was thrown out on the shore
by the storm, I who sing my former hymns.'

In Moscow Pushkin made the acquaintance of the small groups of
young aristocrats, including some talented poets and writers, who challenged the predominant influence of French philosophers. They declared
themselves in favour of the German idealist philosophers Schelling, Fichte
and Hegel. One of these groups, formed in 1823 and prudently dissolved
after the failure of the Decembrist insurrection, was known as the Society
of the Lovers of Wisdom. They were followers of Schelling. A later group
were followers of Hegel. The Russian Hegelians eventually split up into
the conservative Slavophils and liberal Westerners. In 1827 the former
Lovers of Wisdom founded the *Moscow Herald* under the editorship of
Mikhail Pogodin, historian, novelist and journalist. Pogodin as well as the
liberal editor of the *Moscow Telegraph*, Nikolai Polevoy, tried to secure
Pushkin's collaboration on their papers. Pogodin finally succeeded in
signing up Pushkin for a yearly salary of fifteen thousand roubles. Pushkin
hoped that he would be able to direct the policy of the *Moscow Herald*,
but it soon became evident that he did not share the ideas of the Lovers
of Wisdom. On March 2, 1827, he wrote to Delvig:

You reproach me for the *Moscow Herald* and the German Meta-
physics. God knows I hate and despise it, but what can one do about it?
Stubborn, bright young lads have gathered together . . . I say to them,
Gentlemen, why are you so keen on wasting your time? That's all very
well for Germans who are already saturated with positive knowledge,
but not for us . . . The *Moscow Herald* sits in a pit and asks: what is a
rope? (By the way, this metaphysical question could be answered but
N.B.! [an allusion to the five Decembrists hanged in 1826]), but my
time is valuable and I am not going to waste it on any *Herald*. So much
the worse for them, if they do not listen to me.

As it turned out, Pushkin found it difficult to contribute even to the *Moscow Herald* because he could not publish anything without the approval of the Tsar. After the paper became the personal property of its editor Pogodin, Pushkin began thinking of publishing his own journal to which he hoped to attract writers who shared his views. This was only partly realised with the publication in Petersburg of *The Literary Gazette* under the editorship of Anton Delvig.

Pogodin, who met Pushkin for the first time on October 12, 1826, was astonished to find that instead of 'a majestic priest of high art' he saw 'a very short little man with long and somewhat curly hair, a man who seemed to have no pretensions of any kind, with quick, vivacious eyes and rapid movements, a pleasant voice, wearing a black cutaway coat, a dark waistcoat, buttoned to the top, and a casually tied cravat'.

Nikolai Polevoy's brother, Xenophon Polevoy, who was trying to persuade Pushkin not to stop contributing to his brother's paper, first saw Pushkin at his room in a Moscow hotel. He writes in his memoirs:

Before the bureau stood a man whose head came only a little above the bureau. He was thin, with deep wrinkles on his face and large sidewhiskers, which covered the lower part of his cheeks and chin, and a mass of curly hair. His face, which looked anything but young, wore an expression of gloom when not smiling. I was so surprised by this unexpected impression, which did not in any way correspond to my idea of the poet, that I could not recover for some time and had to repeat to myself in astonishment that it was Pushkin who was standing in front of me.

Polevoy saw Pushkin again a few months later in Petersburg:

I went to see him every morning because he always welcomed me pleasantly and I was fascinated by his talk and stories. He occupied two rooms at the hotel Demuth and led a rather odd kind of life. He usually stayed at home all morning which began very late for him. When alone he read in bed and when a visitor arrived he got up and sat down at a table with toilet accessories and, while talking, cleaned and filed his fingernails which were so long that one could describe them as claws. He was extraordinarily clever and pleasant in conversation. Many of his remarks and judgments stuck in my memory. Speaking about the vanity of authors, he said: 'When I read praises of my works I remain indifferent. I do not value them, but spiteful criticism, even if it is stupid, irritates me.' I observed that this merely proved that he was not indifferent to praise. 'No,' he replied, laughing, 'perhaps an author's vanity.'

Pushkin stayed in Moscow till May, 1827. He did little work, most of his time being occupied with visits to theatres, the English Club, the resort of the Moscow aristocratic gamblers, balls and all sorts of other social occasions. Among his new acquaintances was the Polish poet Adam Mickiewicz, who had been exiled from Vilno for being a member of a Polish nationalist group. He was present at one of Pushkin's readings of *Boris Godunov*. In the spring of 1827 Pushkin asked Benkendorf for permission to return to Petersburg. Permission was granted, but Benkendorf warned him that in permitting this 'his Majesty has been so good as to express the view that he did not doubt that a word of honour given by a Russian nobleman to his Emperor – to conduct himself honourably and with decorum – will be carried out.' His departure from Moscow was rather a grim affair. He had suffered his first rebuff in what was to become a frantic attempt during the next three years to find a bride. His reputation had suffered because of his reconciliation with the monarchy, and he had lost at cards most of the annual advance from the *Moscow Herald*. He made a late appearance at a farewell party given in his honour and departed hurriedly after dinner which, Xenophon Polevoy records, 'made a very unpleasant impression on everybody'.

In Petersburg things did not improve. He wrote to Mrs Osipov in June, 1827:

What am I to tell you about my life in Moscow and Petersburg? The insipidity and stupidity of our two capitals are equally great, though different, and since I have pretensions to impartiality, I shall say that if I had been given the choice between the two, I should have chosen Trigorskoye, more or less like Harlequin who, when asked which he preferred: to be broken on the wheel or to be hanged, replied, I prefer milk soup. I am about to leave Petersburg and I am certainly counting on spending a few days at Trigorskoye. . . .

He had been gambling heavily. According to one of his friends, he had lost everything he possessed: seven thousand roubles. Pushkin had by then acquired an almost superstitious belief in autumn as a dispenser of inspiration and he fled to Mikhailovskoye in the hope of repairing his losses at cards by his pen. Alexey Vulf, who visited Pushkin in the country on September 15, 1827, left this record in his diary:

I dined with Pushkin at his mother's estate which had so recently been his place of exile and where he had come intending to take a rest from the dissipations of our capital cities and to write without being disturbed . . . I walked over the rickety front steps into the ramshackle hut of our foremost Russian poet. I found him sitting at his writing table wearing a red Moldavian fez and a dressing gown. On the table were scattered all the appurtenances of the dressing table of a man of fashion. Next to them lay the works of Montesquieu with the *Biblio-thèque de Campagne*, and the Journal of Peter I. I could also see Alfieri (Vittorio), Karamzin's monthlies and a dream book hidden among half a dozen almanacs, and, finally, two writing books in black morocco, the former ledgers of a masonic lodge in which he was now writing his poems. In one of them he showed me two chapters of a prose novel he had just written, in which the chief character was his great-grandfather Hannibal . . .

The 'prose novel' was Pushkin's unfinished novel *The Blackamoor of Peter the Great*, his first attempt at a prose narrative, written between July 31 and August 10, 1827.

Pushkin returned to Petersburg in October. He had been waiting in vain for inspiration. He had begun writing the seventh canto of *Eugene Onegin* in August, but by February, 1828, he had managed to write only twelve stanzas. He finished the canto in November, 1828. Apart from his semi-humorous *Epistle to Delvig*, and his short poems on the anniversary of the foundation of the Lycée – October 19, 1827 – in which he mentions his classmates languishing 'in the gloomy caverns of the earth', the autumn he spent in Mikhailovskoye was poetically unproductive. On the way to Petersburg an incident had occurred which a few days later found its echo in the lines about the gloomy caverns of the earth. Pushkin described it in the only entry in his diary for 1827:

October 15, 1827. Yesterday was a remarkable day for me. On arriving in Borisovichi at twelve o'clock in the morning, I found one of the travellers . . . keeping the bank in a card game with a hussar officer. I had lunch, but finding that I was five roubles short to pay my bill,

I put them on a card and, one card after another, lost one thousand six hundred roubles. I paid up feeling rather disgruntled, borrowed two hundred roubles and left . . . At the next stage I found Schiller's *Clairvoyant* and had hardly time to read a few pages when four troikas with a courier drove up. 'Poles, I suppose?' I said to the landlady. 'Yes,' she replied. 'They are being taken back now.' I went out to have a look.

One of the prisoners was leaning against a post. A tall, pale, thin young man in a frieze greatcoat walked up to him . . . We looked intently at one another and – I recognised Kuechelbecker. We threw ourselves in each other's arms. The gendarmes dragged us apart. The officer in charge seized me by the arms, swearing and uttering threats. I did not listen. Kuechelbecker fainted. A gendarme gave him a drink of water, put him in a cart and galloped off. I drove off. At the next station I found out that they were being brought from Schluesselburg. But where to?

According to the official report of this incident, Pushkin asked the officer's permission to give Kuechelbecker some money. When he refused, Pushkin began shouting at him and threatening to complain to Benkendorf and the Emperor.

Pushkin never saw Kuechelbecker again.

Pushkin spent the last months of 1827 and nearly the whole of 1828 in Petersburg. According to Polevoy, Pushkin was no longer a young man in 1828. He looked exhausted and faded, but he still wanted to appear young. On one occasion Polevoy quoted to him his line from *Eugene Onegin*: 'Am I really thirty?', but he immediately corrected him: 'No, no, what I wrote was: Will I really be thirty soon? I am waiting for that fatal date and have not yet said goodbye to my youth.' On another occasion Polevoy told him that in his works one came across such true gaiety as in no other work by a Russian poet. He replied that basically his character was sad and melancholy and that it was very rarely that he was in a cheerful mood.

If Pushkin no longer looked young in 1828, it was due to some extent to the renewed persecutions by the government. He had been called to account for two of his long forgotten poems: *The Gabriliade* and the extract from *André Chénier*, circulated under the title of *December 14, 1825*, and was finally placed under the surveillance of the secret police. There was, besides, his growing dissatisfaction with what he had described in a letter to Mrs Osipov as his 'disjointed' life. On May 19, 1828, he wrote his famous poem *Memory* in which he speaks of his sleepless nights and how 'in the hours of wearisome vigil' he was 'crushed by anguish' as he watched his memory 'unroll its long scroll before him', saw his years wasted 'in idleness, in frantic feasts, in the madness of wanton freedom, in poverty and exile', heard 'the buzz of slander, the whisper of envy and . . . the reproaches of frivolous vanity'. A few days later, on his birthday, May 26, 1828, he wrote his no less celebrated but more despairing poem, beginning with the lines:

> Useless gift, accidental gift,
> Life, why have you been given me?

and ending with the quatrain:

> There is no goal before me;
> My heart is empty, my mind is idle,
> And the monotonous tumult of life
> Wearies me with its tedium.

Pushkin had been feeling more and more the need for settling down, but so far all his attempts at marriage had failed partly because of his precarious financial position and partly also because of his unfortunate choice of brides-to-be.

2

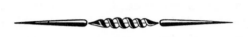

Pushkin had made his first proposal of marriage shortly after his arrival in Moscow in 1826. The girl of his choice was Sofia Pushkin, a girl of twenty and a distant relative of his. He made his proposal through Vasily Zubkov, a friend of his who was Sofia's brother-in-law, and received a reply which he interpreted as acceptance or as half acceptance. At any rate, having gone to Mikhailovskoye to write his paper on education, he wrote to Vyazemsky on November 9 that he would return to Moscow on the first of December because 'she commands it'. At the end of November, he left for Moscow via Pskov, but on December 1 he was still in Pskov from where he wrote a remarkable letter to Zubkov which tells us a great deal about the way Pushkin could fall in love in less than a moment and already plan to marry the girl:

> I wanted to drop in on you like a bomb on the first of December, that is, today, so I left my damned estate five or six days ago by post-horses on account of the disgusting roads. The Pskov coachman had nothing better to do than to overturn me. I have a bruised side, a pain in my chest and I cannot breathe. In my rage I am gambling and losing. But enough of this. I am waiting until I feel a little better before I take post-horses again . . . Since I am here at an inn in Pskov instead of at Sofia's feet, let us talk, that is, let us reason. I am twenty-seven, my dear friend. It is time I began to live, that is, to know happiness . . . But it is not my personal happiness that worries me, for I could be no other than the happiest man on earth beside her. I shudder at the thought of the fate that perhaps awaits her, at the thought that I shall not be able to make her as happy as I should like. My life, so wandering and so stormy up to the present, my character so uneven, jealous, suspicious, violent and weak all at once – it is that which gives me moments of painful reflection. Ought I to unite a being so sweet and so beautiful to a fate so sad, to a character so unfortunate? Good Lord, how lovely she is and how ridiculous my conduct towards her has been.

Dear friend, try to blot out the bad impression it might have given her. Tell her that I am more sensible than I appear to be . . . That vile Panin has been in love with her for two years and is planning to propose to her, while I saw her once in a theatre box, a second time at a ball, and a third time am proposing to her! If she thinks that Panin is right, she must believe that I am mad, mustn't she? . . . I do not think for a moment that I could make her fall in love with me. I have therefore acted well in coming straight to the point, for once one has fallen in love with her, it is impossible to love her more just as it is impossible to find her more beautiful . . . because it is impossible to be more beautiful. My dear fellow, persuade her, entreat her, frighten her with that nasty Panin and marry me off.

Pushkin arrived in Moscow only on December 20, by which time Sofia was already engaged to Panin and, in January, 1827, they were married. But even after he had proposed to Sofia, Pushkin seemed to be hesitating between her and another girl, the twenty-three-year-old Katerina Ushakov. He had been deeply attached to her even while looking elsewhere for a wife. The Ushakov house in Moscow was one of Pushkin's most favourite haunts between 1826 and 1830. He was more than at home there: it was the only house in Moscow where he did not succumb to depression. He liked to talk to Mrs Ushakov and to listen to her singing Russian folksongs which he wrote down. He enjoyed the 'gay and sparkling' conversation of her two daughters, Katerina and her younger sister Elisaveta. He sketched Katerina's profile on his manuscripts. But – she was a little too intelligent for him. She was, like Alexander Raevsky some years before, his 'demon'. On November 3, 1826, he wrote to Vera Vyazemsky from the country: 'S.P. [Sofia Pushkin] is my good angel; but *the other* [Katerina Ushakov] is my demon: this most inconveniently troubles me in my poetic and amorous meditations.' [*S.P. est mon bon ange; mais l'autre est mon démon: cela me trouble dans mes méditations poétiques amoureuses le plus mal à propos du monde.*] In April, 1827, he wrote a semi-humorous poem in Katerina's album in which he reminded her that when an apparition appeared in the old days one had only to say, Amen, amen, get thee behind me, Satan, and it vanished. 'But you, my good or evil genius, when I see your profile or your eyes, or your golden tresses, when I hear your voice and your gay and sparkling talk, I am enchanted, I am on fire, I tremble, and I say to my heart which is full of dreams of you: Amen, amen, get thee behind me . . .'

On May 19, 1827, three days before his departure from Moscow, he wrote in Katerina's album a poem in which he disguised his deep feeling by a jest: 'Away from you I shall be inseparable from you and shall always remember your languorous eyes and languorous lips. Pining away in silence, I do not want to be consoled, but – will you heave a sigh for me when I am hanged?'

In Petersburg Pushkin met Anna Olenin, the daughter of Alexey Olenin, President of the Academy of Arts, at whose house he had met Anna Kern eight years earlier. Anna Olenin was nineteen when she met Pushkin at a ball in the autumn or winter of 1827. She recorded her first impression of the poet in her diary on July 18, 1828:

> Having endowed him with remarkable genius, God did not reward Pushkin with an attractive exterior. His face, of course, was expressive, but a certain malice and sarcasm darkened the intellect which could be seen in his blue and rather glassy eyes. The Negro profile he inherited from his mother's ancestors did not enhance his looks. To this must be added his terrible sidewhiskers, his tousled hair, his long nails which looked like claws, his short stature, his mincing manners, the impudent way in which he stared at the women whom he found attractive, his strange character, and his natural and unlimited vanity. People said that he was a dissolute man, but then all the young men of that time were dissolute.

Their next meeting took place in the spring of 1828. Vyazemsky wrote to his wife on April 18: 'Yesterday we danced a little at the Olenins. Nothing in particular happened. The Olenin girl is a forward little thing. Pushkin calls her, "A sweet little dragoon" and seems to be in love with her.' On May 3, Vyazemsky again wrote to his wife: 'I went to the Olenins where they were celebrating Mrs Olenin's birthday. Pushkin and I played cat and mouse, that is to say, I was flirting with Countess Natalie Zubov, who looks like a cat, and Pushkin was flirting with Anna Olenin, who is small and frisky like a mouse.' On May 7, Vyazemsky sent his wife a description of a ball at the Countess Yekaterina Meshchersky's, Karamzin's youngest daughter: 'I danced a pot-pourri with Anna Olenin and praised her coquetry. Pushkin thinks that he is in love with her and pretends to be jealous.' But Pushkin was not pretending to be jealous. He was already thinking of marrying Anna Olenin. In the rough copy of his narrative poem *Poltava* he jotted down a series of anagrams on her name: 'Eli Enilo, Ettena, Enilo, Olenina, Annette' and above his own surname *Pouchkine*. On the next page of his manuscript he wrote his first poem to Anna Olenin, beginning with the line, 'You are spoilt by nature,' and describing her waist, 'as light as a sylph' and her red lips 'like a harmonious rose'. The poem is dated between April 5 and the beginning of May, 1828. A year later Pushkin slightly revised it and wrote it in the album of Elisaveta Ushakov.

On May 9, 1828, Pushkin went for a trip to Kronstadt with the Olenins, Griboyedov, Vyazemsky, and the English painter, George Dawe, who was at the time painting the portraits of the heroes of the 1812 campaign for the Army Gallery of the Winter Palace. The second poem Pushkin wrote to Anna Olenin bears the note: 'May 9, 1828. The sea. Anna Olenin. Dawe,' and begins with the line: 'Alas, the language of love is garrulous.' It is unusually hesitant in expressing Pushkin's feelings which seems to indicate that Pushkin's avowals of love did not evoke any enthusiastic response. Another poem written at the same time is addressed 'To Dawe, Esq.' It begins with the line, 'Why does your wondrous pencil draw my Negro profile,' and appeals to the artist to draw Anna Olenin instead.

When Vyazemsky arrived in Petersburg he was struck by the 'fiery eyes' of a nineteen-year-old lady-in-waiting, Alexandra Rosset, who was later to become one of Gogol's closest friends. Pushkin, to whom Vyazemsky had confided his admiration of Alexandra Rosset's eyes, admitted in his third poem to Anna Olenin that Alexandra's 'Circassian eyes' could be compared with 'southern stars' but, he went on, 'You must admit that the eyes of my Olenin are more beautiful!' Indeed, 'when she raises them – it is Raphael's angel who thus contemplates divinity.' During May, 1828, Pushkin had 'secret assignations' with Anna Olenin in the Summer Garden. 'They took place in this way,' Anna Olenin told one of her grandnephews. 'I used to drive with my English governess to the Summer Garden and Pushkin used to come there at the same time and we would walk together, the Englishwoman acting as our chaperone.'

In the middle of May the Olenins moved to Priyutino, their estate near Petersburg. On May 20, Vyazemsky wrote to his wife:

I drove down with Mickiewicz yesterday evening to the Olenins' country house at Priyutino. The estate is quite charming especially as it is so near Petersburg: there are quite interesting views, hills, water, woods, but the mosquitoes transform it into a veritable hell. I have never seen so many mosquitoes in my life. You keep on waving your arms. I couldn't stay there for a single day. Mickiewicz said: '*Que c'est une journée sanglante.*' Pushkin who was covered in pimples and besieged by mosquitoes, kept exclaiming tenderly: 'It's sweet.'

Anna Olenin records how one day by mistake she addressed Pushkin as *tu*. Next Sunday he brought her the poem entitled *Ty i Vy* (Thou and you, or, in French, *Tu et Vous*). It ends with the lines: 'Before her I stand lost in thought, unable to take my eyes off her, I say to her, How lovely you are! And think: How I love *thee*!'

Three days after his visit to the Olenins' country house, Pushkin wrote on the page on which, on May 19, he had written the rough draft of *Memory*, the date Anna Olenin had said *tu*: 'May 20, 1828, Priyutino,' and followed it up by his poem *Ty i Vy* dating it May 23. On Sunday, May 27, Pushkin was again at Priyutino where he gave Anna the poem. By that time Pushkin seems to have become obsessed with her. He kept drawing her head and jotting down lines, which seem to be intended as a way of breaking off a relationship with some woman:

> But you, my friend, forget me,
> Forget me as one forgets
> A painful sad dream
> When . . .

He may have written this to Yelisaveta Khitrovo, the forty-five-year-old daughter of Fieldmarshal Kutuzov, who had fallen in love with Pushkin and had been his mistress for a time. The drawings and the lines are written on the page where Yelisaveta Khitrovo had, at his dictation, written the poem *Useless gift, accidental gift*. A few days later Pushkin again drew Anna's portrait in one of his notebooks.

None of Pushkin's poems to Anna Olenin is of great artistic merit, but she was indirectly responsible for one of the finest lyrical poems which Pushkin wrote in 1828. Anna was taking music lessons from Glinka and one day, in Pushkin's presence, she was learning a Georgian tune that Griboyedov had brought to Petersburg and which Glinka had transcribed. Shortly afterwards, on June 12, Pushkin wrote his famous poem:

Do not sing, beautiful girl, in my presence
The songs of mournful Georgia:
They remind me
Of another life and a faraway shore.
Alas, your cruel melodies
Remind me of
The steppe and the night and – in moonlight
The features of a faraway, poor maiden . . .
The dear and fatal spectre
Seeing you, I forget,
But you sing, and before me
I imagine it again.

In the summer of 1828, when Pushkin was contemplating marriage with Anna Olenin, her father, Alexey Olenin, learned that Pushkin was again in trouble with the authorities in connection with the banned passage from *André Chénier*. In his official capacity as State Secretary of the Department of Civil and Ecclesiastical Affairs, he was one of those who on June 28 signed the order which put Pushkin under police surveillance. Thus Alexey Olenin as good as let Pushkin know that he would never give his consent to their marriage. Pushkin must have realised it, for in the poem *Presentiment*, beginning with the line, 'Once more the clouds have gathered over me,' he hastens 'for the last time' to press the hand of his 'gentle angel', and promises that his memory of her 'will replace in my soul the strength, the pride, the hope and the courage of the days of my youth'.

Anna never really thought of marrying Pushkin, though she liked to keep such a famous poet dangling. On July 17 she wrote in her diary that she had had a long talk with Ivan Krylov during which she said to him, 'I hope you do not wish me to marry Pushkin,' to which the fabulist, always candid, replied, 'God forbid!'

On August 11, her twentieth birthday, Anna Olenin wrote in her diary: 'The guests began to arrive . . . as usual, Pushkin, or the Red Rover as I nicknamed him, also arrived. He is in love with Zakrevsky. He keeps talking about her to make me jealous and then says all sorts of sweet nothings to me in a soft voice.' Red Rover, the hero of a best-selling novel by Fenimore Cooper, was, like Pushkin, short, had 'wavy hair' and 'intelligent eyes'.

In between wooing Anna Olenin, Pushkin had a violent affair with the twenty-nine-year-old Countess Agrafena Zakrevsky, the wife of the Minister of the Interior. He wrote several poems to her, including *The Portrait* in which he described her 'with her blazing soul and tempestuous passions' appearing 'like a lawless comet' in Petersburg society. He portrayed her under the name of Zinaida Volskaya, the heroine of his two unfinished stories: *The Guests Arrived at the Country House* and *We Spent the Evening at a Country House*. In an expunged passage of the first story, the following revealing passage occurs:

'I should very much like to fall in love with P.,' said Volskaya.

'What nonsense,' replied Minsky. 'In fashionable society P. is the same kind of a bad imitation of Lord Byron as in his poems. What you think is so original in him is nothing more than a rather mediocre imitation, but then you don't read anything and therefore it is easy to blind you with often repeated ...'

Pushkin scholars have generated a great deal of heat over the identification of Countess Zakrevsky with Nina Voronskaya, the 'Cleopatra of the Neva' whom Pushkin introduces in the Eighth Canto of *Eugene Onegin* as one who by her 'marble beauty' could not eclipse his heroine Tatyana. An expunged passage of the same Canto describes Nina's entry at the ball in a seductive gown that bears a close resemblance to the dresses of Volskaya and Cleopatra in Pushkin's second story. In a letter to Vyazemsky on September 1, 1828, Pushkin described the Countess as 'a bronze Venus'. He wrote: 'I have entered high society because I am homeless. If it were not for your bronze Venus I should have died of boredom, but she is comfortingly amusing and sweet. I am writing poems to her and she has made me into one of her panders ...' Minsky, the hero of *The Guests Arrived at the Country House*, also describes himself and Volskaya in the same terms: 'I am simply her confidant or what you like, but I love her with all my heart: she is killingly amusing.' Pushkin wrote to Yelisaveta Khitrovo approximately at the same time: 'I fear decent women and lofty sentiments most of all. Long live the grisettes! It is much easier and much quicker with them ... Would you like me to be quite frank with you? I may be elegant and *comme il faut* in my writings, but my heart is completely vulgar and my inclinations are completely *tiers-état*. I am fed up with intrigues, sentiments, correspondence, etc., etc. To my misfortune, I am having an affair with a witty, morbid, and passionate woman who drives me to distraction though I love her with all my heart. . . .'

In her memoirs the Countess's niece tells the credible story of how Pushkin, who was with the Countess at a 'rout', was so furious with her for paying more attention to another man that he drove his long nails into her arm so deeply that he drew blood.

Pushkin resumed his courting of Anna Olenin after the satisfactory conclusion of the investigation into his authorship of *The Gabriliade*. In the margin of the rough copy of his poem *Poltava*, he again drew a number of portraits of her. One of them shows her with her head propped on her hand, looking pensively before her. She is wearing a hat and Pushkin has drawn her down to the waist. This is the only portrait of Anna Olenin in which Pushkin tried to draw the eyes he had found so irresistible. Usually he draws her with her hair covering her eyes, but this drawing seems to illustrate the line in his poem 'What pensive genius is in them'. Next to Anna's portrait Pushkin also drew an elderly woman which bears a strong resemblance to her mother. Once more Pushkin jots down anagrams of Anna's name: Olenine, Olenine, Annette, Annette A.P.A.P., repeated a few pages further. He refers to her again in his eight-line poem which sums up his attitude to Petersburg, as a 'sumptuous' and 'poor' city, a city of 'slavery . . . boredom, cold, and granite', ending with the lines: 'I feel a little sorry for you all the same, because here sometimes a little foot is walking and a golden curl is waving.' It was Anna Olenin's little feet that so enchanted Pushkin that at last he made up his mind to make a formal proposal of marriage. He went to see Anna's mother, who soon disabused him of any idea of marrying her daughter. When asked many years later why she did not marry Pushkin, Anna replied: 'Because he had no position in society and because he was poor.' Her mother, no doubt, bluntly told him the same. A good idea of Pushkin's fury can be obtained from his description of Anna Olenin and her father in the expunged lines in Stanza XXVI of the Eighth Canto of *Eugene Onegin*: 'Here was K.M., a Frenchman, married to a sickly, hunchbacked doll [Anna had prominent shoulder blades] and seven thousand serfs! Here with all his decorations was an inflexible member of the Board of Censors (this fierce Cato has recently been removed for taking bribes).' Alexey Olenin became an *ex officio* member of the board of censorship on September 6, 1828, and remained one until 1834. In one of the drafts of Stanza XXVI Anna Olenin appears under the name of Liza Losin (from *los*, an elk, an allusion to *olen*, a stag) and is described as 'so mincing, so diminutive, so slatternly, so shrill, that every guest involuntarily imagined she had both intellect and malice'. The lines about Liza Losin were written in December 1829 after Pushkin's long journey to the Caucasus.

3

On April 26, 1828, Russia declared war on Turkey. The war was generally regarded as a war of liberation, since it decided the fate of the Greek insurrection and Pushkin asked to be allowed to join the army. He was told that there were no vacancies for him. Pushkin then asked to be allowed to go to Paris for six months, but his request was again refused. 'I deeply regret,' Pushkin wrote to Benkendorf on April 23, 'that my wishes [to join the army] cannot be carried out and I accept with veneration the decision of the Emperor . . . As during the next six or seven months I shall most probably have nothing to do, I should have liked to spend them in Paris, which I may not succeed in doing afterwards . . .' However, the authorities soon saw to it that he had plenty to do by subjecting him to constant interrogations and forcing him to sign a statement that he would write no more blasphemous poems. 'The demand for a signed police statement,' he wrote to Benkendorf on August 17, 'humiliates me in my own eyes and I am firmly of the opinion that I do not deserve it and would have given my word of honour to this effect, if I still hoped that it had any value.' The affair with Anna Olenin was no less humiliating and acted as another blow to his *amour-propre*. Pushkin showed how touchy he was about his 'position in high society' by sending a challenge to the secretary of the French Embassy, whom he thought he overheard saying to a woman at a reception, Send him away! It was only on receiving a firm denial from the surprised diplomat, that Pushkin let the matter drop. A year before also, Pushkin had nearly fought a duel in answer to a challenge by another man, who resented his attentions to a young woman with whom he was in love. It was, therefore, with a sigh of relief that he finished the rough draft of *Poltava*, famous for its battle scenes, its apotheosis of Peter the Great, and its melodramatic love affair, and left on October 19 for Malinniki, Mrs Osipov's estate in the province of Tver. The only two people perturbed by Pushkin's decision to go to Malinniki and not to Mikhailovskoye, which he could not face after the death of his nurse, were, strangely enough, Alexey Vulf, who thought that it might harm the reputation of his mother and his sister, and Katerina Karamzin who (in a letter to Vyazemsky) thought that his 'solitude' in Mikhailovskoye would have had 'a greater effect on his imagination than the society of a certain provincial lady, which can only provide him with a few more scenes for his Onegin, which has too many as it is'. But both Alexey Vulf and Katerina Karamzin were wrong. Pushkin seemed to have enjoyed his stay at Malinniki without getting himself involved in any compromising situations. 'I am very happy here,' he wrote to Delvig on November 15, 'I love Praskovya with all my heart; it is a pity that she is ailing and is always worrying. The neighbours come to look at me as at the dog Munito [a performing dog on show in Moscow at the time] . . .' On November 26 he wrote to Delvig again: 'I am having great fun because I love country life very much. Here they think I came to collect stanzas for Onegin and frighten their children with me as a bogey man. I go riding on the newly fallen snow, play whist at 80 kopecks a rubber and in this way am clinging to the charms of virtue and shunning the toils of vice – tell it to our ladies. I shall come to them rejuvenated in body and soul . . .'

This autumn was more productive than the year before. Before leaving for Malinniki he wrote his ghostly folk 'ballad' *The Drowned Man* and in the country he revised *Poltava* and finished the seventh canto of *Eugene Onegin*. He also wrote his poems *Cleopatra*, *The Upas Tree* (*Anchar*), a symbolic attack on the autocracy in which he had to change 'tsar' in the last strophe to 'prince', and *The Poet and the Mob*, in which he replied to the critics who demanded that he should teach 'moral lessons' to his readers by asserting the poet's right to self-expression.

At the end of November Pushkin arrived in Moscow and stayed there until January 7, 1829. In Moscow Pushkin first of all visited the Ushakovs. His absence of a year and a half showed the flimsiness of his affair with Yekaterina, for during his very first visit he learned that she was engaged to Prince Alexander Dolgoruky. 'What am I left with?' cried Pushkin. 'With the stag's horns,' replied Yekaterina, a rather malicious hint at Pushkin's unsuccessful wooing of Anna Olenin. The relationship between Pushkin and the two Ushakov girls remained as amicable as ever. This is proved by the famous list of over thirty names of the women Pushkin had been in love with, which he wrote down in November, 1829, in the album of the younger sister Yelisaveta, and which has been rather humourlessly dubbed The Don Juan List by Pushkin scholars.*

Pushkin's arrival in Moscow was unexpected, but it would appear from Vyazemsky's letters to his wife that he was still looking for a wife. On December 12, 1828, he wrote:

Pushkin is here and I did not expect him at all. He arrived for three weeks he says. He has not fallen in love with anyone yet, and his old loves somehow won't have anything to do with him. Yesterday he should have visited the Korsakovs [Alexandra Rimsky-Korsakov's visit to the Caucasian Mineral Waters with her mother in May, 1827, created a sensation because of a rumour that she had been kidnapped by the Circassians. In 1831 Pushkin planned to write a novel based on her visit. According to Vyazemsky, Pushkin was not indifferent to her in 1827–1828], I don't know what their meeting was like. I am trying to persuade him to come to Penza with me, but I don't think he will, particularly as he will probably have fallen in love by that time. He has not changed at all, though he does not seem to be so cheerful.

On December 19, Vyazemsky wrote again:

Yesterday we dined at Vasily Pushkin's with the Ushakov girls, but do not think it is a betrothal, though he does fall in love on old yeast. But here is Alexander Dolgoruky and it looks as though there is going to be a wedding. Pushkin began to take himself off to the Korsakovs, but I was not there with him and I don't know how things are there.

*The list is divided into two columns, the first includes the names of the women Pushkin had been seriously in love with, and the second the names of those of less permanent involvements. The first column includes: Natalia I (probably the serf actress of Count Tolstoy's theatre in Tsarskoye Selo, though it might also be Countess Natalia Kochubey), Katerina I (Yekaterina Bakunin), Katerina II (Yekaterina Karamzin), N N (Countess Sofia Potocki-Kiselev), Princess Avdotya (Princess Eudoxie Golitsyn), Nastasia (the name is difficult to decipher and it may refer to the Nastasia who served as a box office girl in the Petersburg Zoo, with whom Pushkin seems to have had an affair in 1819), Katerina III (Katerina Raevsky, the wife of General Orlov), Aglaya (Davydov, wife of General Alexander Davydov, the owner of Kamenka), Calypso (Polychrony), Pulcheria (Varfolomey), Amalia (Riznich), Eliza (Vorontsov), Euphraxie (Vulf, with whom Pushkin had a brief affair in 1829 and who married Baron Vresky in 1831), Katerina IV (Yekaterina Ushakov), Anna (Olenin), Natalia (Pushkin's wife). The other column includes: Maria (unknown, probably Maria Smith), Anna (Anna Vulf), Sofia (Pushkin), Alexandra (Osipov, Praskovya Osipov's stepdaughter), Varvara (unknown), Vera (probably Vera Vyazemsky, Prince Vyazemsky's wife), Anna (Vulf, Praskovya Osipov's daughter), Anna (Kern), a third Anna (Olenin?), Varvara (unknown), Yelisaveta (Khitrovo), Nadezhda (unknown), Agrafena (Zakrevsky), Lyubov (unknown), Olga (Kalashnikov), Yevgenia (unknown), Alexandra (Rimsky-Korsakov), Yelena (unknown), Tatiana, Avdotya (unknown).

He says he is beginning to feel like falling in love again. In general, he does not look as depressed as before and he is not playing the fool so much . . .

But Pushkin was certainly not his cheerful self when he left Moscow on January 7, 1829. 'Pushkin left the other day,' Vyazemsky wrote to his wife on January 9. 'He did not seem to be very happy. I can't explain or guess what had or had not happened to him, *mais il n'était pas en verve.* He went mostly to see the Korsakovs and the gipsies; I saw him quite often in both places and I just could not recognise our old Pushkin . . .'

What happened was that in his quest for likely brides Pushkin went to a ball given by his old dancing master Iogel, in whose house at the age of nine, he had met the love of his 'golden childhood years', the eight-year-old Sofia Sushkov. This time he saw a beautiful sixteen-year-old girl in a white chiffon dress and a gold circlet on her head and, as was all too usual with him, he fell violently in love. The girl was Natalie Goncharov, whom he was to marry two years later. But in her case, as in the case of Anna Olenin, his doubtful social status and his unsatisfactory financial position made him realise that it was quite hopeless to expect Natalie's mother (her father was an incurable lunatic) to consent to her daughter's marriage to him. On his return to Petersburg, 'he became unpleasantly gloomy in society', Karamzin's eldest daughter Sofia wrote to Vyazemsky from Petersburg on March 30, 1829. 'He spent days and nights gambling with a sombre kind of fury, I am told,' she added. Pushkin was back in Moscow in mid-March, after receiving from Benkendorf oral permission to go to Tiflis to see his brother Lev who was on active service in the Caucasus. (At the same time Benkendorf sent an order to the local authorities for a surveillance of Pushkin in the cities where he stopped.) In Moscow Pushkin made a formal proposal for the hand of Natalie through Count Fyodor Tolstoy, the 'American'. Her answer was neither a refusal nor an acceptance. On May 1, 1829, the day he left for the Caucasus he wrote to Natalie's mother:

> On my knees, shedding tears of gratitude, that is how I should have written to you now after Count Tolstoy has brought back your answer to me. This answer is not a refusal. You allow me to hope. Do not accuse me of ingratitude, if I still murmur and if sadness and bitterness are mixed in my feeling of happiness: I quite understand a mother's prudence and tender solicitude, but do forgive the impatience of a

heart that is sick and deprived of happiness. I am departing at once and I am carrying away in the depth of my soul the image of a celestial being who owes her existence to you. If you have any commands to give me, please direct them to Count Tolstoy who will see that they reach me.

This sentimental effusion, of which Pushkin was only too capable when in the throes of a great passion, he tried to explain in a letter to Mrs Goncharov on April 5, 1830:

. . . When I saw her for the first time her beauty had hardly begun to be noticed in society. I fell in love with her. My head was in a whirl. I made a proposal, and your answer, vague as it was, nearly made me lose my reason. The same night I departed for the army. You ask me whatever for. I swear to you that I do not know, but a kind of involuntary anguish drove me out of Moscow. I would not have been able to bear either your or her presence there. I wrote to you. I hoped. I waited for an answer. It did not come. The mistakes of my early youth presented themselves to my imagination; they were too violent by themselves and calumny has added to them further; the talk about them has become unfortunately widespread. You might have believed it. I dared not complain, but I was in despair.

Pushkin loved 'to pile it on'. He showed little despair during his journey across the Caucasus. Indeed, he enjoyed his trip immensely, had a rather unlucky encounter with a pretty eighteen-year-old Kalmuck girl and, only six days after his arrival in the army, a breathless, if brief, encounter with the enemy on the way to Erzerum.

4

Pushkin described his trip to the Caucasus in great detail in his *Journey to Erzerum*. On the way he made a detour to visit General Alexey Yermolov, the famous conqueror of the Caucasus who had fallen into disfavour and lived in retirement in Oryol. Pushkin spent two hours with him, listening to his bitter criticisms of the army command and especially of General Ivan Paskevich, the Commander-in-chief of the Russian armies. Next he visited a Kalmuck village where he had his encounter with the reluctant Kalmuck girl on May 22. He described it in an expunged passage of his *Journey*:

The other day I went to inspect the Kalmuck tents. In one of them I came across a Kalmuck family; a pot was boiling in the middle of the tent, the smoke rising through a hole in the top. A young, rather good-looking Kalmuck girl was busy sewing, while smoking a pipe. Her face was swarthy, of a darkish red complexion, her lips were red, her teeth as white as pearls . . . I sat down beside her. 'What's your name?' I asked. She told me her name. 'How old are you?' 'Ten and eight.' 'What are you sewing?' 'Trousers.' 'For whom?' 'For me.' 'Kiss me.' 'I can't. I am ashamed.' Her voice was extremely pleasant. She gave me her pipe and joined the rest of her family who were having a meal. In the pot they had cooked tea with mutton fat and salt. I don't think the cuisine of any people could have produced anything more nauseating than that. She offered me her little jug and I . . . I gulped down a mouthful, doing my best not to inhale. I asked for a bite of something and they gave me a small slice of the dried meat of a mare. I swallowed it with great pleasure. After this feat I fancied that I deserved some reward, but my proud beauty hit me over the head with one of their musical instruments that reminded me of a balalaika. This example of Kalmuck courtesy did not particularly please me and I left the tent and continued my journey.

1. Nadezhda Pushkin,
née Hannibal,
the poet's mother.
From a miniature by
K. de Maistre, 1810

2. Sergey Pushkin,
the poet's father.
Portrait by an
unknown artist

3. View of Petersburg

5. Alexander Pushkin as a boy. Engraving by E. Heitman

6. Tsarskoye Selo: The gardens of Catherine the Great

7. Tsarskoye Selo: Pushkin's sketch of the Lycée
from the Eighth Canto of *Eugene Onegin*

8. A view of Moscow

9. Odessa where Pushkin stayed during his exile

10. Countess Sofia Potocki. Portrait by P. A. Hall

11. Count and Countess Vorontsov.
Pushkin's sketch from his MS of *Eugene Onegin*

12. Mikhailovskoye—the family estate to which Pushkin was exiled in 1824

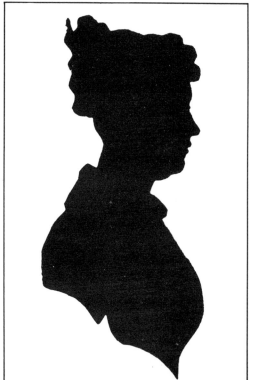

13. Anna Kern in the 1820s

14. The Hanged Decembrists (1826):
    Pushkin's sketch from
    his MS of *Poltava*

15. Self-portrait from the
    margin of the fifth canto
    of *Eugene Onegin*

16. Self-portrait

17. Pushkin. Portrait by A. O. Kiprensky, 1827

18. Pushkin. Portrait by V. Tropinin, 1827

19. Self-portrait: Pushkin with a Cossack pike
in skirmish against the Turks, 1829

20. An illustration by Pushkin for his
poem *The Little House in Kolomna*

21. A group of Russian writers in the 1830s: *from left to right—*
Nicolai Gneditch, Vasily Zhukovsky, Pushkin, Ivan Krylov

22. Natalie Pushkin,
née Goncharov,
the poet's wife. An
engraving by V. Gay

23. Natalie Pushkin.
Water colour by
A. Bryulov, 1831

24. Autograph of *The Bronze Horseman*
with four lines crossed out by Nicholas I, 1833

25. Georges d' Anthès who killed Pushkin in a duel

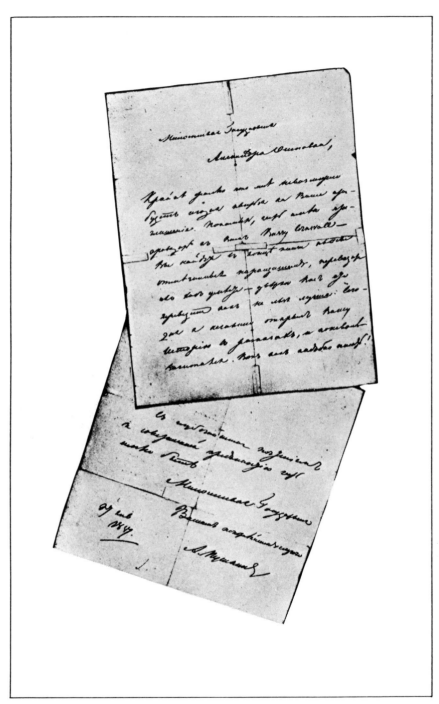

26. Autograph of Pushkin's last letter
written on January 27th, 1837,
shortly before the fatal duel

Pushkin's epistle to the Kalmuck girl draws a parallel between civilised society women and the native girl, whose 'eyes and wild beauty' enchanted his mind and his heart. 'Is it not one and the same thing,' he asks, 'to lose oneself in a reverie in a brilliant ballroom, a fashionable theatre-box or in a nomadic tent?'

Pushkin visited the hot springs he had visited with the Raevsky family. 'I was sorry not to find the steep, rocky path, the bushes and unfenced precipices over which I used to clamber,' he writes. At one of the inns on the road, he found a soiled copy of his *Caucasian Captive* and re-read it with great pleasure. 'All that was weak and young and incomplete,' he thought, 'but a great deal had been divined and well expressed.' Further on Pushkin was introduced to a Persian poet, a member of the suite of a Persian prince who was travelling to Petersburg to conduct peace negotiations with the Russian government. Pushkin writes:

> With the help of an interpreter, I began a florid oriental greeting, but I felt ashamed when, in reply, the Persian poet made a simple intelligent and courteous speech which one would expect a decent man to make. He hoped to meet me in Petersburg and expressed his regret that his acquaintance with me was so brief, etc. Ashamed, I was forced to give up my gravely facetious tone and have recourse to the usual European phraseology. Here is a lesson for our Russian sarcasm. In future, I shall not judge a man by his tall sheepskin papakha (as the Persian hats are called) and his painted finger-nails.

In the baths in Tiflis Pushkin was somewhat surprised to find more than fifty women, young and old, half dressed or completely undressed, taking no notice of him. It made him feel that he had entered the room as an invisible man. Many of them were beautiful and reminded him of a few lines from Thomas Moore's *Lalla Rookh*:

> A lovely Georgian maid,
> With all the bloom, the freshen'd glow
> Of our country maidens' looks,
> When warm they rise from Tiflis' brooks.

He was left in the care of a noseless Tartar bath attendant, who jumped on his shoulders and performed a Cossack dance on his back, rubbed him with a wool mitten and, after pouring warm water over him, began washing him down with a soapy cotton flannel, 'a most inexplicable

sensation: the hot soap pours over you like air!' After washing him down
with the cotton flannel, he lowered him into the bath, which was the end
of 'the ceremony'.

Pushkin spent two weeks in Tiflis, but did not find Nikolai Raevsky
and his brother who had joined the advancing Russian army. Pushkin had
only been permitted to go as far as Tiflis, but as soon as he got a letter
from Raevsky asking him to hurry up and join him in Kars, he left Tiflis.
He describes how on the way to Kars he met a cart drawn by two
oxen:

> Several Georgians accompanied the cart. Where are you from? I
> asked. From Teheran. What are you carrying? Griboyedov. It was the
> body of Griboyedov, killed by the Persian mob in Teheran, which they
> were taking to Tiflis. I never thought of meeting our Griboyedov again!
> I said goodbye to him last year in Petersburg before his departure for
> Persia. He looked depressed and had strange forebodings. I tried to
> reassure him, but he said to me: *Vous ne connaissez pas ces gens-là: vous
> verrez qui'll faudra jouer des couteaux.* He thought that the reason for
> the bloodshed would be the death of the Shah and the internecine strife
> between his seventy sons. The aged Shah is still alive, but Griboyedov's
> prophetic words came true. He perished under the daggers of the
> Persians, a victim of ignorance and perfidy. His mutilated body, which
> had for three days been the sport of the Teheran mob, was recognised
> only by a bullet scar on his arm.

On arriving at the Turkish frontier, Pushkin suddenly realised that he
had never before seen a foreign country:

> A frontier was something mysterious for me. From my childhood
> travels were my favourite dream. For a long time afterwards I had led a
> nomadic life, wandering sometimes in the south, sometimes in the
> north, but never had I escaped from the borders of boundless Russia.
> Now I cheerfully rode into the forbidden river and my good horse
> brought me out onto the Turkish bank, but that bank had already been
> conquered; I was still in Russia.

On his arrival at the front on June 13 Pushkin met Nikolai Raevsky and
some of his 'old friends', who had been involved in the Decembrist
uprising and whom the authorities were anxious that he should not meet.
He greatly enjoyed camp life. 'In the morning,' he writes, 'we were roused

by a salvo from the guns. I found sleep in a tent extremely healthy. At dinner we washed down our Asiatic shashlik with English beer and champagne.'

On June 19 Pushkin's wish was fulfilled and he actually took part in the fighting. According to the official history of the war, Pushkin 'in a poetic impulse rushed out of the tent of the Commander-in-Chief, mounted his horse and immediately found himself in the front line'. A major Raevsky sent after the poet 'was just in time to overtake him and bring him out of the front line of the Cossacks at the moment when, seizing a pike of one of the killed Cossacks, Pushkin was about to hurl himself against the enemy cavalry'. Mikhail Pushchin, younger brother of Pushkin's Lycée classmate, had been exiled to the Caucasus for his part in the Decembrist uprising. He met Pushkin at the front and left the following description of this incident:

We had just finished dinner at Raevsky's with Pushkin, his brother Lev and Major Semichev, when we were informed that the enemy had appeared before our front lines. We all rushed to our horses, which had been saddled since morning. As soon as I rode out, I found myself in the midst of an engagement between our Cossacks and the Turkish cavalry. It was there that I came across Semichev who asked me whether I had seen Pushkin. I galloped off with him to look for Pushkin and found him separated from the Cossacks and galloping against the Turks who were riding straight towards him. Our approach together with the approach of a detachment of Uhlans forced the Turks to retreat and, though dissatisfied, Pushkin did not leave us any more, particularly as the attack of the Turks had been repulsed and our cavalry had returned to its former position at nightfall . . . A few days later one of our patrols came upon the whole Turkish army . . . When Pushkin heard it, he got very excited and began jumping about and waving his arms, saying that this time he was quite determined to come to blows with the Turks. But however much Pushkin might have wanted to fight the Turks, he could not do so because the Turks were in full retreat. Every time I met Pushkin he was furious with the Turks who did not wish to accept the battle which he craved for.

Pushkin entered Erzerum after the city had surrendered to the Russians and left this description:

The streets of the town were narrow and twisting, the houses were rather tall, there were crowds of people everywhere but the shops were closed. After spending about two hours in the town I returned to our camp. The Turkish Commander-in-Chief and four Pashas who had been taken prisoner were already there. One of the Pashas, a thin old man, who was talking animatedly to our generals, saw me wearing a frockcoat and asked who I was. Told that I was a poet, the Pasha put his hand on his chest and, bowing to me, said through an interpreter: 'Blessed is the hour when we meet a poet. A poet is the brother of the dervish. He has neither country nor earthly possessions and while we, poor wretches that we are, worry about glory, about power and about treasures, he stands equal to the rulers of the world, and men worship him.' The oriental greeting of the Pasha pleased all of us very much. I then went to have a look at the Turkish Commander-in-Chief. On entering his tent, I came across his favourite page, a black-eyed boy of fourteen wearing a rich livery. The Commander-in-Chief, a white-haired old man of very ordinary appearance, was sunk in deep gloom. He was surrounded by a crowd of our officers. On leaving his tent, I saw a half-naked young man who was wearing a sheepskin hat, and carrying a cudgel in his hand and a waterskin on his back. He was shouting at the top of his voice. I was told it was my brother, the dervish, who had come to welcome the conquerors. He was chased away.

After a visit to the palace of one of the Pashas where he was not allowed into the harem, Pushkin was summoned to General Paskevich. 'Mr Pushkin,' the Commander-in-Chief said, no doubt on the Emperor's orders, 'your life is dear to Russia, you have nothing more to do here and I advise you to go back . . .' On saying goodbye to the poet, Paskevich made him a present of a Turkish sabre. Pushkin left the army and was back in Tiflis on August 1.

The following description of Pushkin in the army was left by Mikhail Yuzefovich, one of Nikolai Raevsky's aides-de-camp:

I met Pushkin in 1829 under conditions very favourable for making friends with people. Although I spent with him only about five or six weeks, I was with him all the time. He lived with Nikolai Raevsky and I lived with his brother Lev in the next tent.

I can see him now just as he was, full of life, simple in his manner, always laughing, extremely agile, even over-vivacious, with a pair of wonderful large, clear and bright eyes, with gleaming white teeth, of which, like Byron, he took very good care. He was not dark at all, but white-skinned with wavy chestnut hair. His features were pleasant and his general demeanour very sympathetic. While with us he wore an elegant black frockcoat and a gleaming top hat; not knowing who he was, the soldiers took him to be the regimental padre and called him 'the dragoon priest'.

Pushkin had brought with him a few books, including the works of Shakespeare. One day he read and translated a few scenes from Shakespeare to his brother and to Yuzefovich, who was struck by Pushkin's curious pronunciation which sounded so absurd that he began to suspect his knowledge of the language. He invited a relative of his who knew English fluently to listen to Pushkin read and translate a passage from Shakespeare. 'My cousin,' Yuzefovich writes, 'burst out laughing at the very first words Pushkin read out in English. "Tell me," he asked Pushkin, "what language are you reading?" Pushkin, too, burst out laughing and explained that he read English just as if it were Latin. My cousin, though,' Yuzefovich concludes a little too rashly, 'found his translation to be absolutely correct and his understanding of the language irreproachable.'

In Tiflis Pushkin spent a few days 'in amiable and cheerful company'. In Vladikavkaz he came across Pushchin and Dorokhov, an army officer, both on their way to the hot springs to recover from the wounds they had received in the campaign. Pushkin writes:

In Pushchin's room I found a number of Russian journals on the table. The first article I came across was a criticism of one of my poems. In it the author abused me and my poem mercilessly. I began reading it aloud. Pushchin stopped me and demanded that I should read it with greater expression. I must point out that the article was written in the form of a dialogue between a deacon, a woman who baked holy wafers and a proof-reader. Pushchin's request seemed so amusing to me that the vexation aroused by the reading of the article disappeared completely and we burst out laughing. Such was the first welcome I received in my dear native land.

After quarrelling with Dorokhov for beating up his batman, Pushchin went on alone to Vladikavkaz where he had to wait a few days until the arrival of a convoy.

Pushchin records:

On the eve of my departure from Vladikavkaz together with the convoy, Pushkin rushed into my room and told me that he had specially overtaken me in order to travel with me to Piatigorsk and asked me to take Dorokhov with us. I agreed on condition that both promised not to play cards before our arrival in Piatigorsk. They promised and Pushkin told his servant to fetch his and Dorokhov's things, including a box of excellent hock which Raevsky had given him. We at once drank a few bottles. Everything went swimmingly during our slow progress from Vladikavkaz to Piatigorsk. We travelled in my carriage, though sometimes Pushkin mounted his Cossack horse and galloped away from the convoy in search of adventures or a meeting with mountaineers, which he intended to entice near enough for our gun to be fired: but he found neither adventures nor mountaineers. During our stops on the road and our stay at the inns at night, Pushkin and Dorokhov found it very difficult to keep their promise. Dorokhov did not dare to strike his batman and Pushkin did not dare to mention cards, though he did try to induce me to go back on our agreement . . . On arriving in Piatigorsk I went to see the sights . . . and on returning after sunset, found Pushkin playing cards with Dorokhov and an army officer. '*La glace est rompue,*' said Pushkin to me. 'We are no longer under your wardship, so won't you put something on a card.' I refused. Pushkin won two gold roubles that evening. Pushkin and the army officer finished the game looking very pleased with themselves, while Dorokhov left the table looking gloomy. They promised to join me in Kislovodsk and when at last they did join me they both had lost everything they possessed. Pushkin lost the thousand gold roubles he had borrowed from Raevsky. He told me that he was now firmly determined to lead an exemplary life and to work a lot. He asked my batman to bring him one of my horses every morning because he intended to go for a ride. I soon learnt that the army officer to whom Pushkin had lost all his money had settled on the outskirts of Kislovodsk and Pushkin rode over to play cards with him every morning. On his return from his ride one morning, Pushkin flung a few gold coins on the table and admitted that he had been gambling with the army officer.

Altogether he had won twenty gold coins, but he was taking a very long time to win back his lost thousand gold coins.

Pushchin had in the end to lend Pushkin enough money to take him to Moscow, but on the way to Moscow Pushkin again lost five thousand roubles.

5

By 1830 Pushkin had to admit that he was no longer popular with the Russian reading public. His reconciliation with Nicholas I lost him the support of the Russian radicals. (Nikolai Turgenev, who had been sentenced to death *in absentia* for his part in the Decembrist plot, reacted violently to Pushkin's *Stanzas* by describing him in a letter to his brother Alexander as 'a barbarian'.) The Emperor, on the other hand, never really believed in Pushkin's change of heart. His distrust increased when Pushkin disobeyed his orders and left Tiflis for the army where he was known to have associated with some of the former Decembrists. On his return, Benkendorf wrote to ask him who gave him permission to go to the army and why he 'broke his word' by going to Trans-Caucasia. In his reply (on November 10, 1829), Pushkin expressed his 'profound sorrow that his Majesty was displeased with my trip to Erzerum', but his excuse of wishing to see his brother was rather thin. Still more so was his explanation for taking part in the fighting:

> Once there it seemed embarrassing to avoid taking part in the engagements which were about to take place and it so happened that I participated in the campaign, half soldier and half traveller. I realise now how false my position was and how heedless my conduct, but at least it was only heedlessness. The idea that any other motive might be attributed to me would be unendurable. I'd rather suffer the most severe disfavour than be thought an ingrate by him to whom I owe everything and for whom I am ready to sacrifice my life. This is not just a phrase. . . .

The exaggerated way in which Pushkin professed his loyalty to the throne merely increased the Emperor's suspicions. When, on January 7, 1830, Pushkin wrote to Benkendorf asking for permission to go to France or Italy, or even to China as a member of the Russian mission to Peking while, as he ingenuously put it, 'I am still neither married nor attached to the Service,' he was curtly told that a trip abroad would take him away from his work and embarrass his financial position still further. 'My relations with the government,' Pushkin wrote to Afanasy Goncharov, his future wife's grandfather, on September 9, 1830, 'are like our spring weather: one moment it rains, another the sun is shining. Now a cloud has appeared. . . .'

The 'cloud' was the growing opposition of the authorities to Pushkin's new journalistic venture, *The Literary Gazette*, edited by Delvig. The journal appeared once in five days. It was not particularly successful in its competition with Faddey Bulgarin's *Northern Bee*, which was published three times a week and was considered to be the official organ of the government. At first a close associate of Ryleyev and Griboyedov, Bulgarin went over completely to the side of the government after the events of December 14, 1825, and became closely associated with the secret police. A fierce opponent of *The Literary Gazette*, he became a bitter enemy of Pushkin whom he rightly considered to be the chief inspirer of the new journal. From its very first number (published on January 1, 1830) *The Literary Gazette* encountered all sorts of difficulties. Pushkin and his friends were surrounded by ill-wishers, among whom was Nikolai Polevoy, the publisher of *The Moscow Telegraph*. In 1830 the political events in Europe, notably the July revolution in France; the exile of Charles X to England which brought many French legitimists, including the man who was eventually to kill Pushkin, to Russia; the dissolution of the Holy Alliance; the insurrection in Warsaw, followed by the Russo-Polish war and the capture of Warsaw, and, finally, the cholera epidemics in 1830, resulting in the 'cholera disturbances', during which the peasants massacred army doctors and many high ranking army officers – all had repercussions on the attitude of the Russian authorities to Pushkin. In the autumn of 1830 Benkendorf, at the instigation of Bulgarin, banned *The Literary Gazette* for publishing a French poem by Casimir Delavigne, dealing with the revolution in France. The journal was reissued later but on condition that Delvig was no longer its editor.

Bulgarin began his attacks on Pushkin with the publication of the so-called *Anecdote* on March 12, 1830. He subtitled his article 'From an English Journal' and described Pushkin as 'A French rhymester' who 'aped Byron whom he did not understand in the original' and then lost his popularity. The 'Frenchman' (an all too transparent allusion to Pushkin's nickname at the Lycée) 'did not reveal a single thought in his works, nor

a single lofty feeling, nor a single useful truth . . . like the obsessed in
the fable of Pilpay, he threw stones at everything sacred, boasted about his
freethinking to the mob while grovelling at the feet of the mighty . . . he
scribbled on white sheets of paper for gain, and then gambled away the
money on marked playing cards . . . he possessed only one ruling passion –
vanity'. Pushkin replied by an epigram in which he declared that it did
not matter that Bulgarin was a Pole, for Kosciusco and Mickiewicz, too,
were Poles, but it did matter that he was a 'Vidocq Figlyarin', Vidocq
being the chief of the French secret police and *figlyar* the Russian for a
mountebank and a toady. Bulgarin published this epigram, substituting
his own name for 'Vidocq Figlyarin'. Pushkin then published a review
On the Memoirs of Vidocq (Vidocq's memoirs were greatly in vogue at the
time) in *The Literary Gazette* of April 6, 1830, in which he drew so faithful
a portrait of Bulgarin, hinting at his service in the French army during the
1812 campaign, his political denunciations and the dubious past of his
wife, that Bulgarin felt obliged to launch an even more vicious attack on
Pushkin in the August number of *The Northern Bee*. Here, without
mentioning Pushkin's name, he derided Pushkin's claim to be a descendant of an old aristocratic family by referring contemptuously to Pushkin's
Negro great-grandfather who, he wrote, 'was bought by a drunken skipper
for a bottle of rum'. Pushkin was well aware that Bulgarin would never
have dared to publish so personal an attack if he had not made quite sure
beforehand that it would be favourably received by Benkendorf, Bulgarin's chief, as well as by Nicholas I. Its full implication took some time
to sink in, for it was only on November 24, 1831, that Pushkin thought it
necessary to make his position clear to Benkendorf, who was a Baltic
German and, like the Pole Bulgarin, might take a dim view of Pushkin's
pride in his aristocratic descent. Pushkin wrote to Benkendorf in formal
French:

About a year ago a satirical article was published in one of our
journals in which a certain writer was mentioned who pretended to be of
noble birth while in fact he was only a *bourgeois-gentilhomme*. It was
added that his mother was a mulatto, whose father, a poor Negro boy,
had been bought by a sailor for a bottle of rum. Though Peter the
Great bears little resemblance to a drunken sailor [Pushkin must have
been very well aware that by 'the skipper' Bulgarin did not mean Peter
the Great but the captain of the slaver that plied between the African

coast and Constantinople, a centre of slave traffic], it was quite clearly meant to be me, for among Russian writers I alone have a Negro amongst my ancestors. Since this article was published in an official paper and since impropriety had gone so far as to mention my mother in a column which should have been purely literary and since our journalists do not fight duels, I considered it my duty to answer the *anonymous* satirist, which I did in a poem, and very sharply, too. [A reference to *My Pedigree*, written on December 3, 1830, in which Pushkin admitted that he was 'a bourgeois in the nobility', but asked what 'inspired Figlyarin' was in his 'respected family', except a 'nobleman in Meshchanskaya', that is 'Bourgeois', Street in the red light district, a rather unchivalrous reminder that Bulgarin was married to a former prostitute.] I sent my reply to the late Delvig [who died on January 14, 1831] . . . who advised me not to publish it . . . because it would be ridiculous to defend myself against such an attack and flaunt aristocratic sentiments when, as a matter of fact, I am only a *gentilhomme-bourgeois*, if not a *bourgeois-gentilhomme*. I accepted his advice and that was the end of the matter: meanwhile a number of copies of my reply were circulated. I was not sorry for this, since I do not disavow anything in it. I confess that I am not ashamed of what people call prejudices. I am not ashamed of being as good a nobleman as anyone, though there is little profit in it for me; I am certainly not ashamed of my ancestors' name, for that is the only inheritance they have left me. But since my poem could be taken as an indirect satire on the origin of certain prominent families, if one did not know that it was a very moderate reply to a provocation that deserved extreme censure, I consider it my duty to give you this frank explanation and to enclose the poem in question.

Whether or not Pushkin implied that Benkendorf was also a member of 'certain prominent families', there can be little doubt that the chief of the Third Department was behind Bulgarin's attacks on Pushkin. Benkendorf, even more than Bulgarin, was one of Pushkin's bitterest enemies and was indirectly instrumental in bringing about Pushkin's death five years later. It was not only Bulgarin who was in full cry after Pushkin's blood. Count Vladimir Sollogub, a writer of some distinction belonging to the younger generation, records in his memoirs that 'Pushkin's literary enemies never gave him any peace and constantly hurt his self-esteem by

their announcements that Pushkin had written himself out, that he had
become old-fashioned, that he had weakened . . . Pushkin replied with
crushing sarcasm, but he did not know how to acquire the necessary
indifference to published insults.'

In the Eighth Canto of *Eugene Onegin* (Stanza XXV), written in 1830,
Pushkin refers to his waning popularity in passing:

> The almanacks and the journals
> Where they keep lecturing us
> Where they abuse me so much today
> And where such compliments
> Used to be paid to me now and then . . .

A much more thorough analysis of the reasons for his unpopularity will
be found in the autobiographical introduction he wrote on October 26,
1830, to an unwritten story:

In spite of the great advantages enjoyed by poets, they are subject
to great disadvantages and unpleasantnesses. I am not referring to their
normal social insignificance or to their poverty . . . but to the envy and
calumny of their fellow-writers if they should happen to achieve fame,
and to the contempt and derision which descend upon them from every
side if their works fall out of favour . . . His vocation, the soubriquet
with which he is branded and which stays with him forever, is the most
bitter, the most unendurable thing to a poet. His readers regard him
as their property and think they have a right to make him account for
every trifle. They believe that he is born for their delectation and draws
breath only for the sake of spinning rhymes. If circumstances demand
his presence in the country, every man he meets on his return asks him:
What new little thing have you brought back for us? If he pays a visit
to the army to see some friends and relations, the public demands
that he should write a poem on the last victory, and journalists are angry
with him for making them wait so long for it. If he worries about his
straitened circumstances, or some family difficulty, or an illness of
someone dear to him, a vulgar smile immediately accompanies a no
less vulgar explanation: 'I suppose you are writing something!' If he
falls in love with some beautiful girl, she immediately buys herself an
album and expects him to write an elegy in it . . . One of my friends,

a famous poet, confessed to me that he is so infuriated by these greetings, questions, albums, etc., that he has to force himself not to be
rude and keeps telling himself that the dear people probably have no
intention of exasperating him.

My friend is a very simple and ordinary man. When the stupid fit
(so he calls his inspiration) takes possession of him, he locks himself
up in his room, goes to bed and writes from morning to late at night,
dresses hurriedly to have dinner at a restaurant, goes out for a walk
for an hour or two, and goes back to bed and writes till daybreak. This
goes on for two or three weeks, at most for a month, and happens once
a year, always in the autumn. My friend assures me that only then does
he know true happiness. [This is an exact description of the way Pushkin
wrote *Poltava*, as related by Yuzefovich in his memoirs.] The rest of
the year he does nothing . . . but still hears the inevitable question:
How soon will you make us a present of a new work? Our estimable
public would have to wait a long time for his presents, if the booksellers did not pay him so much for his poems. Being always in need
of money, my friend keeps publishing his works and has afterwards the
pleasure of reading the reviews which, in his energetic vernacular, he
calls eavesdropping in a pub to hear what the grovelling louts are
saying about him.

My friend derives his descent from one of our oldest families and is
proud of it . . . except for this little weakness which we attribute to his
wish to imitate Lord Byron, who, too, sold his works for a good
price, my friend is *un homme tout rond*, as the French say, *homo
quadratus*, as the Latin expression has it, or simply a very good man.
He dislikes the literary fraternity with very, very few exceptions . . . he
prefers the society of women and men of good social standing who . . .
do not indulge in literary conversations with him and never ask him the
famous question: Are you writing anything at the moment?

A more general explanation of his growing unpopularity is contained
in one of Pushkin's prose fragments in which he discusses the relationship
between the poet and his reader:

The ideas and feelings of an eighteen-year-old poet are still near and
familiar to everyone. Young readers understand him and recognise
excitedly their own feelings and thoughts in his work, which are
expressed clearly, vividly and harmoniously. But years pass, the young

poet matures, his talent grows, his ideas become loftier and his feelings
change. His poems are no longer the same, but his readers are still the
same except that, perhaps, they have become colder at heart and more
indifferent to life's poetry. The poet separates himself from them and
little by little retires completely into his shell. He still creates, but he
does so for himself alone and if, occasionally, he publishes his works,
their reception is cold, he encounters complete lack of attention, and
finds an echo to his sounds only in the hearts of a few admirers of
poetry who are as lonely and lost to the world as he is.

In his essay *A Few Words about Pushkin* (1832) Gogol's comment on the
decline in Pushkin's reputation is almost identical.

The true poet is faced with two alternatives: he has either to pitch
his style as high as possible and win the acclaim of the public [a reference to the pseudo-sublime school of writers who enjoyed a short-lived
popularity in the thirties] or he has to remain faithful to truth alone . . .
It is an undeniable fact that the more a poet becomes a poet, the more
he expresses feelings that are only known to poets, the more does the
crowd round him dwindle and at last becomes so small that he can
count his true admirers on the fingers of one hand.

The first sign of decline was the complete failure of his new poem
Poltava, his first historical poem, in which the narration is entirely
objective and the narrator does not intrude into the action. Pushkin
described it as 'a completely original creation'. But it was not only
Poltava. Every other new work by Pushkin, including the last cantos of
Eugene Onegin, was condemned by the critics, who were perhaps too near
to him in time to be able to appreciate his genius. Only thirteen years
later did the critic Visarion Belinsky publish the first of his famous eleven
essays, which finally established Pushkin's reputation as one of the
greatest Russian poets.

6

Pushkin's marriage began as a farce and ended as a tragedy.

The farce centred round the dowry a bride was by custom obliged to bring to her husband, and the trousseau which the bride's mother was supposed to provide. Natalie had neither, for both her mother, who was supposed to provide the dowry, and her grandfather, who undertook to provide the trousseau, were on the verge of bankruptcy, or as Pushkin charitably put it, 'in serious financial difficulties'. For a dowerless girl like Natalie, the only hope was marriage to an elderly rich nobleman, preferably a general, as was illustrated by Anna Kern and by Pushkin's own heroine, Tatyana. Therefore when, on his return from the Caucasus, Pushkin paid a visit to the Goncharovs with the intention of renewing his suit for the hand of Natalie, his reception was decidedly cool: Mrs Goncharov was obviously still hoping for a rich elderly suitor for her daughter, who would also relieve her own financial anxieties. 'Your silence, your coldness, and Natalie's indifferent and inattentive reception,' Pushkin was to write later to Mrs Goncharov, 'robbed me of any desire to explain myself and I left for Petersburg with death in my soul. I felt that I played a rather ridiculous part. For the first time in my life I felt timid and timidity in a man of my age could hardly have pleased a young girl of your daughter's age.'

Pushkin did not leave for Petersburg, though, no doubt, deeply hurt, he left for Malinniki where, as he expressed it in a poem written on January 18, 1829, during his earlier visit, he had earned the reputation of a 'vampire' from the ladies of the Tver province and where he felt anything but timid. He had gone there, he wrote to Alexey Vulf from Malinniki on October 16, 1829, 'to collect certain arrears', by which it is conjectured he had meant a successful, though brief, affair with Euphraxie Vulf, who was twenty at the time and whom he had always admired. Indeed, Euphraxie was the only daughter of Mrs Osipov for whom he preserved a genuine affection all through his life. In his letter to Vulf, Pushkin described his visit to the Staritsa district, which included Malinniki and other Vulf family estates, with a somewhat exaggerated nonchalance which was apparently meant to allay Vulf's suspicions.

On his return to Petersburg, Pushkin helped to found *The Literary Gazette*. Having failed to obtain permission to go abroad, he tried again to forget Natalie by reviving his old passion for Countess Carolina Sobansky. But this attempt to go back to 'the old yeast', as Vyazemsky described it, failed. In the spring of 1830 Pushkin received a message that Mrs Goncharov had undergone a change of heart about his marriage to her daughter. The Moscow marriage market had obviously failed to produce the rich elderly general, for whom the hearts of all the mothers of dowerless daughters yearned. Meanwhile Mrs Goncharov's financial position became so desperate that she was ready to marry her daughter off even to Pushkin, provided she could be sure that he was not in serious trouble with the authorities and, what was much more important, that by his marriage to her daughter she could raise some money to tide her over her difficulties. She knew that Pushkin's father owned estates in the Nizhny-Novgorod province. If Pushkin could get his father to agree to let him have an estate of his own, he could mortgage it, or rather the serfs on it, and she could then cheat him out of a considerable part of the mortgage money. All she had to do was to insist that her daughter must have a dowry and that, since she could not give her one, he would have to *lend* her the dowry, which she would then give back to him. She was shrewd enough to realise that Pushkin was the only man to fall for such a scheme. 'My mother-in-law,' Pushkin wrote to his friend Nashchokin on June 20, 1831, 'is keeping quiet [that is, about returning him the money he had lent her for her daughter's dowry] and is glad that God has sent her Tashenka [Natalie's pet name] such a meek husband.' Pushkin was *meek* enough to write to his father on April 6, 1830, the day of his 'tentative' engagement to Natalie, asking his parents for their formal consent to his marriage and pointing out that since Mrs Goncharov's financial affairs were in a 'sad state', that is to say, since he could not hope to receive any dowry from her, his parents would have to 'come to my aid'. He soon received a reassuring reply from his father who agreed to give him the small estate of Kistenovo, adjoining his larger estate of Boldino. Pushkin thus became the owner of two hundred serfs, which, he wrote to Vera Vyazemsky on April 28, 1830, he intended to mortgage.

'My marriage to Natalie, who,' he added parenthetically, 'is my one hundred and thirteenth love, has been decided.'

When he arrived in Moscow in early spring, he was shocked to receive a letter from Benkendorf, who demanded to know Pushkin's reasons for going to Moscow 'without permission' and threatened 'unpleasant' consequences if he could not produce a good reason. In his answer on March 21, 1830, Pushkin pointed out that he had received permission 'to live in Moscow' from the Emperor and that he had told Benkendorf himself about his impending trip to Moscow, when he met him in the street. 'You were even so good as to say to me: *vous êtes toujours sur les grands chemins.*' He now thought it wise to inform Benkendorf of his engagement to Natalie Goncharov, whom both the Emperor and Benkendorf had met in Moscow earlier that year. 'Madame Goncharov,' Pushkin wrote in formal French on April 16, 1830, 'is afraid that she might be giving her daughter to a man who has the misfortune of incurring his Majesty's disfavour. My happiness depends on a word of goodwill from a person to whom my devotion and gratitude are already pure and unbounded.' He then went on to ask for 'another favour', namely the removal of the ban on the publication of *Boris Godunov*, for which he had been offered two thousand roubles by Alexander Smirdin, the Petersburg bookseller and publisher. The true reason for the ban, he revealed for the first time, was that 'two or three passages' in the play seemed to Nicholas I to allude 'to more recent events', that is, to the Decembrist insurrection. Pushkin wrote:

All seditions resemble each other. A dramatic author cannot be held responsible for the words he puts into the mouths of his historical personages. He must make them speak according to their known character. One must therefore pay attention only to *the spirit in which the entire work is conceived*, to the impression which it has to produce. My tragedy is a work of good faith and I cannot in all conscience suppress what appears to me to be essential.

Safe in the knowledge that Pushkin was unaware that he was under the surveillance of the secret police, Benkendorf did not hesitate to send the false assurance that he had not been then, or at any other time, under police surveillance. He also conveyed to Pushkin the Emperor's permission to publish *Boris Godunov* on his own responsibility. 'His Majesty,' he wrote to Pushkin, 'received the news of your impending marriage with gracious satisfaction and expressed the hope that you have carefully

considered the step undertaken by you and have found in your heart and
character qualities necessary to ensure the happiness of a woman, especially a woman so worthy and charming as Mademoiselle Goncharov.' This
claptrap was not likely to have impressed Pushkin, except perhaps that
it contained an ominous hint of the favourable impression made on
Nicholas I by Natalie's beauty. It was a danger signal, but too far distant
to worry Pushkin. What did worry him greatly was Mrs Goncharov's
systematic campaign to wear down his resistance to parting with more
than a third of his mortgage money for a 'dowry' for his bride. She seems
to have made it quite clear that he could not expect her seventeen-year-old
Natalie to reciprocate his love and that, as Pushkin realised very well,
'only habit and long intimacy' could eventually win him Natalie's affection. She vented her disappointment by expressing her conviction that it
was only 'unfortunate fate' that prevented her daughter from forming
'ties more brilliant, more fitting and more worthy of her beauty' and that
if he failed to make Natalie's position in society 'as brilliant as she
deserves', he must not be surprised if she would regard her husband 'as an
obstacle' to her happiness and 'as a fraudulent ravisher'. Pushkin sum-
marised all these objections to his marriage in a letter he wrote to Mrs
Goncharov on April 5, 1830. But all he could say in reply was that he was
not ready to die in order to leave Natalie 'a dazzling widow' free to choose
a new husband the next day. 'This thought,' he wrote in unconscious
anticipation of what was actually to happen, 'is hell to me.'

A month after his engagement (on May 6, 1830) Pushkin formulated
his own less violent objection to his forthcoming marriage in an autobiographical sketch beginning with the lines: 'My fate has been decided,
I am going to be married.' The girl he was in love with and whom his
eyes had been looking for everywhere, Pushkin wrote, was 'almost' his.
The expectation of the final answer was 'the most painful feeling' of his
life. Pushkin continued:

The expectation of the last card dealt by the banker, pangs of
conscience, sleep before a duel, all this seemed nothing to me in
comparison . . . To marry! It is easily said: the majority of people see
in marriage shawls taken on credit [Pushkin got one, probably also on
credit, from a Tartar he knew: 'Find out where my Tartar lives,' he
asked his friend Pavel Nashchokin a month before his marriage], a new
carriage, a pink dressing-gown. Others – a dowry and a quiet life . . .

Others still get married because everyone gets married, because they [like Pushkin] have reached the age of thirty . . . I am getting married, that is to say, I am sacrificing my happy-go-lucky existence, my expensive habits, my aimless wanderings, my solitude, my inconstancy. I am about to double a life which is incomplete anyhow. I never worried about happiness. I could do without it. Now I shall have to have enough happiness for two, and where am I to get it? While I am still unmarried what do my obligations amount to? I have an ailing uncle whom I practically never see. If I visit him, he is very glad, if not, he finds an excuse for me: the rascal is young, he has other things to think of. In the morning I get up when I like . . . I go for a ride on my intelligent, gentle Jennie . . . When I return home, I look through my books and papers, put my dressing-table in order, dress casually if I am going to see friends or with painstaking care if I am dining at a restaurant where I proceed to read the journals or a new novel; if Walter Scott or Fenimore Cooper have not written anything new and if there is no murder trial in the papers, I order a bottle of champagne on ice, watch my glass go cold, drink slowly, happy in the thought that the dinner only cost me seventeen roubles and that I can permit myself such luxury. I go to the theatre, search for some wonderful dress in a box, for a pair of black eyes, I start a flirtation that keeps me busy till the end of the play. The evenings I pass either in noisy society where the whole town seems to be present, where I can see everyone and everything, where no one pays any attention to me, or in a selected circle of friends where I keep talking about myself and where everyone listens to me. I return home late and doze off reading a good book . . . That's what my bachelor life is like . . . At that moment I am handed a note . . . My proposal has been accepted . . . All my sad doubts disappear before this heavenly thought. . . .

Alas, only to reappear again all too soon.

On May 21, 1830, Pushkin and Natalie paid a visit to Afanasy Goncharov, Natalie's grandfather, on his estate of Polotnyany Zavod ('Cotton Mill', a name derived from a paper and cotton mill that once upon a time provided a considerable income to the Goncharovs but was no longer a going concern at the time of Pushkin's visit). The estate in the province of Kaluga was very large and terribly neglected. The visit only lasted seven days: the meeting with Natalie's mad father, who was allowed to roam all over the estate, was hardly likely to make the visit particularly happy; neither was the grandfather's support of Mrs Goncharov's demands for the dowry, nor the old man's insistence on Natalie's trousseau, which he undertook to provide himself on condition that Pushkin lent him the money first. Afanasy Goncharov also tried to fob off on Pushkin a colossal statue of Catherine II. He had inherited it from his father who had intended to erect it on the estate in honour of the Empress's visit in 1775. Pushkin promised to find a purchaser for the statue, but was not so forthcoming about the trousseau. In the end, however, the wily old man extracted from Pushkin a promise to lend him twelve thousand roubles for the trousseau, which like the dowry was never repaid. 'Grandfather,' Pushkin wrote to Nashchokin on October 22, 1831, 'is a swine. He is marrying off his third concubine and giving her a dowry of ten thousand roubles, but he can't pay me back my twelve thousand and he doesn't give anything to his granddaughter.'

On Pushkin's return to Moscow, Mrs Goncharov found a new way of tightening her pressure on the recalcitrant poet. Pushkin wrote to Pletnyov on September 29, 1930, from Boldino:

> My mother-in-law was postponing the wedding because of the dowry . . . She began to treat me badly every time I paid them a visit and to start stupid quarrels with me and that infuriated me. I felt depressed and black thoughts took possession of me . . . I was already anticipating a refusal . . . I was hurrying my mother-in-law, while, she, like a stupid peasant woman, kept worrying me about the dowry – the devil take it!

Pushkin was afraid that although his engagement had been publicly announced, it might still be broken off by Mrs Goncharov. She continued to raise objections to the marriage in order to get Pushkin in the right frame of mind to hand over the eleven thousand roubles she desperately needed. Meanwhile, Pushkin's own financial affairs were in a perilous state: he had lost twenty-four thousand roubles at cards and, after desperate pleas, could raise only one thousand eight hundred roubles from Pogodin.

In July he left Moscow for Petersburg to discuss his financial affairs with his father. On July 30 he wrote to Natalie: 'Everyone is awaiting you with impatience in society. Beautiful ladies ask to see your portrait and do not forgive me for not having one. I console myself by spending hours in front of a fair-haired Madonna who is as much like you as two drops of water. I would have bought her if she did not cost forty thousand roubles.' The painting was Perugino's *Madonna and Child* (now in the Pushkin State Art Museum in Moscow). It inspired Pushkin's first poem to Natalie, the sonnet *Madonna*, written on July 8, 1830, which ends with the three lines:

> My desires have been fulfilled. The creator
> Has sent you to me, you, my Madonna,
> The purest example of purest loveliness.

He was having a good time in Petersburg, he wrote to Vera Vyazemsky on August 4. This, it is conjectured, was a hint about the news of the July revolution in France, which was an exciting topic of conversation in Petersburg high society and which Pushkin received at first hand in the salons of Yelisaveta Khitrovo and her daughter Daria (Dolly) Ficquel-mont, wife of the Austrian ambassador. Back in Moscow, he was asking Yelisaveta Khitrovo for the latest news of Europe. 'Here, no one receives journals from France,' he wrote on August 21, 1830, 'and it is among these orang-outangs that I am condemned to live at the most interesting moment of the century. On top of all these troubles and unpleasantnesses my poor uncle Vasily has just died. I must say that never did an uncle die at a more inopportune moment. Because of it my marriage has to be postponed for another six weeks . . .' To Pletnyov Pushkin wrote on September 9, 1830, from Boldino: 'Poor uncle Vasily. Do you know what his last words were? I went to see him. I found him in a coma. When he came to he recognised me, looked mournfully at me, and after being silent for a little while, said: "How boring Katenin's articles are!" and not another word did he utter. How do you like that? That's what it means to die a soldier's death at one's post, *les cris de guerre à la bouche.*'

The postponement of his wedding made him feel 'terribly depressed' he wrote to Pletnyov on August 31 from Moscow:

> The life of a thirty-year-old fiancé is worse than thirty years of a gambler's life . . . Meanwhile I am cooling off. I am thinking of the worries of a married man and of the delights of bachelor life. Besides, Moscow gossip is reaching the ears of my fiancée and her mother, giving rise to tiffs and all sorts of sarcastic insinuations, shortlived reconciliations. In short, if not unhappy, I am not particularly happy, either. Autumn is approaching, my favourite season, when my health

usually becomes more robust and the time of my literary labours approaches, but I have to worry about the dowry and the wedding, which goodness only knows when we shall celebrate. . . .

The continual postponements of Pushkin's wedding became a topic of conversation in Moscow. 'Here people keep wondering whether Pushkin will marry or not,' Vyazemsky wrote to his wife. 'I shouldn't be surprised if they didn't start laying bets on his wedding in the same way as bets are laid on the day when the Neva will be free of ice.'

Pushkin arrived at Boldino on September 9. He intended to spend only a few weeks there, but was forced to stay for three months by the outbreak of cholera. Before leaving Moscow he wrote to Natalie in French: 'If your mother has decided to break off our engagement and if you obey her, I shall accept all the reasons which she chooses to give, even if they are as reasonable as the scene she made yesterday and the insults she heaped on me. Perhaps she is right and I have been wrong in believing for one moment that happiness was made for me. In any case, you are perfectly free.'

Pushkin also mentioned his quarrel with Natalie's mother in a letter to Vera Vyazemsky: 'On the day after the ball she made the most ridiculous scene you could imagine. She said things to me which in all conscience I could not endure. I still do not know whether my engagement has been broken off or not, but there is good reason to believe that it has. I have left the door wide open . . . Oh, what a cursed thing is happiness!' On arriving in the country, however, he wrote to Pletnyov on September 9, that his 'gloomy thoughts' had dispersed:

I have arrived in the country and am resting. All round me is cholera morbus. Have you any idea what kind of a wild beast it is? Before you know it may come to Boldino and bite us all and – I shall go off to pay a visit to Uncle Vasily and then you'll be writing my obituary . . . You can't imagine [he went on characteristically] what fun it is to run away from one's fiancée and just sit down and write poems. A wife is quite a different thing from a fiancée. Good heavens, yes! A wife is part of you. You can write as much as you please in her presence, but a fiancée is worse than the censor . . . She binds you hand and foot. Today I received a most charming letter from her: she promises to marry me even without a dowry –

– a dowry, that is, that she was supposed to bring him!

Boldino was situated on a flat, treeless plain. The village was dirty and depressing. It consisted of a pothouse, a church and offices in the centre, surrounded by small thatched cottages. Pushkin wrote on October 10, 1830, in a poem addressed to his 'red-faced critic':

Look, this is the view you see from here: a row of wretched cottages, behind them the black earth, the sloping descent to the plain, over them the thick line of grey clouds. Where are the bright meadows? Where are the dark forests? Outside, by the low fence, two poor trees stand to delight your eyes, only two trees, and one of them, too, has been completely bared by the rainy autumn . . . There is not a live dog in the yard. There is, it is true, a peasant, followed by two peasant women, hatless, who carries a coffin of a child under his arm and shouts from a distance to the lazy son of the priest to call his father and open the church. Quick! No time to wait! He should have been buried long ago!

He spent his days scribbling and fuming, Pushkin wrote to Natalie in one of his curiously impersonal letters in French. In the meantime his father wrote to tell him that his engagement had been broken off. 'It is enough,' Pushkin wrote to Natalie on November 4, 'to make me hang myself.'

Pushkin returned to Moscow on December 5, 1830, but his wedding to Natalie did not take place till February 18, 1831. 'The wedding of Beauty and the Beast,' quipped the Moscow wits.

Pushkin's first disappointment with Natalie seems to have occurred on their wedding night. On January 19, 1830, when his marriage to Natalie was still in the balance, Pushkin wrote one of the finest erotic poems in the Russian language. In it he declared that he no longer valued 'the passionate rapture, the sensuous ecstasy, the madness, the frenzy, the moans and shrieks of a young bacchante' when 'writhing like a serpent in my arms . . . she hastens the moment of my last spasms': a thousand times more dear to him was his 'meek darling' when, yielding to his 'long supplications' she gave herself to him at first 'without rapture', but later on became 'more and more and more animated' and at last 'shares my ardour in spite of herself'. The 'meek darling' seems to refer to his young mistress, the serf girl Olga Kalashnikov, for whom he had a special warm place in his heart, though he was forced to treat her as many other Russian noblemen, including Tolstoy, treated their serf mistresses. But the poem also reveals certain anticipations of his marriage to Natalie, who failed to do justice to them. Indeed, on the day after their wedding Natalie ran crying to her mother and Princess Vera Vyazemsky because, according to the princess, 'the moment Pushkin got out of bed, she never saw him again the whole day. She found herself alone in a strange house and cried bitterly.' A month later, in a letter to an old friend of his family, Pushkin quite frankly expressed his disappointment with his marriage and tried to justify himself for so conventional a step in his tumultuous career:

I have calmly weighed the advantages and disadvantages of the married state. My youth has passed tempestuously and fruitlessly. Till now I have lived differently from the way people usually live. There has been no happiness for me. *Il n'est de bonheur que dans les voies communes.* I am over thirty. At thirty people usually get married. I do as people usually do and I shall probably not regret it. Besides, I am marrying without rapture, without childish enchantment. The future does not appear in roseate hues to me, but in all its austere nakedness. Misfortunes will not surprise me; they are included in my family budget. Any joy will be something I did not expect.

As for Pushkin's budget, it amounted, as he explained to Pletnyov on February 16, to 38,000 roubles, which he received after mortgaging his two hundred serfs. Of this sum, he gave 11,000 to his mother-in-law 'who insisted that her daughter must have a dowry, but I may as well say goodbye to it'. Another 12,000 roubles he was obliged 'to lend' to Natalie's grandfather for her trousseau, and 10,000 roubles he had to send to a friend to pay off some of his gambling debts. He was thus left with practically no money and, as he wrote to Pletnyov: 'There is nothing that can be done about it: I shall have to publish my tales.'

The rows with his mother-in-law continued with increased ferocity after his marriage. Mrs Goncharov seemed to have been shocked to discover that Pushkin actually expected her to give him back the 'dowry'. She also began interfering in her daughter's private life. Pushkin decided to take Natalie away from her family and in the middle of May he left Moscow for Tsarskoye Selo, where Pletnyov had rented a small house for them near the Lycée. On June 26, 1831, he wrote a furious letter in French to Mrs Goncharov explaining his reasons for leaving Moscow.

I was forced to leave Moscow to avoid the unpleasant scenes which in the long run would have jeopardised more than my peace of mind:

I was being represented to my wife as an odious man, as a greedy and vile usurer. She was told, 'You are a fool to permit your husband' etc. You must admit that that meant preaching divorce. A wife cannot with decency allow it to be said that her husband is a man without honour. It is the duty of my wife to submit to whatever I permit myself to do. It is not for a girl of eighteen to govern a man of thirty-one. I have shown a great deal of patience and delicacy, but it would seem that neither was of any use. I value my peace of mind and I shall know how to make sure of it. When I left Moscow you did not think fit to discuss business with me. You preferred to make a joke about the possibility of a divorce or something of the kind. It is nevertheless absolutely necessary that I should know definitely what you have decided about me. I am not speaking about what has been intended to be done for Natalie – that is not my business, and I have never thought about it in spite of my rapacity. I mean the eleven thousand roubles which I advanced to you. I am not asking for their return and I am not pressing you in any way. All I want to know is what arrangement you intend to make so that I may make mine accordingly.

Pushkin's next letter to Mrs Goncharov is dated August 25, 1834. By that time he had become reconciled to the loss of his 'dowry'. He had other worries. Not the least of them were caused by Natalie's headlong plunge into the world of fashion and her breathless climb to the dizzy heights of the Imperial Court.

7

Pushkin's uncanny ability to separate his creative from his private life is best illustrated in the remarkable output of verse and prose during the three months of his enforced stay in Boldino. The Boldino autumn was indeed his *auctumnus mirabilis*. Pushkin wrote to Delvig on November 3, 1830:

'This autumn has been procreative, my master, and your humble vassal is not going to succumb to this saracen epidemic, cholera by name, brought back by the crusaders, I mean the Volga boatmen, and that in your castle, that is to say, *The Literary Gazette*, the songs of the troubadour will not be silent the whole year.' On December 9, 1830, Pushkin wrote to Pletnyov from Moscow:

> Let me tell you a secret: in Boldino I wrote as I have not written for a long time. This is what I have brought back: the two last Cantos of *Onegin*, the eighth and the ninth completely ready for the press, a narrative poem written in octaves about four hundred lines in length [*The Little House in Kolomna*], which will be published anonymously. Several dramatic scenes or little tragedies, namely, *The Covetous Knight, Mozart and Salieri, Feast in the Time of the Plague* and *Don Juan* [*The Stone Guest*]. In addition, I have written about thirty small poems. Good? That is not all. (Very secret, for you alone.) I have written five prose tales [*The Tales of Belkin*] which we shall also publish anonymously.

The four 'little tragedies' are Pushkin's most remarkable contribution to dramatic art. Pushkin finished *The Covetous Knight* on October 23, *Mozart and Salieri* on October 26, *The Stone Guest* a week later, and *The Feast in the Time of the Plague* on November 6. In these tragedies Pushkin concentrates on the psychological analysis of a man's mind seized by all-absorbing, egoistic and destructive passions – covetousness, envy, lust. The characters personifying these passions are men of great intellect and will-power, but insofar as their passions are completely selfish, they inevitably lead to crime. *The Covetous Knight* erects the edifice of his power on the foundation of human 'tears, blood and sweat'. Salieri, 'the priest of pure art', who is passionately in love with music for its own sake, murders Mozart in the play, and tries to justify the murder by claiming that he had committed it in the name of the restoration of 'violated justice', in the name of 'the salvation of art'. In 1832 Pushkin added the following note to *Mozart and Salieri*:

> During the first performance of *Don Giovanni*, when the whole theatre, full of astonished aficionados, were revelling in Mozart's harmony, somebody hissed – everyone turned indignantly to the man – and the famous Salieri left the auditorium in a fit of rage, eaten up by envy. Salieri died eight years ago. Some German journals stated that on his deathbed he confessed to having committed a terrible crime – he had poisoned the great Mozart. An envious person who could hiss *Don Giovanni* could very well have also poisoned its creator.

Pushkin's Don Juan, the hero of *The Stone Guest*, is a recreation of a man of the Renaissance who boldly challenges the beliefs and prejudices of the Middle Ages. He is arrogant and proud, passionate and fearless. He tears himself away from the embraces of his mistress Laura to accept the challenge of Don Carlos, whose brother, the Commodore, he had killed earlier in a duel and who was to come back as the Stone Guest and kill him. According to Pushkin, Don Juan is a mixture of spontaneity and guile, frivolous thoughtlessness and sincerity.

The Feast in the Time of the Plague is a free adaptation of a scene of John Wilson's *City of the Plague*. Having chosen this scene, which forms the climax of the work, and the situation, which reminded him of the cholera epidemic which raged throughout Russia while he was confined in Boldino, Pushkin created an original work of art which is remarkable both for psychological insight and artistic perfection. The chief idea of this play is the triumph of man's spirit over death.

The remarkable thing about *Eugene Onegin* is its perpetual freshness: the essence of life itself seems to be distilled in it. Pushkin invented a special stanza, fourteen lines of iambic pentameter, for it and this neat division into stanzas with a carefully fashioned sequence of rhymes makes the elegiac or ironic digressions in this novel in verse less obvious than they would have been in a prose narrative. The reader is always aware of

Pushkin's stimulating presence, narrating the story, passing judgment, introducing all sorts of autobiographical details and a great number of topical allusions, and even mentioning contemporary figures. All this tends to increase rather than to diminish the interest of the reader in spite of the fact that the world Pushkin describes has ceased to exist. This is because Pushkin's comments on life and men are based on a profound understanding of humanity and a sympathy for the tragic undercurrent of life, which grew and deepened during the eight years he was engaged in writing this poem. The plot of the poem changed gradually as Pushkin worked on it. According to his first plan, Onegin should have fallen in love with Tatyana at their first meeting. In the Fourth Canto, Pushkin seemed to have contemplated Tatyana's immediate departure for Moscow after her meeting with Onegin. The whole of the Fifth Canto as well as the episode of Onegin's duel with Lensky occurred to Pushkin much later.

In reply to critics who complained that in the last cantos of *Eugene Onegin* he was lagging behind the age, Pushkin, in an introduction to the Eighth and Ninth Cantos, claimed that

if science, philosophy, and sociology may change and improve with the passing of time, poetry neither ages nor changes. Its aim remains the same and its means are the same. While the ideas, the works and the discoveries of the great representatives of ancient astronomy, physics, medicine, and philosophy are out of date, the works of true poets remain fresh and eternally young. If a poetic work is weak, unsuccessful and full of faults, it is the talent of the poet that is at fault. It is not the age that has left him behind.

During his second journey to the Caucasus in 1829 Pushkin had told some of his old Decembrist friends that according to his 'first plan' Onegin 'should either have been killed in the Caucasus or have joined the Decembrists'. The Tenth Canto of *Eugene Onegin*, which Pushkin burnt on October 19, 1830, was dedicated to the Decembrist revolt. Pushkin, finally, left out the Eighth Canto of *Eugene Onegin*, describing Onegin's travels through Russia. 'The author candidly confesses,' Pushkin wrote in his introduction to *Extracts from Onegin's Journey*, 'that he cut out a whole canto from his novel, in which Onegin's journey across Russia was described . . . and numbered the last canto eight instead of nine . . . The author has decided to leave out this canto for reasons that are important to him and not to the public.'

The Little House in Kolomna is a humorous story of Petersburg low life written in octaves because, as Pushkin admits in the first lines of the poem, he was bored with 'the iambic pentameter'. Pushkin meant this poem to be a challenge to the critics who objected to 'the insignificance and the low character' of the subjects of his poetry and who were mainly responsible for the disastrous decline in his reputation.

Among the thirty lyrical poems Pushkin wrote in Boldino, *The Devils* is interesting for a number of reasons. To begin with, it is a most wonderful description of a blizzard overtaking travellers in the open country. It also reflects Pushkin's thoughts about his life which occasionally reminded him of the aimless wanderings of travellers lost in a blizzard on an endless plain. The poem reveals Pushkin as the greatest master of sound suggestion in Russian. The meaning of the words in a line of the poem, as indeed in many of Pushkin's other poems, is of subsidiary importance to the emotions evoked by their mere sound. Its function is not only to arouse emotion, but also to deepen it to a point where the reader is actually made to experience the same kind of sensation of heat, cold, terror, etc. In the first four lines of *The Devils* Pushkin uses only eleven words to convey the feeling of horror, loneliness and mysterious foreboding of evil by a description of the scudding clouds, of fleeting glimpses of the moon and the eerie light in which the whirling snowflakes can be seen. He achieves his effect by the marvellous use of assonance and caesuras, of short and long vowels, of double consonants, impeding and slowing down the rhythm of the last line with its unusual double caesura, and suddenly bringing it to a stop with an ominous crash.

Pushkin's prolific and masterly use of the adjective and adverb is another feature of his mature poetry. It can be said that it is this use of the adjective that most reveals his greatness as a poet. Pushkin's mature poetry, besides, shows a miraculous clarity and compactness of imagery, the fullest possible integration of idea and character, an ability to bring everything he touches to life, a profound understanding of the human heart, a humane, warm kind of humour. Above all, there is a mastery of language that seems astonishing in its simplicity and profundity, a combination of qualities which makes Pushkin the great and unsurpassed poet that he is.

The cycle of prose stories, *The Tales of Belkin*, include *The Shot*,

The Blizzard, *The Undertaker*, *The Stationmaster* and *The Young Lady-Peasant Girl*. It is Pushkin's first attempt to write a number of prose tales in simple and clear prose. *The History of the Village of Goryukhino*, an unfinished story also written in Boldino, is a graphic attempt to paint a true picture of the conditions of serfdom in a Russian village.

As early as 1822 Pushkin had referred, in the Third Canto of *Eugene Onegin*, to the possibility of taking up prose in his 'declining days'. After criticising the popular novelists of his day for their flamboyant style, he declared himself quite willing to 'descend to humble prose' in order to reproduce 'the simple speech of the common people, the innocent love stories of their children, their jealousies, partings, reconciliations, lovers' quarrels and, finally – the happy ending, their weddings'. Pushkin had to wait eight years before 'the new devil of prose' took hold of him. The most characteristic feature of Pushkin's prose is its precision and brevity, which, Pushkin wrote, 'are the first virtues of prose. Prose demands thought, thought and thought – without thought the most brilliant style is of no use.' Pushkin's ideal of creative prose was 'the ability to bring a character to life in a few words'. In fact, Pushkin's way of describing a character is precise but sparse. The supposed author of *Belkin's Tales* is thus described by Pushkin: 'Ivan Petrovich was of medium height, he had grey eyes, dark brown hair, a straight nose: his face was lean and white.' This is the portrait of the station-master: 'While he was copying my order for posthorses, I looked at his grey hair, the deep wrinkles on his unshaven face, his bent back – and I could not help being astonished to see a hale and hearty man transformed into a feeble old man in three or four years.' The little peasant boy who takes the narrator of *The Stationmaster* to the cemetery, is 'a ragged boy, red-haired and cross-eyed'. All Pushkin's prose characters are described in this precise, objective manner.

Pushkin was the first Russian prose writer to make a deliberate use of fiction as a social force, all the more effective because he never obtrudes his own political opinions and convictions upon his readers. In this, too, he was a great innovator and was followed by the Russian writers of the nineteenth century who used fiction as a pulpit for their social and political ideas, either directly, like Dostoevsky, or indirectly, like Chekhov, Turgenev and Tolstoy. Pushkin's insistence on the dignity of man, however humble his origins or circumstances, is another feature of his stories which he introduced into Russian literature. Vyrin, the hero of *The Stationmaster* and the prototype of Gogol's Akaky Akakievich in

The Overcoat and of Dostoevsky's Devushkin in *Poor People*, is the type of humble man whose dignity no calamities can crush.

Pushkin was the first Russian fiction writer to create characters who are true to life in the sense that they are never wholly good or wholly evil. It is this many-sidedness, this multiformity of the human character that Pushkin introduced for the first time into Russian literature. Pushkin never tries to shape the ultimate fate of his characters. In this respect, too, he was an innovator and the direct precursor of Tolstoy and Chekhov. Action, events and the inter-relationship between the characters of the story, throwing light on their future, are the main elements Pushkin uses for the development of his prose tales. His later tales, with the exception of *The Queen of Spades* (1833) and *The Captain's Daughter* (1836), but including his popular Robin Hood story *Dubrovsky* (1834), all remained unfinished.

PART SIX

1831-1837
Last Years

I

Pushkin was looking forward to his life in Tsarskoye Selo, where, he wrote to Pletnyov on March 26, 1831:

I hope to spend the summer and the *autumn* in inspirational solitude near the capital and in the midst of sweet memories and similar comforts. I don't expect the houses there are expensive: the hussars have gone, the court is not there – lots of empty apartments. I should see you, my dear fellow, every week, Zhukovsky too – Petersburg is next door – living is cheap, no need to keep a carriage. What could be better?

Pushkin found life in Moscow unbearable not only because of his mother-in-law. He hated the whole atmosphere of the place and not the least the intellectual pretensions of the young disciples of Schelling and Hegel, who were soon to split up into violent revolutionaries and ultra-nationalist reactionaries. 'Moscow,' Pushkin wrote to Yelisaveta Khitrovo on March 26, 1831, 'is a city of nonentities. On its gates is written: Abandon all intelligence, o ye who enter here.'

Towards the end of May Pushkin and Natalie with half a dozen servants moved into the little, two-storied wooden house Pletnyov had rented for them not far from the Lycée. Vyazemsky let them have his furniture. On the first floor was their dining room, Natalie's boudoir and the servants' quarters; on the second floor was Pushkin's study: a long, oval room with a large round table, piled high with books and manuscripts, a large sofa against one of the walls and a little table with a decanter of water and a jar of Pushkin's favourite gooseberry jam. In the morning Pushkin worked and received his friends; in the afternoon he and Natalie went for a walk in the Tsarskoye Selo park. It was in the park that Vladimir Sollogub met them one day shortly after their arrival. 'Pushkin,' Sollogub writes in his memoirs, 'had only recently married and he was walking arm in arm with his wife, the foremost European beauty, as he told me afterwards. He introduced me to his wife and, in reply to my question whether he knew Gogol, said that he did not know him, but had heard of him and wished to meet him.'

It was Pletnyov who had first mentioned Gogol to Pushkin. 'I must introduce you to a young writer who shows great promise,' he wrote to Pushkin on February 22, 1831. 'Zhukovsky is in raptures over him. I am impatient to introduce him to you.' The introduction took place some time at the beginning of June, 1831, in Petersburg at one of Pletnyov's literary parties. Pushkin's short trip to Petersburg is a bit of a mystery. According to Vyazemsky, Natalie suddenly came to see his wife in a state of utter despair: her husband had not been home for the last three days. It seems, Vyazemsky claims, that while out on a walk he met some court lamplighters who were going to Petersburg. He joined them and in Petersburg he chanced to meet his old schoolfellow Danzas, who had just returned from his regiment in Poland, and 'spent three days having a riotious time with him.' Pushkin was certainly in Petersburg at the beginning of June, for he wrote two letters from Petersburg dated June 9. One was to Yelisaveta Khitrovo, in which he thanked her for lending him Hugo's *Notre Dame de Paris* and Stendhal's *Le Rouge et Le Noir* (which he found 'a good novel in spite of its false rhetoric in a few places and some remarks of bad taste'). The other was written to Nashchokin, to whom he forwarded a thousand roubles (for the repayment of a gambling debt?) and whom he asked whether Vyazemsky (who was in Moscow at the time) wanted him to send 'his thousand roubles'. In his letter to Mrs Khitrovo Pushkin apologised for not being able to call on her that evening because 'a very boring duty' forced him to go and 'yawn' somewhere, which might well have been Pletnyov's literary party where he met Gogol. In that case, Vyazemsky's surmise that Pushkin was having 'a riotous time' in Petersburg seems, to say the least, a little exaggerated. At any rate, on June 11 Pushkin was back in Tsarskoye Selo and from there he wrote to Nashchokin: 'We are living here quietly and happily as though in the depths of the country.' But the halcyon days were soon over: 'I am without a carriage and without dessert,' he wrote to Nashchokin on June 26, 'but the money disappears all the same.' On the same day he wrote the furious letter to his mother-in-law demanding the return of the eleven thousand he had 'lent' her for his wife's 'dowry'. He was beginning to wonder whether the acquisition of a small estate near Trigorskoye would solve his financial difficulties by curbing his wife's expensive taste for the latest fashions. But the arrival on July 11 in Tsarskoye Selo of the Court, driven out of Petersburg by the cholera epidemic, put an end to Pushkin's dreams of burying himself in the country. Nicholas I cast his roving eye on Natalie and decided that she would be an important acquisition at his court. To cover the expenses of such a preliminary move in his pursuit of Natalie, he offered Pushkin a job. 'The Tsar,' Pushkin wrote to Pletnyov on July 22, 1831, 'has taken me into his service, not into an office or the court or the military. No, he has given me a salary, has opened the archives to me so that I may rummage there and do nothing. Very nice of him, isn't it? He said: *Puisqu'il est marié et qu'il n'est pas riche, il faut faire aller sa marmite.*' The pot, indeed, had to be kept boiling, though Pushkin's salary of five thousand roubles a year was certainly insufficient to cover the expenses of Natalie's court wardrobe. Pushkin obtained permission to work in the State archives for his projected history of Peter the Great and his successors up to Peter III. His appointment was to start on November 14, 1831.

During the summer of 1831 Gogol and Pushkin met almost daily. 'All summer,' Gogol wrote to a friend on November 2, 1831, 'I lived in Pavlovsk near Tsarskoye Selo . . . Almost every evening we met: Zhukovsky, Pushkin and I. If only you knew the delightful things that have appeared from the pens of these two great men!' Pushkin was revising his *Tale of a Priest* and his *Labourer Balda* and writing his *Tale of the Tsar Saltan*, while Zhukovsky, too, was writing his *Sleeping Princess* and his *Tale of Tsar Berendey*, as well as translating innumerable ballads from German and English, including a canto from *Marmion*. Zhukovsky's enormous output made Pushkin feel a little vexed. 'Zhukovsky's poetic diarrhoea has ceased,' Pushkin wrote to Vyazemsky on August 14, 'but he is still squirting hexameters.'

On August 15 Pushkin sent his *Tales of Belkin* by Gogol to Pletnyov. The first volume of Gogol's *Evenings on a Farm near Dikanka* was being printed just then. Gogol described the effect his stories had had on the compositors in a letter to Pushkin on August 31. As soon as he thrust his head in at the door, Gogol wrote, the compositors burst out laughing and, snorting and spluttering into their hands, turned to the wall. In his reply, Pushkin congratulated Gogol on his 'first triumph'. Pushkin also reviewed the first volume of the *Evenings* in the *Literary Supplement of the Russian Disabled Soldier (Russky Invalid)*:

Molière and Fielding would probably have been glad to set *their*
compositors roaring with laughter . . . These stories amazed me. This
is real gaiety, straightforward, unforced, without affectation and without prudishness and what poetry in places! What sensitivity! This is so
unusual in our literature that I still cannot come to my senses . . . I
congratulate the public on a diverting book and I wish its author many
more successes.

Another person whose company Pushkin enjoyed in Tsarskoye Selo
(to his young wife's great chagrin) was the twenty-two-year-old lady-in-
waiting Alexandra Rosset, whom he had first met in 1828, and whom he
described in his letters as 'the southern swallow' and 'our dark, rosy-
cheeked beauty'. Alexandra Rosset writes:

When the court was in Tsarskoye Selo, I used to go to see Pushkin
at eleven o'clock in the morning when I was not on duty and went up
with his wife to his study. It was terribly hot there. He loved the heat.
Every morning he used to take a cold bath and then dressed except for
his cravat. His curly hair was still wet. He was writing his fairy tales,
crossing out and revising them so many times that it was impossible
to read his corrections. On the floor lay books and in his hands he had a
pencil. 'I've got something new to read to you,' he would say, but he
read his poems very badly.

His wife was jealous of me. I used to say to her, 'Why are you jealous
of me? Zhukovsky, Pushkin, Pletnyov are all the same to me. Don't
you realise that I am not in love with him or he with me?'

'I realise that very well,' she would reply, 'but I am vexed because
he is so cheerful with you while he yawns with me.'

In the mornings Alexandra Rosset, Natalie and Pushkin would go for
a drive in a long cart, Alexandra and Natalie sitting at the back and
Pushkin on the transom. Every time, Alexandra records, Pushkin would
break into one of the most disloyal songs of that time in which Nicholas I
was described as 'a Prussian Sergeant-Major' wearing 'a tight uniform'
and pretending to be 'a Greek Orthodox Emperor'.

In mid-October Pushkin and Natalie left for Petersburg where they
eventually rented a large apartment in a four-story house in the centre
of the city. Six months later they moved again to a smaller house and in
December, 1832, to still another where they stayed till the summer of

1833. Life in Petersburg entailed a considerable increase in expenses. Pushkin had to get a carriage and horses and more and more fashionable dresses for his wife. In December he hurried off to Moscow in an unsuccessful attempt to settle his gambling debts. On his return he attempted to raise a loan of 25,000 roubles since, as he wrote to a friend, 'the expenses of my wedding, setting up my household, combined with the payment of my gambling debts have brought me to the verge of bankruptcy.' He now made another appeal to the Emperor for permission to publish his works at his own discretion and received an answer from Benkendorf that permission to publish *Boris Godunov* did not apply to any of his other poems. Benkendorf added a stern reprimand for the publication of Pushkin's short poem, *Anchar – The Tree of Poison*, without the Emperor's knowledge.

'I am the only one of all our writers,' Pushkin replied, 'to be subjected to the most cramping censorship, a censorship,' he added for once in an attempt to let Benkendorf and Nicholas I know what he thought of them, 'that regards me with prejudice and finds everywhere all sorts of hidden meanings, allusions and difficulties, and these accusations of hidden meanings and their implications have neither limit nor justification if the word *tree* is taken to stand for constitution and the word *arrow* for autocracy.' But in view of his precarious financial position Pushkin decided that it would be wiser not to send this letter, only a rough copy of it in French has been preserved. On May 16, 1832, he wrote to Mrs Osipov: 'I am living a completely worldly and absurd mode of life.' On May 19, 1832, his first child, christened Maria after his late grandmother, Maria Hannibal, was born. 'My wife,' Pushkin wrote on June 4, 1832, to Vera Vyazemsky, 'has had the tactlessness to give birth to a little lithograph of me. I am in despair in spite of all my self-conceit.' In September Pushkin again went on business to Moscow where he stayed till October 10. He tried unsuccessfully to mortgage his Kistenovo serfs for fifty additional roubles each. On his return to Petersburg he wrote to Nashchokin on December 2, 1832: 'I found great disorders in my house and I was forced to discharge some servants, to change cooks and, finally, to rent a new apartment, and as a consequence I had to use sums which would otherwise have remained untouched.' In the same letter he told Nashchokin that he had made arrangements for paying his debts by selling the second edition of *Eugene Onegin* to Alexander Smirdin.

It was earlier that year that Smirdin moved his business to new premises and to celebrate the occasion gave a dinner at which Pushkin, Zhukovsky, Krylov, Vyazemsky and Gogol were present. At the end of the dinner the guests decided to publish an almanack in appreciation of their host's hospitality under the title of *Housewarming*. Pushkin contributed his poem *The Little House in Kolomna*. Smirdin's bookshop became a kind of literary club where most Russian writers met. It was there that twenty-year-old Ivan Panaev met Pushkin. Together with Nekrasov he was eventually to take over Pushkin's *Contemporary* and make it into a fighting organ of the Russian radicals. Panaev writes in his memoirs:

At the same time as I, two other men entered Smirdin's bookshop. One was a tall, stout, fashionably-dressed man with a reddish goatee, and the other a man of under medium height, dressed simply, even casually, with curly hair and a somewhat Negroid profile, thick protruding lips and unusually lively and intelligent eyes. I recognised Pushkin. He asked Smirdin for a book and, turning its pages, said something to his companion.

It was at this time, too, that Pushkin and Gogol frequently met at Gogol's flat. Gogol read his works to Pushkin and Pushkin read his own poems to Gogol. Pushkin followed Gogol's progress lovingly and kept telling him constantly: 'Write, write!' He laughed a lot at Gogol's stories and always left in a cheerful mood. Gogol wrote in his *Author's Confession*:

Pushkin made me take a serious view of my writing. He had long been trying to persuade me to undertake a big work and at last one day after I had read him a short description of a small scene, he said to me: 'How can you with this ability to divine a man's character and display him as if he were alive – how can you possibly fail to write a big work? It's simply scandalous!' After that he began talking to me about my weak constitution and my illnesses, which might put an early end to my life. He mentioned Cervantes who, though he had written several very remarkable and excellent stories, would not have occupied the place he now occupies in world literature if he had not written *Don Quixote*. In conclusion he presented me with his own subject which he wished to make into some sort of a poem and which, according to his own words, he would not have given to anyone else. This was the subject of *Dead Souls*. The idea of *The Government Inspector* was also his.

The idea was the result of an incident during Pushkin's trip to Orenburg and Kazan to get accounts from eye-witnesses of the Pugachov rebellion in 1733. While collecting the material for his life of Peter the Great, Pushkin came across some secret documents about the Pugachov rebellion. The peasant disorders which had led to that rebellion reminded Pushkin of the serious peasant disorders following the outbreak of cholera in the Novgorod district as well as in Petersburg. He immediately asked for permission to study the official documents of the Pugachov rebellion. His new researches eventually resulted in his *History of Pugachov* and his short novel *The Captain's Daughter*.

Meanwhile Pushkin was getting more and more dissatisfied with his life in Petersburg. He wrote to Nashchokin on February 2, 1833:

My life in Petersburg is neither one thing nor another. Worries about living prevent me from being bored, but I haven't the leisure, the freedom of bachelor life that is so necessary to a writer. I am rushing about in high society. My wife is a leader of fashion and all this requires money, money, money, and money I can obtain only through my work and my work requires solitude. This is what I am planning to do. After my wife's confinement in the summer, I shall send her off to their Kaluga estate to her sister's and I shall myself make a trip to Nizhny and perhaps to Astrakhan.

Pushkin's second child, Alexander, was born on July 6, 1833.

On July 22, 1833, Pushkin asked Benkendorf for permission for a trip to Orenburg and Kazan to visit the scenes of the Pugachov rebellion as he was anxious to collect material for a book which he had begun long before and which would provide him with the money he was so badly in need of. He was referring to *The Captain's Daughter*, the preface to which is dated August 5, 1833, but which was not completed till 1836. He wrote on July 20 to one of Benkendorf's subordinates:

I feel ashamed to waste time on such vain pursuits, but ... they alone provide me with my independence and enable me to live with my family in Petersburg where, thanks to the Emperor, my labours have a more important and useful purpose. Except for my salary, granted to me by the generosity of His Majesty, I have no fixed income, while life in the capital is expensive, and with the increase in my family, expenses increase too. The action of the novel I am writing and which I hope to finish in the country, takes place in Orenburg and Kazan and that is why I should like to visit both provinces.

On August 17, 1833, Pushkin left Petersburg for Orenburg, his wife and children remaining in their summer villa in the fashionable suburb of the Black River. Pushkin arrived in Torzhok on August 19 and on the way to his mother-in-law's estate of Yaropolets, he decided to visit the Vulfs and in the evening of August 20 he arrived at the estate of Pavlovskoye owned by Pavel Vulf, Mrs Osipov's brother-in-law. Of his old 'girl friends', he wrote to Natalie on August 21, he found only the white mare on which he had ridden to Malinniki during his last visit. In Malinniki, too, instead of all the 'Annettes, Euphraxies, Sashas, Mashas, etc. there was only Mrs Osipov's manager.'

In Yaropolets his mother-in-law received him quite amicably. He spent a day with her and she let him borrow some books from the library. He arrived in Moscow on August 25 and left on August 29. In Moscow he met Nikolai Raevsky in a bookshop. '*Sacré chien,*' Raevsky said, '*pourquoi n'êtes-vous pas venu me voir?*' Pushkin answered, *with feeling*: '*Animal, qu'avez-vous fait de mon manuscrit petit Russien?*' (The manuscript is unknown.) After which they drove off and dined together.

On September 2 Pushkin arrived in Nizhny-Novgorod and paid a visit to General Mikhail Buturlin, the military and civil governor of the province. Buturlin suspected Pushkin of being a government inspector sent by Nicholas I to report on the state of the provinces he was travelling through. He therefore sent a letter to Count Vasily Perovsky, governor of Orenburg and an old friend of Pushkin's, warning him of Pushkin's arrival and telling him of his suspicions. Pushkin later told Gogol about this and Gogol used it as the subject for *The Government Inspector*. While Pushkin was being taken for a government inspector by one official, Benkendorf sent instructions to the local police to keep Pushkin under surveillance, but those instructions did not catch up with Pushkin while he was in the Pugachov country.

He left Simbirsk for Orenburg on September 12, but on the way a hare ran across the highway and, taking it as a bad omen, he turned back. 'The devil take it,' he wrote to Natalie from Simbirsk on September 14. 'I'd give a lot to be a borzoi: I'd have found that damned hare. Now I am off on another road.'

Pushkin arrived in Orenburg on September 18. There he met Vladimir

Dahl, a medical man who was to attend him during his last illness, who later won fame as a lexicographer and author of Cossack folk tales. Dahl took Pushkin round the city and showed him the Georgievsk belfry in the suburb on which Pugachov had tried to hoist a cannon to bombard the city. He also saw what remained of the trenches between the gates of the town ascribed by legend to Pugachov, as well as the wood from which Pugachov tried to enter the fortress by marching across the ice-bound river.

Next day (September 19) Dahl took Pushkin to the Cossack village of Berdy, where Pugachov had his headquarters during the six months' siege of Orenburg. He introduced Pushkin to an old woman who had known, seen and remembered Pugachov. Pushkin talked to her all morning. He was next shown the site of the cottage which Pugachov covered in copper and which was known as the 'golden palace', and the top of the hill, where Pugachov is said to have buried a huge treasure, sewn in a shirt and covered with a dead body to remove suspicion and deceive any future treasure hunters who, finding the body, would assume that it was an ordinary grave. The old woman sang him a few songs about the buried treasure and he gave her a golden coin before leaving. Dahl writes in his memoirs:

We left the town but the golden coin created an upheaval. The old woman and the old men of the village could not understand why a stranger should have shown such interest in a brigand and a pretender with whose name so many terrible memories were connected in that region. They could understand even less why that man should have given the old woman a gold coin. The whole thing seemed highly suspicious to them. They were afraid that they might be called to answer for talking to the stranger. Next day they took the old woman and the gold coin to Orenburg and informed the authorities that the day before a stranger came to their town who had the following distinctive features: he was short, he had dark curly hair and a swarthy complexion, and he tried to rouse the people just as Pugachov had done by giving them gold coins. They further surmised that he was probably the anti-Christ because instead of fingernails he had claws. Pushkin laughed a lot about that.

Pushkin next travelled to Uralsk where the local head of the Cossacks and the Cossacks themselves gave two dinners in his honour and gave him all the information he wanted. He left Uralsk on September 23 in the evening. It began to rain and in half an hour the road became impassable. 'On top of that,' he wrote to Natalie on October 2 from Boldino, 'it began to snow and I broke in the winter road by driving about thirty-five miles on a sleigh.' In Boldino another shock awaited him. 'As soon as I arrived at Boldino,' he wrote to Natalie on October 8, 1833, 'I met some priests and I became infuriated with them as I did with the Simbirsk hare. All these encounters bode ill.' But this time he need not have worried: his second autumn in Boldino proved almost as fruitful as the first. In addition to *The History of Pugachov*, Pushkin wrote *The Bronze Horseman*, *The Tale of the Fisherman and the Fish*, *The Tale of the Dead Empress and the Seven Heroes*, *Angelo* (an adaptation of Shakespeare's *Measure for Measure*) and a number of shorter poems including *The Hussar*, *Budryis and His Sons*, *The Voevoda* and his famous story of a compulsive gambler, *The Queen of Spades*.

On his return to Petersburg in November, 1833, Pushkin was about to conclude an agreement with Alexander Smirdin, who offered to pay him 15,000 roubles a year provided he published all his new works in Smirdin's new journal, *A Library for Reading*, which was to appear in 1834.

Pushkin wrote to Benkendorf on December 6, 1833:

> The bookseller Smirdin is publishing a journal to which he has asked me to contribute. I can agree only if he undertakes to send my works to the [ordinary] censorship as he does with the works of other writers. I did not wish to tell him anything definite without your knowledge. Although I have tried to burden the attention of the Emperor as infrequently as possible, I venture now to request his Majesty's gracious permission to publish *The Bronze Horseman*. I also wrote a history of the Pugachov rebellion which I venture to request permission to present for his Majesty's examination.

But Nicholas I objected to the publication of *The Bronze Horseman*. Pushkin resumed writing his diary on his return from Orenburg and on December 14 he noted that Benkendorf had asked him to go and see him on December 11:

> I went. He returned me my *Bronze Horseman* with the Emperor's remarks. The word *idol* was not passed by the highest censorship, and the lines:

And before the younger capital
Old Moscow was eclipsed,
As before a new Empress
A purple clad dowager Empress –

have been crossed out. In many other places a question mark has been put. All this makes a great difference to me. I was forced to change the conditions of my agreement with Smirdin.

'Here I have all sorts of financial difficulties,' Pushkin wrote to Nashchokin on December 10, 1833. 'I came to an agreement with Smirdin, but was forced to break the contract because the censorship would not pass *The Bronze Horseman*. This is a great loss to me. If they don't pass my *History of Pugachov* I shall have to go and live in the country . . .' But Nicholas I was getting too involved with Natalie to let Pushkin go. He raised no objections to the publication of the History. 'By permitting the publication of this work [*The History of Pugachov*],' Pushkin wrote to Benkendorf on February 10, 1834, 'his Majesty has assured my fortune. The money which I shall be able to realise from it will make it possible for me to accept an inheritance [his late uncle Vasily's estate], which I have been forced to give up for lack of some forty thousand roubles . . .'

He goes on to make two requests: (1) To be permitted to publish his work at his own expense and (2) a two-year loan of 15,000 roubles, 'a sum which would permit me to devote all my time and care to the publishing of my work.'

As a result of this letter and a visit to Benkendorf, Pushkin received a loan from the Tsar of 20,000 roubles. 'The Tsar gave me a loan of 20,000 for the publication of *Pugachov*. Thanks,' Pushkin wrote in his diary on February 28, 1834.

Pushkin offered no thanks for the Tsar's more obvious move to keep Natalie near his person by appointing Pushkin (on December 31, 1833) Junior Gentleman of the Bedchamber. Pushkin recorded this in his diary on January 1, 1834:

> The other day I was appointed a Junior Gentleman of the Bedchamber, which is rather unbecoming considering my age, but the Court wished that Natalie should dance at Anichkov Palace. I am satisfied because the Emperor intended to confer a distinction on me and not to make me look ridiculous. So far as I am concerned, he could

have appointed me a page provided he did not force me to learn French
vocables and arithmetic . . .

'The Emperor said to Princess Vyazemsky,' Pushkin wrote in his diary
on January 7, 1834: ' *"J'espère que Pouchkine a pris en bonne part sa
nomination. Jusqu'à présent il m'a tenu parole, et j'ai été content de lui,"*
etc., etc. The Grand Duke [Mikhail] congratulated me the other night in
the theatre. "Thank you very much, your Highness," I said, "Till now
everyone laughed at me, you are the first to congratulate me." '

On January 17 Pushkin noted in his diary that he had been at a ball
at which the Emperor spoke to him about his *History of Pugachov*, but
did not mention his appointment. 'I did not thank him,' Pushkin added.
Nicholas I expressed his annoyance with Pushkin a few days later when
Pushkin arrived at a ball in Anichkov Palace in uniform and was told that
all the guests were in evening dress. 'I left,' Pushkin wrote in his diary on
January 26, 'leaving Natalie and, after changing, went to a party at
Saltykov's. The Emperor was dissatisfied. He said: *"Il aurait pu se donner
la peine d'aller mètre un frac et de revenir,"* the Emperor remarked to
several of his guests. *"Faites lui des reproches."* '
Pushkin continues:

On Thursday I attended a ball at Prince [Vasily] Trubetskoy's [one
of the heroes of the war of 1812]. They were all in mourning for some
royal prince. Ladies in black. The Emperor arrived unexpectedly. Was
there for half an hour. He said to my wife: '*Est-ce à propos de bottes ou
de boutons que votre mari n'est pas venu dernièrement?*' [Was it because
of his boots (that is to say, without any reason) or because of his
buttons that your husband did not make an appearance last time?]
(Uniform buttons. The old Countess Bobrinsky excused me because
the buttons had not been sewn on my uniform.) Baron d'Anthès and
the Marquis de Pina, two *chouans* [royalist rebels of Brittany, Nor-
mandy and the Vendée], will be accepted in the Guards as officers.
There is murmuring among the guardsmen.

This is Pushkin's first mention of d'Anthès, the man who was to kill
him three years later.

2

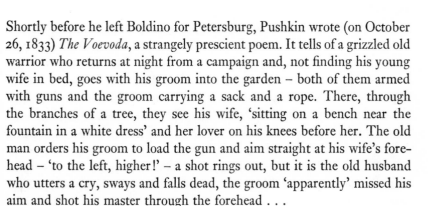

Shortly before he left Boldino for Petersburg, Pushkin wrote (on October 26, 1833) *The Voevoda*, a strangely prescient poem. It tells of a grizzled old warrior who returns at night from a campaign and, not finding his young wife in bed, goes with his groom into the garden – both of them armed with guns and the groom carrying a sack and a rope. There, through the branches of a tree, they see his wife, 'sitting on a bench near the fountain in a white dress' and her lover on his knees before her. The old man orders his groom to load the gun and aim straight at his wife's forehead – 'to the left, higher!' – a shot rings out, but it is the old husband who utters a cry, sways and falls dead, the groom 'apparently' missed his aim and shot his master through the forehead . . .

This is a free adaptation of a ballad by Mickiewicz. Pushkin wrote it when he was getting more and more worried by his wife's flirtations with Nicholas I, and was beginning to wonder whether he might not be confronted with a crisis, the consequences of which would be too disastrous to contemplate. The crisis had been mounting steadily ever since Natalie's first visit to the Palace in the autumn of 1831. It is reflected in almost all of the sixty-four tender, cajoling, beseeching letters Pushkin wrote to her between December 6, 1831, and May 18, 1836. The letters, written in marvellously simple and direct Russian, reveal Pushkin's fairness and weakness in dealing with his wife's social ambitions and her selfish pride in her easy conquests.

The best description of Natalie is to be found in Count Sollogub's memoirs:

I have seen many beautiful women in my life and I have met women who were more charming than Mrs Pushkin, but I have never seen a woman who combined such perfect classically regular features and so perfect a figure. She was very tall with a fabulously slender waist and beautifully developed shoulders and bosom. Her small head, like a lily

on its stem, swayed gracefully on her slender neck; I have never seen
such a beautiful and regular profile in my life; and her skin, her eyes,
her teeth, her ears – yes, she was a real beauty and other women, even
the most charming ones, dimmed in her presence. She always looked
restrained to a point of frigidity and, generally, did not talk a great deal.
In Petersburg . . . she was always to be seen in high society and at
court. . . .

She was intelligent enough not to 'talk a great deal', but not intelligent
enough to realise Pushkin's greatness as a poet. It is doubtful whether she
even bothered to read his works. She even tried to emulate him in
writing some poetry of her own. 'I am not reading your poems,' Pushkin
had written to her with curt finality on December 16, 1831, from Moscow.
'What the hell! I'm fed up even with my own.' The general
admiration her beauty aroused must have made her even more resentful
of Pushkin's contempt for her intellect and she knew instinctively how
to hurt him. She was pregnant when Pushkin left her for the first time
after their marriage for his short trip to Moscow in December, 1831.
'Since I left you,' he wrote to her on December 8, 'I can't help being
afraid for you. You won't stay at home, you will go to the Palace and I
fear you will have a miscarriage on the one hundred and fifth step of the
grand staircase . . . If you go to a ball don't for heaven's sake dance anything except quadrilles . . .' Two days later: 'I beg you not to go to the
Palace and not to dance at balls.' On his return to Petersburg he wrote to
Nashchokin (on January 10, 1832): 'My wife dances at balls, flirts with the
Emperor, jumps off the front steps. I must take the hussy in hand.' Her
flirtations were now worrying him constantly and when in Moscow in
September 1832 he received an 'indulgent' and 'amusing' letter from her,
he got really upset. 'What does it mean?' he wrote anxiously to her on
September 30. 'I am not a cuckold, am I? Take care . . .' On October 3
he wrote to her: 'You are at fault because you get all sort of nonsense into
your head . . . because you flirt with the entire diplomatic corps . . .' Next
August, at the beginning of his trip to Orenburg, he implored her again
not to flirt on her nameday, August 26, the date also of the annual ball
commemorating the Battle of Borodino, which was postponed that year
because of the Emperor's absence abroad. 'You'll say,' Pushkin wrote,
'there's no one to flirt with. Still do not flirt.' As for himself, he assured
her that he was quite 'harmless' in every respect. 'I am not paying court

to young ladies,' he wrote from Orenburg on September 19, 1833. 'I am not pinching stationmasters' wives, I am not flirting with Kalmuck girls, and the other day I refused to have anything to do with a Bashkir girl in spite of my curiosity which is very forgivable in a traveller, for you know the Russian proverb: in a foreign country even an old woman is a gift of God.' She knew very well how anxious he was, but that merely increased her desire to hurt him. '. . . Don't frighten me,' he wrote to her on October 8 from Boldino. 'Don't say you are flirting in good earnest. I'll come back to you without having succeeded in writing anything and without money we shall be in real trouble. You'd better leave me in peace and I'll work and hurry. If the Tsar will allow me to publish my notes [the historical materials he had compiled] I'll get about 30,000 in cash and pay back half of our debts . . .' On October 11 he begged her again not to 'frighten' him. 'Look after the children,' he wrote, 'and do not flirt with the Tsar. I am writing, I am very busy. I do not see anyone and I shall bring back lots of all sorts of things.' Ten days later: 'I don't mind your flirting but I demand of you coolness, propriety, dignity, not to mention irreproachability of conduct which has nothing to do with *tone* but is something much more important . . . How's red-haired Sashka? Where did he get his red hair from? Thank my priceless Katerina Ivanovna [Zagryazhsky, Natalie's old aunt] for not letting you do as you like in the box at the theatre. I beg her for God's sake not to leave you at the mercy of your adorers.' On October 30, he wrote:

'You seem to have overdone your flirtations. Take care! It's not for nothing that flirtation is not in fashion and is considered to be a sign of bad breeding. There's little sense in it. You are happy when male dogs run after you as after a bitch with their tails up in the air and sniffing your arse. What a thing to be happy about! Not only you, but even Praskovya Petrovna [probably Vyazemsky's daughter] can easily train some unmarried ne'er-do-wells to run after her. All you need do is trumpet it abroad that you are willing. That is the whole secret of coquetry. Where there's a trough, there'll be swine. Why should you receive men who want to make love to you? You never know whom you may run into. Read Izmaylov's fable about *Foma and Kuzma*. Foma stuffed Kuzma on caviare and herrings. Kuzma began to ask for a drink, but Foma wouldn't give him one. So Kuzma gave Foma a thrashing for being a rascal. From all this the poet draws the following

moral: Pretty women, don't feed men on herrings if you do not intend
to give them anything to drink or you might run up against a Kuzma.
You see? I beg you not to give these academic lunches at my house
[Pushkin was dissatisfied with the luncheons at the Russian Academy
because vodka was served there instead of wine]. Now, my angel, I kiss
you as though nothing had happened and I thank you for describing
your dissolute life so frankly to me. Have a good time, darling, only
don't overdo it and do not forget me. I would like very much to see
your headdress à la Ninon. I expect you must look lovely. Why didn't
you think of that old whore before and borrow her headdress from her?
Describe your appearance at balls which, as you write, have probably
begun and please, my angel, do not flirt. I am not jealous and I know
that you will not go too far, but you know how I dislike everything . . .
that is not *comme il faut*, everything that is *vulgar*. If I find on my
return that your charming, simple, aristocratic manners have changed,
I shall divorce you and join the army as a private from sheer misery.
You ask me what I am doing and whether I have grown better looking.
To begin with, I have grown a beard. I wake up at seven, have a cup of
coffee and lie in bed till three o'clock. Not so long ago I began writing
and I have already written a prodigious lot. At three o'clock I mount my
horse and go riding. At five I take a bath and then dine on potatoes and
buckwheat porridge. I read till ten. There's my day for you and they
are all alike.

Finally, he wrote in his last letter to her from Boldino on November 6,
1833:

Let me repeat to you a little more gently that flirting leads to nothing
good and, though it has its pleasant moments, nothing deprives a
young woman so quickly of the things without which there is no family
happiness nor tranquillity in her relationships to society: *respect*. There
is nothing for you to be pleased about in your conquests. Ninon, the
whore from whom you borrowed your headdress (N.B. You must be
very pretty in that headdress. I was thinking of that last night) used to
say: *Il est écrit sur le coeur de tout homme: à la plus facile*. After that, be
proud, if you like, of stealing men's hearts. Think it over carefully and
do not worry me needlessly . . . My dear, dear, dear wife, I am travelling
along highways, living three months in the wilds, stopping in horrible
Moscow which I detest, and all for what? For you, darling, so that you

should not be worried and shine in society to your heart's content as befits a beautiful woman of your age. But, please, take care of me, too. Do not add to the worries which are inseparable from a man's life, family troubles, jealousy, etc., etc., not to mention *cocuage*, about which I read a whole essay in Bartôme's *La Vie des Dames Gallantes* a few days ago.

On his return to Petersburg he found that Natalie was at a ball. 'I went to get her,' he wrote to Nashchokin on November 24, 1833, 'and then took her away like a Uhlan abducting a provincial Miss from a mayoress's birthday party.'

Three months later, on March 4, 1834, on the last day of the Shrove-tide carnival, Natalie had a miscarriage during a dance at the Palace. In mid-March Pushkin wrote to Nashchokin:

Just imagine, my wife nearly died the other day. Balls were particu-larly numerous this winter. During shrovetide they were even dancing twice a day. At last the Sunday before Lent came. I thought to myself, thank goodness, that's the end of the balls. My wife was at the Palace. Suddenly I noticed that she was feeling ill. I took her away and after we got home she had a miscarriage. Now she is – touch wood – thank God, well, and in a day or two she's going to the Kaluga estate to her sisters, who are suffering terribly from the caprices of my mother-in-law.

He had more troubles with his parents, who were penniless and quite incapable of managing their estate, but at least he got his wife away from the temptations of the court. He saw her off on April 15 and on his return found an order from Count Julius Litta, the Court Chamberlain, to go and see him, for he had deliberately abstained from taking part in the celebra-tions on the occasion of the coming of age of the heir to the throne, the future Alexander II. He wrote in his diary on April 16:

I found a summons to go and see Count Litta next day. I realised that he was going to haul me over the coals for not having been at morning mass. Indeed, the same evening I learned from Zhukovsky, who dropped in to see me, that the Emperor was dissatisfied with the absence of many Chamberlains and Junior Gentlemen of the Bed-chamber and that he ordered that we should be told about it. In the Palace Litta harangued us with great warmth saying: *Il y a cependant pour les Messieurs de la Cour des règles fixes*, and repeated *des règles fixes* . . . I sent my apologies in writing. I am told we are going to march in pairs like high-school girls. Just imagine me with my grey beard marching alongside some eighteen-year-old Bezobrazovs or Remers. Not for anything in the world! *J'aime mieux avoir le fouet devant tout le monde*, as Monsieur Jourdain says [I'd rather be whipped before everybody – from Molière's *Le Bourgeois Gentilhomme*].

Though not whipped in public, he was in hot water again a few days later. A veritable storm broke over his head as a result of his letter to Natalie on April 22, 1834:

I sent your letter to your aunt because I am officially ill and afraid of meeting the Tsar. I have no intention of going to see the heir to the throne with congratulations and greetings; his reign is yet to come and I shall probably not live to see it. I have seen three Tsars: the first ordered my cap to be taken from my head and told my nurse off on my account; the second did not like me very much, and though the third did confer the rank of Junior Gentleman of the Bedchamber upon me in my old age, I have no wish to exchange him for a fourth: I prefer to leave well alone. Let us see how our Sashka will get on with his namesake. God preserve him from following in my footsteps and from writing verses and quarrelling with emperors! He would not excel his father in poetry, but neither would he chop wood with a penknife. But enough of this nonsense. . . .

But it was no nonsense. Pushkin must have forgotten the Moscow postmaster's predilection for opening his letters. Finding in his letter (as Pushkin remarked in his diary on May 10) 'an account of the oath of allegiance taken by the Grand Duke, written apparently in an unofficial style', the Post Office informed the police and the police sent the letter on to Nicholas I, who flew into a rage, summoned Zhukovsky and told him to warn Pushkin of the dire consequences his disloyal sentiments might cause.

Pushkin wrote in his diary on May 10:

A few days ago I received a note from Zhukovsky. He informed me that a certain letter of mine was circulating in town and that the Emperor had spoken to him about it. I imagined that it must be some obscene poems, which the public had graciously and indulgently attributed to me. But it was not at all what I thought. The Moscow

Post Office opened a letter I had written to my wife and informed the police about it. Without attempting to make any sense of the letter, the police presented it to the Emperor who in a fit of anger did not understand it, either. Fortunately, the letter was shown to Zhukovsky who explained it. Everything quietened down. The Emperor did not like that I should refer to my appointment as Junior Gentleman of the Bedchamber without an expression of tender emotion and gratitude. I can be a subject and even a slave, but I shall not be a flunkey and a clown even before the King of Heaven. Yet what profound immorality in the habits of our government! The police open letters from a husband to his wife and take them to be read by the Tsar (a well-bred and honourable man), and the Tsar is not ashamed to admit it and to set in motion an intrigue worthy of Vidocq and Bulgarin. Say what you like, but it is certainly hard to be an autocrat.

'The thought that someone is eavesdropping on us,' he wrote to Natalie on June 3, 1834, 'drives me to a frenzy *à la lettre*. It is quite possible to live without political liberty, but without the sanctity of the family [*inviolabilité de la famille*] it is quite impossible: hard labour in Siberia is infinitely better. This is not written for you . . .' 'Now they look upon me as a flunkey,' he wrote again to Natalie on June 8, 'whom they can treat as they like. Disgrace is better than contempt. Like Lomonosov, I do not want to be a clown even before the Lord God.' And to make sure that the Emperor was in no doubt about what he thought of him, he wrote to Natalie on June 11: 'I am no longer angry with *him* because, *toute réflection faite*, he cannot be blamed for the swinishness around him. If you live in a privy, you cannot help getting used to shit, and its stench won't disgust you even though you are a *gentleman*. Oh, if only I could run off to where the air is fresh . . .' He even blamed the Emperor when he lost all his money at cards. 'I had the money,' he wrote to Natalie on June 28, 'and I lost it at cards. What was I to do? I was in such a mood that I had to do something to distract myself. He is to blame for everything, but let that pass. If only he would let me go free.'

On June 25, Pushkin sent Benkendorf a formal letter of resignation from the civil service. 'Family matters,' he wrote in French, 'necessitate my presence now in Moscow and now in the interior of the country and I find myself forced to retire from the service and I beg your Excellency to obtain this permission for me. I would ask as a last favour that the permission which his Majesty has been so good as to grant me to visit the archives should not be withdrawn from me.' On June 30, Pushkin received Benkendorf's reply. 'His Imperial Majesty,' Benkendorf wrote, 'does not wish to keep anyone against his will.' Pushkin might retire, if he wished, but permission to use the archives would not be granted, for this right belonged solely to people enjoying the especial trust of the authorities. It was a threat calculated to make Pushkin withdraw his resignation, for Pushkin was still hoping to publish his life of Peter the Great. But Nicholas I was for obvious reason anxious not to lose control over Pushkin and he empowered Zhukovsky to act as a go-between and try to persuade Pushkin to withdraw his resignation. 'On receiving your first letter,' Pushkin wrote to Zhukovsky on July 4, 'I immediately wrote to Count Benkendorf asking him to cancel my resignation, *ma démarche étant inconsidérée*, and I said *que j'aimais mieux avoir l'air inconséquent qu'ingrat*. After that I received an official notification that my resignation would be accepted, but that access to the archives would be refused to me. That was a great blow to me in every respect.' He immediately wrote another letter to Benkendorf, expressing his deep concern that his 'unconsidered' petition, forced on him 'by unpleasant circumstances and petty worries', should have been interpreted as a sign of insane ingratitude and opposition to the will of him who had till then been his 'benefactor' rather than his Emperor.

Pushkin followed this up by another letter to Zhukovsky in which he stressed how much the Emperor's anger had grieved him and expressed his willingness to ask the Emperor's forgiveness; in a third letter to Benkendorf he laid it on rather thick about his being broken-hearted at the idea of losing an all-powerful protector, who had showered him with favours and whom he had always regarded as his Providence. Benkendorf pointed out in his report to Nicholas I that it was much safer to keep Pushkin as a State official than to let him do as he liked as a private person. Nicholas I scribbled on Benkendorf's report: 'I forgive him, but ask him to see you so that you can explain to him the whole senselessness of his behaviour and point out to him what it can end in, and that what can be forgiven to a twenty-year-old madman, cannot be forgiven to a married man of thirty-five with a family.' Pushkin understood the hint. He wrote in his diary on July 22: 'The last month has been stormy. I have nearly quarrelled with the court, but everything came right in the end. However, I won't get away with it.'

3

Pushkin did not get away with it. Nicholas I was quite determined to keep Pushkin, or, rather, Natalie in Petersburg. In June Pushkin asked again for a lengthy leave of absence, going so far as to hint that to keep his wife in Petersburg for the delectation of the Emperor would eventually mean financial ruin to him.

He wrote to Benkendorf on June 1, 1835:

At the moment, I am compelled to put an end to the expenses which force me to incur debts and are preparing for me a future of anxiety and worries and perhaps destitution and despair. Three or four years of life in the country would make it possible for me again, on my return to Petersburg, to resume the pursuits for which I am still indebted to the favours of his Majesty. I have been showered with benefactions by the Emperor and I would be in despair, if his Majesty suspected that I wished to leave Petersburg for any other motive than that of absolute necessity.

Nicholas I rejected Pushkin's request in a threatening note recalling Pushkin's attempt to retire a year earlier. Pushkin wrote to Benkendorf on July 4, 1835:

The Emperor was so good as to write a note on my letter to you to the effect that I could not go to the country for several years unless I first resigned. I commit my future completely to the Tsar's will and I only wish that the decision of his Majesty is not a sign of disfavour towards me and that the access to the archives will not be forbidden me when circumstances permit me to be in Petersburg.

On July 22, 1835, Pushkin wrote again to Benkendorf. He had incurred debts of close on sixty thousand roubles and if he could not retire to the country, he would have to borrow a large sum of money. Nicholas I offered Pushkin a loan of ten thousand roubles and six months' leave of absence 'to see whether he needed to go into retirement or not.' But ten thousand was not enough even to repay his gambling debts. He wrote again to Benkendorf four days later:

I am sorry that at the moment when I am receiving an unexpected favour I should have to ask for two more, but I have resolved to appeal in all frankness to one who has deigned to be my Providence. Of the 60,000 roubles I owe, half are debts of honour. In order to pay them I see myself under the obligation of borrowing money from money-lenders, which will increase my difficulties, or force me once more to appeal to the generosity of the Emperor. I, therefore, beg his Majesty to do me a full and complete favour: first by granting me the possibility of paying off these 30,000 roubles and, secondly, of permitting me to regard this sum as a loan and accordingly to have the payment of my salary suspended until my debt is paid off.

Nicholas I was only too glad to grant this request, for now Pushkin was completely in his power, at least till his loan was paid back and that, at five thousand roubles a year, would take six years. But the relationship between them was getting more and more strained in spite of all the attempts at reconciliation, in which Zhukovsky took a leading part. 'The Emperor,' Pushkin wrote to his wife on June 30, 1835, 'promised to give me permission to publish a journal and then withdrew it; he forces me to live in Petersburg and does not give me the means to live by my work.' On December 31, 1835, Pushkin wrote to Benkendorf for permission to publish four volumes of 'purely literary, historical and scientific articles, as well as critical reviews of Russian and foreign literature, something on the lines of the English quarterly review.' This time permission was granted on condition that no political articles were included in the review, which was eventually published under the title of *The Contemporary*.

In his letter to Benkendorf Pushkin, purposely or not, greatly under-estimated his indebtedness. After his death sixteen months later, it was established that he owed a total of 138,988 roubles and 33 copecks, of which 95,600 roubles was owed to private persons and about 40,000 to the exchequer. There can be no doubt that a considerable amount of this debt was due to Natalie's extravagance, which Pushkin was too weak to stop. 'As a nobleman and as a father of a family,' Pushkin wrote on February 5, 1836, to 'a great nobleman and a representative of our ancient and genuine nobility', he had to watch over his honour and the name he was to leave to his children. Natalie could destroy both. She knew it and the knowledge made it possible for her to exercise great power over him. Alexander Smirdin has left this illuminating glimpse into Pushkin's subservience to his wife during the last years of his life:

I once had occasion to talk to her [Natalie Pushkin]. I came to see Pushkin to collect a manuscript and to give him some money. He made it a condition that I should always pay him in gold because his wife refused to take any money except gold coins. As I entered his study Pushkin said to me: 'My wife has taken away my manuscript. Go to her room. She wants to see you herself.' He took me to her room and knocked on the door. 'Come in,' she answered. Pushkin opened the door, but did not go in himself. I did not dare to cross the threshold because I saw a lady standing in front of her dressing table with one knee on a stool, while her maid was lacing her satin corset.

'Come in,' Mrs Pushkin repeated. 'I am in a hurry to get dressed. I asked you to come and see me because I wanted to tell you that you would not get the manuscript from me unless you brought me a hundred instead of fifty gold roubles. My husband has sold his poems to you much too cheaply. Bring the money at six o'clock and you will get the manuscript. Goodbye.'

She spoke very rapidly without turning her head to me, looking in the mirror and arranging her long hair, which hung in curls down her cheeks. I bowed and went back to Pushkin. I found him sitting at his desk, drawing lines on a piece of paper with a pencil. 'Well, you see,' he said to me, 'it is much more difficult to do business with a woman than with a man. I'm afraid you'll have to humour my wife. She has just ordered a new ball dress and I have to raise the money to pay for it. I'll settle with you later.'

4

The *Contemporary* was chiefly responsible for the final rift between Pushkin and Gogol. At first Gogol was enthusiastic about Pushkin's new journalistic venture. In his article 'On the Contemporary Review', written in 1846, Gogol declared that he had prevailed on Pushkin to carry on with the quarterly and promised to be 'a loyal contributor' to it. Pushkin, Gogol further asserted, found in his articles a great deal that could impart 'liveliness' to the journal. In fact, it was the conflict between them about Gogol's contributions that brought their friendship to an end. Gogol, who had always resented any changes made by editors in his articles, could not forgive Pushkin for unceremoniously correcting, cutting and even refusing to publish some of his articles. A clash was inevitable, even more with the publication in the *Moscow Telegraph* of a long article by the twenty-four-year-old Visarion Belinsky, in which the critic rightly foresaw the eclipse of poetry and the dawn of prose in Russian literature and hailed Gogol as 'the head of Russian literature' who 'occupied the place vacated by Pushkin'. This article had made a tremendous impression on Gogol, who was only too conscious of what he was later to describe in a letter to Zhukovsky as 'the lion's strength' in his soul and of his ability 'to do something no ordinary man could do'. The effect Belinsky's article had made on Gogol could not have escaped his mentor Pushkin, who, though a voluminous correspondent, only wrote four short hastily written notes to Gogol without even bothering to address them.

Pushkin never really understood the true significance of Gogol's writings. He saw in them merely a merciless exposure of the gross vulgarity of Russian life. Commenting on Gogol's story *The Nose*, which together with *The Carriage* he published in his *Contemporary*, Pushkin described it as 'a joke' and found a great deal that was 'surprising, hilarious and original' in it. What he overlooked was that Gogol's exposure of the corruption and stupidity of Russian officialdom and the snobbish self-complacency and selfishness of the Russian upper classes was to have a devastating effect on the whole structure of Russian autocracy.

Pushkin was not in Petersburg when *The Government Inspector* had its première at the Alexandrinsky Theatre on April 19, 1836. His opinion of the play can be only surmised from a reference to it in a letter to Natalie from Moscow on May 6, 1836. In it he mentions a discussion about the play he had with Mikhail Shchepkin, one of Russia's foremost actors and producers at the Maly Theatre. 'Send for Gogol,' Pushkin wrote with revealing peremptoriness, 'and read him the following: I have seen the actor Shchepkin who begs him in Christ's name to come to Moscow to read *The Government Inspector*. Without him the actors find it difficult to rehearse the play. He says that otherwise the comedy will be a caricature and *dirty* (to which Moscow has always had a sneaking propensity). For my part, my advice to him is the same. *The Government Inspector* must not turn out to be a failure in Moscow where they love Gogol more than in Petersburg.' There is no evidence that Gogol obeyed Pushkin's summons. Pushkin seems to have lost touch with Gogol completely. He did not even know that Gogol, shocked and disgusted with the reception of his play in Petersburg, had made up his mind to quit Russia. In fact, their relationship had deteriorated so much that Gogol did not even think it necessary to take his leave of Pushkin before his departure. 'I had no time and could not take leave of Pushkin,' he wrote apologetically to Zhukovsky from Hamburg on June 28, 1836. 'Anyway, that was his own fault.'

During his last trip to Moscow in April–May, 1836, where he had gone to get more subscriptions for *The Contemporary*, Pushkin wrote to Natalie: 'I fear the booksellers may take advantage of my soft-heartedness and wheedle some concessions from me in spite of your strict instructions.' But it was not only *The Contemporary* that failed to bring in the money he had hoped for. His *History of the Pugachov Rebellion* was also a failure and, what was much worse, his financial and personal worries seemed to have affected his inspiration. In 1834 his last autumn in Boldino was completely unproductive. Next autumn in Mikhailovskoye he saw the moon over his left shoulder, a portent, he felt, of despair and desolation, which made him worry about Natalie (as well he might) and made any writing out of the question. His despondency was deepened by the thought that he was growing old. On September 25, 1835, he wrote to his wife from Trigorskoye:

I have not written a single line till now and all because I do not feel
at ease in my mind. In Mikhailovskoye I found everything as in the old
days except that my nurse is no longer there and that near the old
familiar pines a young pine family has grown up during my absence
and I feel vexed to look at it as sometimes I feel vexed to see young
cavalry guardsmen at balls at which I no longer dance. But I'm afraid
there's nothing to be done about it. Everything around me tells me that
I am growing old. Sometimes even in plain Russian. Yesterday, for
instance, I met a peasant woman I know and I couldn't help telling her
that she had changed. She, in turn, said to me: 'Why, you, too, sir,
have grown old and ugly.' Though I can say with my late nurse that I
never was goodlooking, I *was* young once.

His looks worried him a great deal now that Natalie was dancing, as he
rightly surmised, with some handsome cavalry guardsman. In a letter to
his wife from Moscow on May 16, 1836, he told her of a plan to sculpt his
bust to which he objected because he was afraid that his 'Negro ugliness'
would be committed to immortality in all its dead immobility'. As for
Natalie's 'flirtation' with Nicholas I, Moscow was just then full of rumours
that Natalie had become his mistress and Pushkin thought it was time he
scotched them at the source by warning Natalie and, at the same time,
conveying to Nicholas I through his loyal Post Office, if not through
Natalie herself, that he (Pushkin), too, was a dab hand at spreading
rumours that might not be very pleasant to His Majesty. 'Some gossip
here concerns you, my dear,' he wrote to Natalie on May 6, 1836, 'though
as husbands are always the last in town to discover something about their
wives, I have heard only part of it. However, it seems that you have driven
a certain person [i.e. Nicholas I] to such despair by your coquetry and
cruelty that, as a consolation, he has established a harem of young
actresses. That is not good, my angel: modesty is the best adornment of
your sex.' To make quite sure that the full implication of his message
was understood, he purposely distorted another story of a certain Savelyev,
a cavalry guards officer, who had been demoted for striking a superior
officer, a Major Gorgoli, into a love drama: 'You have in Petersburg a
certain Savelyev, a cavalry guardsman [like d'Anthès], an excellent young
man. He is in love with Idalie Poletika [a close friend of Natalie's who
arranged clandestine meetings between Natalie and d'Anthès] and on
account of her he slapped Gruenwald [the C.O. of the regiment]. Savelyev

is to be shot in a day or two. Imagine how miserable Idalie must be!'
Natalie knew that there was no truth whatever in the story and, no doubt,
Pushkin's lighthearted 'Savelyev is to be shot' conveyed quite a different
meaning to her, whether the shooting applied to d'Anthès or to the
Emperor himself. Natalie was just then more likely than at any other time
to take Pushkin's hints more seriously, for she was about to give birth to
their fourth child (a girl, christened Natalya, born on May 23, 1836, their
third child, Grigory, had been born a year earlier, on May 14, 1835).

5

Natalie met Georges d'Anthès shortly after her return with her children and her two sisters from her mother's estate in the autumn of 1834. A year earlier the Dutch ambassador in Petersburg, Baron Louis Beveriwaert van Heeckeren, met d'Anthès, an impecunious native of Colmar and a former student of the military college of St Cyr, at an inn in France. Heeckeren, a homosexual, was forty at the time. He fell violently in love with the nineteen-year-old d'Anthès. He took him to Petersburg where they arrived by steamer in October, 1833. It did not take long for d'Anthès, who had remained loyal to Charles X, to win the favour of Nicholas I and to be received into the cavalry guards. He was a great success in Petersburg high society and his popularity increased after Heeckeren had adopted him as his son and heir, for now he was not only 'young, handsome, insolent, self-confident, gay and witty', as Sofia Karamzin described him in a letter to her brother, but also rich. Pushkin, of course, was well aware that d'Anthès was in love with his wife and that his wife was not unresponsive to his advances, but he preferred to bide his time, particularly as his closest friends, such as the Karamzins, were, if not encouraging, then at least looking on benevolently at the growing intimacy between the two young people (Natalie and d'Anthès were of the same age). In January, 1836, the inevitable declarations of love were exchanged. D'Anthès wrote to Heeckeren on January 20, 1836: 'I am madly in love . . . but the terrible thing is that she, too, loves me, but at the moment we cannot see each other because her husband is disgracefully jealous.' A month later, he wrote: 'We had a talk together . . . This woman is usually thought to be silly, but during our talk she showed extraordinary tact and intelligence . . . She said to me:"I love you as I never loved anyone before, but you can demand only my heart from me, as everything else does not belong to me and I can only be happy by doing my duty."

Natalie's 'tact and intelligence' were soon shown by her attempt to distract Pushkin's attention from her affair with d'Anthès by involving him in a duel with Count Sollogub. She accused Sollogub of spreading a rumour that she was in love with a certain government official famous for his prowess in dancing the mazurka. Having laid this false trail, Natalie naturally expected that Pushkin would immediately challenge Sollogub in defence of his own and his wife's 'honour'. She was right, of course. At the time, however, Sollogub was away in Tver on government business. Pushkin, according to Sollogub, began saying that he (Sollogub) refused his challenge. Sollogub at once wrote to Pushkin to say that he was entirely at his service, though he did not feel that he was at fault in any way. Pushkin seemed to be satisfied with his letter, but (apparently at the instigation of Natalie) he wrote to him at the beginning of February, 1836, in French:

> You have put yourself to unnecessary trouble in giving me an explanation which I have not demanded of you. You have permitted yourself to address improper remarks to my wife and you have boasted of having *uttered impertinencies* to her. Circumstances do not permit me to come to Tver before the end of the month . . . The name which you bear and the society which you frequent force me to demand satisfaction from you for the impropriety of your conduct. . . .

In the meantime Pushkin's mother died in Petersburg (on March 29, 1836). Pushkin took her body to Mikhailovskoye, where she was buried on April 8 in the Svyatogorsk Monastery next to the graves of her father and mother. Pushkin bought a plot of land for his own grave beside his mother's. On his return to Moscow his meeting with Sollogub at last took place. Sollogub describes it in his memoirs:

> I expect Pushkin's anger had long cooled off and he probably realised the inappropriateness of a duel with a young man who was almost a child at the time 'as a result of some society gossip'. I had, besides, found out that a French royalist by the name of d'Anthès had appeared in Petersburg and was causing a great deal of worry to Pushkin . . . In Moscow, where I arrived at daybreak, I went to his friend Nashchokin's where Pushkin always stayed when in Moscow. They were still in bed at the time. I went into the drawing room and asked the servant to waken Pushkin. A few moments later he came into the room in his dressing gown, not yet fully awake, and began cleaning his extraordinarily long fingernails. Our first exchanges were very

frigid . . . Pushkin apologised for letting me wait so long and . . . our conversation became a little more animated. We began to discuss his new review, *The Contemporary*. 'The first volume was very good,' said Pushkin 'and I shall try to make the second volume a little more boring, for one must not spoil the public.' Here he laughed and our conversation became almost friendly . . . I agreed to apologise to Mrs Pushkin and wrote a most flowery letter in French, which Pushkin took and at once held out his hand to me after which he became extremely cheerful. . . .

Pushkin's attitude towards duelling at this time becomes clear from his remark to Sollogub: 'You don't think it is fun for me to fight duels, do you? But what can I do? I have the misfortune to be a public man and, you know, that's much worse than to be a public woman ['a public woman' means a prostitute in Russian]'.

In the summer of 1836 the Pushkins lived in a villa in the fashionable holiday resort of Stone Island, the 'swamp' as Pushkin contemptuously called it. Pushkin went for long walks and paid frequent visits to the nearby cemetery. There, as he wrote in his elegy, beginning with the line, 'When beyond the city pensive I wander,' and dated 'Aug. 14. St Isl', he meditated on the contrast between a country churchyard with its 'unadorned graves', where he was to be buried so soon himself, and the crowded cemetery where under vulgar monuments with their lying tributes 'all the dead of the city rot side by side like greedy guests at a beggarly dinner'. On Stone Island, too, Pushkin wrote the famous self-appraisal of his work as a poet. The poem (a free adaptation of Derzhavin's grandiloquent attempt to emulate Horace) has no title and bears the Horatian epigraph: *Exegi monumentum*. It is dated: '1836, Aug. 21, St Isl.' In it Pushkin returns to his earlier claim of having 'glorified freedom in a cruel age' and 'called for mercy to the fallen' and hints at the more recent attacks on him by an appeal to his Muse to accept 'praise and calumny with indifference' and 'not to dispute the fool'.

Natalie was otherwise engaged. One day, accompanied by d'Anthès and her elder sister Catherine, she paid a brief call on Count Vyelgorsky. One of the count's guests left the following description of Natalie: 'On a tall horse which kept pawing the ground with its hoof, Pushkin's incomparable wife was swaying gracefully. The Count invited her to come in. "Awfully sorry, we're in a hurry," Natalie replied, whipping her horse, and the small cavalcade galloped off and vanished behind the birches of the avenue.'

Countess Dolly Ficquelmont, one of Pushkin's close Petersburg friends, wrote in her diary:

Natalie Pushkin enjoyed the role of one of the most beautiful women in Petersburg society . . . D'Anthès was in love with her for a whole year and, meeting her constantly in society, he showed his feelings towards her more and more openly. One of the sisters of Mrs Pushkin [Catherine, who was three years older than d'Anthès] had the misfortune to fall in love with him and did not realise what the consequences of it might be for her sister. She tried to arrange meetings with d'Anthès [she had, in fact, been d'Anthès's mistress] by taking advantage of the Frenchman's infatuation with her sister. In the end, we were all witnesses of the growing danger of this situation. Whether it was Mrs Pushkin's vanity that was aroused and flattered or whether it was d'Anthès who really did succeed in making an impression on her heart, the fact remains that she no longer repulsed him or did anything to stop the manifestations of his uncontrolled passion. Soon d'Anthès, forgetting every delicacy of a sensible man and violating all social proprieties, manifested in public his admiration for Mrs Pushkin to an extent that was completely inadmissible in the case of a married woman. She looked pale and trembled every time he fixed her with his gaze and it was quite evident that she had completely lost any power to curb the feelings of that man and that he had made up his mind to drive the affair as far as he possibly could.

Pushkin's sister Olga, Sofia Karamzin and Vyazemsky have left illuminating descriptions of Pushkin's state of mind during the six months before his fatal duel with d'Anthès. Olga met her brother in June, 1836. 'He was very thin,' she writes, 'his face was yellow and his nerves were on edge. He did not seem to be able to carry on a conversation for long. He could not sit still. He started at the ringing of the doorbell and could not bear the noise of the children or of music. "If only you knew," he said to me, "what a burden life is to me. I hope it will not be prolonged. I feel it won't." '

Sofia Karamzin described Pushkin at her nameday party in a letter to her brother in September, 1836, as 'sad, pensive, and worried. His wandering, wild, distracted gaze,' she wrote, 'was fixed on his wife and d'Anthès, who . . . kept on casting tender glances at Natalie with whom, in the end, he danced the mazurka. It was pitiful to see Pushkin's face. He stood opposite us in the doorway, pale and menacing.'

'In the winter of 1836–1837,' Vyazemsky recalls, 'I happened to walk along Nevsky Avenue with Natalie Pushkin, her sister Catherine Goncharov, and young Heeckeren. At that moment Pushkin rushed passed us like a whirlwind. He did not look back and immediately vanished in a crowd of people on the pavement. The expression on his face was terrifying. For me it was the first sign of the coming storm.'

The storm broke on November 4, 1836, when Pushkin and a number of Pushkin's friends in Petersburg received, by the newly inaugurated city mail, anonymous letters conferring upon Pushkin 'the order of the cuckold', which, in a coded but sufficiently transparent form, hinted that Natalie was the mistress of Nicholas I. The letters, which seem to have been a copy of the letters with which some gay sparks in Vienna had been amusing themselves, read as follows:

> *Les Grands-Croix, Commandeurs et Chevaliers du Sérénissime Ordre des Cocus, réunis en grand Chapitre sous la présidence du vénérable grand-Maître de l'Ordre, S.E.D.L.Narychkine, ont nommé à l'unaminité Mr Alexandre Pouchkine coadjuteur du grand Maître de l'Ordre des Cocus et historiographe de l'Ordre.*

> *Le sécrétaire perpétuel: Cte L. Borch.*

Dmitry Naryshkin was the husband of the mistress of Alexander I, and the mention of his name in the certificate and the description of Pushkin as historiographer could be interpreted as a scarcely concealed hint, for Pushkin was receiving a salary from the government for doing historical research and attending court functions where his wife, as Alexander Turgenev wrote, eclipsed all the other women not only by her beauty but also by her dresses. Pushkin suspected that Heeckeren was, if not the author, then the inspirer of the letters (they were actually written by Prince Peter Dolgorukov, a close associate of Heeckeren's homosexual set). Pushkin sent d'Anthès a challenge on November 5 and sent a letter to Count Kankrin, Minister of Finance, on November 6, suggesting that the Treasury should take over his estate in settlement of the money he owed to the State. Heeckeren immediately asked Pushkin to postpone the duel for two weeks, to which Pushkin agreed. On November 17 Pushkin

withdrew the challenge on the ground that d'Anthès had proposed to
Catherine Goncharov, his mistress, who was at the time five months with
child. The announcement of the marriage came as a big surprise to
everybody.

Sofia Karamzin wrote to her brother Andrey on November 20, 1836:

. . . Well, yes, it is d'Anthès, young, handsome, insolent d'Anthès
(now rich) who is about to marry Catherine Goncharov and I assure
you he looks extremely contented. He even seems to be obsessed by a
kind of feverish gaiety and thoughtlessness. He visits us every evening
because he only sees his betrothed in the mornings at her aunt's the
Countess Zagryazhsky. Pushkin does not receive him at his house. He is
extremely irritable . . . Natalie is nervous, withdrawn and at the mention of her sister's marriage her voice falters. Catherine is so happy that
she seems to be walking on air. The public is surprised, but as the story
of the anonymous letters is not generally known it explains this marriage
very simply. Pushkin alone arouses suspicions and conjectures by his
excited appearance, his enigmatic exclamations and his manner of
cutting d'Anthès and avoiding him in society. Vyazemsky says: 'He
seems to be offended for his wife because d'Anthès is no longer paying
court to her.'

Pushkin, according to Sollogub, did not believe that the wedding would
actually take place. He saw in d'Anthès's intention to marry Catherine
Goncharov merely a subterfuge for escaping a duel. He was obsessed by
the thought of a revenge which, he told Vera Vyazemsky, would completely expose Heeckeren as a villain. On November 21, soon after the
announcement of the marriage, he invited Sollogub into his study.
Sollogub recorded this meeting:

He locked the door and said, 'I am going to read to you my letter
to old Heeckeren. I have finished with the son. It is now the turn of
the old man [Heeckeren was only five years older than Pushkin].'
Then he read to me his well-known letter to the Dutch ambassador. His
lips trembled and his eyes became bloodshot. He was so terrifying that
it was only then that I realised that he really was of African descent.

On the same day Pushkin wrote a long letter to Benkendorf, in which
he mentioned the anonymous letter and his suspicions that Heeckeren was
its author:

I strongly object to seeing the name of my wife associated on this occasion with the name of anyone whatsoever. I let M. d'Anthès know about it. The Baron de Heeckeren came to my house and accepted a duel for M. d'Anthès, asking for a postponement of fifteen days. It turned out that during that interval, M. d'Anthès fell in love with my sister-in-law and asked her hand in marriage. Having learned about it indirectly, I told M. d'Archiac [Vicomte Auguste d'Archiac, secretary of the French embassy and d'Anthès's second] that my challenge should be regarded as not having taken place.

Two days later, on November 23, Pushkin had an audience with Nicholas I in the presence of Benkendorf. Nicholas I apparently persuaded Pushkin not to send his letter to Heeckeren. Pushkin tore up the letter, but included some of its phrases in his second letter to Heeckeren which resulted in his duel with d'Anthès.

Meanwhile Pushkin, Sofia Karamzin wrote to her brother on December 29:

... continues to conduct himself in a most stupid and absurd fashion. He is getting to be more and more like a tiger and he gnashes his teeth every time he discusses the marriage ... He still continues to declare that he will never allow his wife to be present at the wedding or to receive her married sister. Yesterday I tried to convince Natalie to make him give up his absurd decision which would again start all the tongues in town wagging. She does not conduct herself straightforwardly! When her husband is present, she pretends not to bow to d'Anthès and even not to look at him, but when her husband is not there, she resumes her former flirtation with her dropped eyes, her nervous embarrassment in conversation, while he again gazes long at her and seems to forget about his fiancée who changes countenance and is tormented by jealousy. In short, it's a kind of never ending comedy, the meaning of which no one seems to understand properly ... Meanwhile, poor d'Anthès has been through a serious illness ... The other day, he again made an appearance ... looking very thin, pale and interesting and was again very gentle with us, which always happens when a man is very agitated or, perhaps, very unhappy. Next day he came again but this time with his fiancée and what is worse with Pushkin. Once again, there began the expressions of rage and poetic anger; dark like the night and scowling like Jupiter in anger, Pushkin interrupted his gloomy and em-

barrassing silence only by a few abrupt ironic words and from time to
time by demonic laughter . . . To change the subject, [Sofia concludes]
I can tell you that the fourth volume of *The Contemporary* was published a few days ago containing Pushkin's novel *The Captain's Daughter*
which people say is marvellous. . . .

A week before the wedding of d'Anthès and Catherine, Pushkin wrote
to his father:

> We are having a wedding. My sister-in-law, Catherine, is getting
> married to Baron Heeckeren, the nephew and adopted son of the
> ambassador of the King of Holland. He is a very handsome and fine
> fellow, very much in fashion, rich, and four years younger than his
> fiancée. Preparations for the trousseau are occupying and amusing my
> wife and her sisters very much, but they are driving me mad, for my
> house has the air of a *boutique de monde* and a lingerie shop.

The wedding took place on January 10, 1837. Countess Ficquelmont
wrote in her diary:

> Society learned with surprise and scepticism of this unexpected
> marriage. Bets were laid against the proposed wedding and the whole
> thing was regarded as a subterfuge. Pushkin, however, seemed to be
> highly satisfied. He took his wife out everywhere, to balls, to the theatre,
> to the court, and the poor woman now found herself in an extremely
> false position; she dared not talk to her future brother-in-law, she dared
> not look at him while being watched by everybody and she was in a
> state of constant panic since she did not believe that d'Anthès had
> preferred her sister to herself. In her extreme naivety, or rather her
> quite amazing simplicity, she kept arguing with her husband about the
> possibility of such a change in the feelings of a man whose attentions
> she enjoyed perhaps out of vanity. Pushkin did not want to be present
> at the wedding of his sister-in-law. He also refused to see the newly
> weds, though their common friends hoped to bring about a reconcilia
> tion between them and did their best to bring them together almost
> daily. Soon d'Anthès, albeit married, renewed his former attentions to
> Pushkin's wife and finally at one ball he so compromised her by his looks
> and innuendos that everyone was horrified and Pushkin finally made
> up his mind to seek satisfaction. The cup was full to the brim and there
> was no possibility of stopping the disaster. Next day he wrote to

Heeckeren accusing him of complicity and using highly insulting
expressions about him.

Pushkin wrote this fateful letter, which was far more than insulting, in
French to Heeckeren on January 26, 1837:

My dear Baron, Permit me to summarise what has just taken place.
The conduct of your son has been known to me for a long time and it
could not be a matter of indifference to me. I contented myself with the
role of an observer, waiting to intervene at the proper time. An incident
that at any other time would have been highly disagreeable to me
came, fortunately, to rescue me from my predicament: I received anonymous letters. I realised that the time had come for me to act and I took
advantage of it. You know the rest: I made your son play a role so
pitiful that my wife, surprised at so much cowardice and baseness, could
not refrain from laughing and the feeling which, perhaps, this great and
sublime passion had aroused in her, wilted into the most calm contempt
and the most deserved disgust.

I must admit, Baron, that your role was not entirely seemly. You,
the representative of a crowned head, have acted paternally as the
pander of your son. You, it appears, have been directing his conduct
(which was clumsy enough, I must say). I suppose it was you who
dictated the vulgar jokes which he used to make and the absurd things
which he had the impudence to write. Like an obscene old woman,
you would go and lie in wait for my wife in every corner in order to
tell her of the love of your bastard or so he claimed to be; and when,
ill with syphilis, he had to stay at home, you would say that he was
dying of love for her; you would murmur to her: Give me back my
son.

You must realise, Baron, that after all this I cannot permit my family
to have anything to do with yours. It was only on that condition that I
consented not to pursue this filthy business and not to dishonour you
in the eyes of our court and yours, as I had the power and the intention
of doing. It does not matter to me that my wife still listens to your
paternal exhortations. I cannot allow your son, after his contemptible
conduct, to dare to speak to my wife and still less to tell her barrack-
room jokes and pretend devotion and unrequited passion, for he is
only a coward and a scoundrel. I am, therefore, obliged to address
myself to you to ask you to put an end to all this farce if you wish to

avoid a new scandal, from which I shall most certainly not shrink.
I have the honour to be, my dear Baron,
Your most humble and most obedient servant,
Alexander Pushkin.

This time there was no escape. D'Anthès accepted the implied challenge
and the duel took place next day, on January 27, 1837. Three days before,
the Pushkins and the Heeckerens had met at a 'rout' given by Princess
Yekaterina Meshchersky, Karamzin's younger daughter. Sofia Karamzin
sent this description to her brother on January 27:

The Pushkins and the Heeckerens (who continue to perform their
sentimental comedy to the delight of society) were there. Pushkin
gnashes his teeth and assumes his constant expression of a tiger. Natalie
dabs her eyes and blushes at the long and passionate gaze of her
brother-in-law. This is beginning to be much more than the ordinary
kind of immorality. Catherine directs on both of them a jealous
lorgnette . . . On the whole, all this is very strange and uncle Vyazemsky
asserts that he prefers to cover his face and turn away from the house
of the Pushkins. . . .

'Pushkin,' Vyazemsky wrote in his memoirs, 'did not conceal from his
wife that he was going to fight a duel with d'Anthès. He asked her whom
she would weep over. "I'll weep over him who'll be killed," was her calm
reply. Such a reply infuriated him.' Two days before the duel, Ivan
Turgenev, at the time a student of Petersburg University, saw Pushkin at
the morning concert of the Philharmonic Society. Pushkin, Turgenev
writes in his memoirs,

was standing at the door, leaning against the lintel and, crossing his
arms on his wide chest, looked around him with a dissatisfied air. I
remember his small swarthy face, his African lips, the white line of his
large teeth, his drooping sidewhiskers, his dark jaundiced eyes beneath
a high forehead, almost without eyebrows, and his curly hair. He
glanced at me and the unceremonious attention with which I stared at
him must have made an unpleasant impression on him: he shrugged as
though with vexation – he did not seem to be in a good mood – and
walked away.

6

The only detailed and trustworthy account of the duel between Pushkin and d'Anthès on Wednesday, January 27, 1837, was left by Lieutenant-Colonel Konstantin Danzas, Pushkin's second and a Lycée classmate. According to Danzas, the duel had not been stopped by the police because Benkendorf hated Pushkin. The most recent clash between Pushkin and Benkendorf followed Pushkin's violent attack on Sergey Uvarov, the Minister of Education, in his poem *On the Recovery of Lucullus*. Uvarov was the heir of Count Dmitry Sheremetev, one of the richest men in Russia. When Sheremetev fell gravely ill, Uvarov took all the necessary precautions to safeguard what he thought would soon be his own property. But the Count recovered and Pushkin could not let so wonderful an opportunity pass without holding up to derision the man who had described his *History of Pugachov* as a 'subversive book'. In the poem he speaks of Uvarov as 'a raven fond of carrion' who put his 'avaricious sealing-wax' on the Count's 'offices'. Benkendorf, who must have wondered how long it would be before he too would be made the laughing-stock of Russia, at once demanded an explanation of this attack on a Cabinet Minister, and Pushkin's feeble attempt to extricate himself by claiming that he did not have any particular person in mind must have struck him as anything but convincing. Benkendorf, Danzas states positively, sent his gendarmes to Yekaterinhof 'as though by mistake' instead of to the Black River near the commandant's summer residence. Since the actual location of the duel was agreed upon by the two seconds, Danzas and d'Archiac, only a few hours before it took place, somebody must have informed Benkendorf about it. Who was it? It seems very likely that it was Danzas himself, for Danzas was very anxious to avoid the duel (d'Anthès was well known to be a crack shot) and was desperately thinking of some way of doing so. Did Benkendorf consult the Emperor before sending the gendarmes to the wrong place? Whether he did or not, he knew very well that, whatever the outcome, Nicholas I would be only too